Together We *Will* Save America

THE
WORLD
AWAKENS

What the hell just happened
- and *what lies ahead*

VOL 2

JOHN MICHAEL CHAMBERS

outskirts
press

Author Disclaimer

Table of Contents

1. **John Michael Chambers:** If It's Not Okay, It's Not the End (Part Three)... 1

2. **Patrick Byrne:** An Unlikely Insider's View of the Stolen 2020 Election and Intriguing History about How America Came to This... 14

3. **Graham Ledger:** Calling Out the COVID Scam from Its Inception 33

4. **James Grundvig:** Scenario A—America Restored (1871 to 2021)... 52

5. **Sean Morgan:** Trump, Devolution, and the Vax....................... 57

6. **Lt. Scott Bennett:** Notice of Unlawful Orders of Biden Administration and Treason 62

7. **Maria Zack:** Prominent Italians Helped Steal the 2020 US Election for Biden, and Average Brave Citizens from Italy Came Forward to Expose It! 66

8. **Jaco Booyens:** An Honest and Urgent Plea for *Your* Intercession with *Our* Children and Grandchildren................. 73

9. **Sam Sorbo:** Why You Too Should Home Educate Your Child [or Grandchild] 97

10. **Simon Parkes:** Unique Insights on Patriot Intelligence 112

11. **Mike Adams:** Social Media Censorship and Luciferase.......... 129

12. **Jovan Pulitzer:** Expert Information about How They Rigged Our 2020 Vote 134

13. **Mike Lindell:** Introducing Colonel Phil Waldron's Damning Video that Explains How, Why, and Who Stole America's 2020 Elections...................................... 143

14. **Patel Patriot and Praying Medic:** Evidence for "Devolution," the Probable Detailing of Trump, and the Q-Team's Plans..... 151

15. **Mel K and Benjamin Fulford:** Unlocking Historical Truths You Probably Do Not Know.. 159

16. **Alexandra Bruce:** Chinese Warfare 163

17. **Doctor Steve Greer:** The Coming UFO Cosmic Hoax.......... 169

18. **Alexandra Bruce:** Was January 6, 2021, a False Flag FBI Operation on Our Washington, DC, Capitol, as a Way to Implicate Innocent Patriots? 172

19. **Donald S. McAlvany:** Undercurrents of Globalism, including World Wars, Surveillance, and the Rising Populist Awakening 175

20. **Cyrus A. Parsa:** God, China, America, and Artificial Intelligence.. 196

21. **Mary Fanning:** Stealing America 211

22. **Amapola Hansberger:** Legal Immigrants for America 220

23. **Laura Logan:** A Veteran Mainstream Reporter Gives Some New-Media-Type Truth about the Global Threat.......... 225

24. **Editor's Supplement:** Lord Willing, After We Have Helped God Stomp Out Much Evil in Our Time, What Comes Next Biblically? 227

25. **John Michael Chambers:** If It's Not Okay, It's Not the End (Part Four) 238

1

John Michael Chambers: If It's Not Okay, It's Not the End (Part Three)

With my more recent updates included, like parts one and two, much of this book's parts three and four are taken from me being interviewed in May 2021 by Mary Woods, an online-show host and strong, patriot voice in Nevada:

Another piece of this information war are the cabal's Agenda 21 and Agenda 2030, plots Trump exposed so they've had to escalate their time frame for bringing the whole world under complete deep state control. Juan O Savin essentially stated that part of those plans were to involve cryptocurrency—another black hat operation—period. Can some make lots of cash with cryptos? Yes, just like gamblers can in Las Vegas, but most lose and everyone does over enough time. I don't invest in cryptocurrency because I put my savings into more traditional, tangible assets like gold, silver, and reasonably priced real estate, while also investing in my media outlet and the people involved who help get the truth out.

The deep state started their crypto-world scam with Bitcoin, which was supposedly invented by a man named Satoshi Nakamoto. But that's another lie, and AMP's James Grundvig was one of the first to point that out. The fictitious name is just a cleverly crafted phrase combining the corporate names of four deep state tech giants who probably helped create and sponsor that unbacked fiat currency: Samsung, Toshiba, Nakamichi, and Motorola. Their idea was to pour boatloads of money into cryptos like Bitcoin, prompting the public to do the same with their savings. But then when Hillary would win the presidency, they planned to trigger their usual trap that they have pulled so many times with other markets like stocks, bonds, and real estate. Those schemes always allow the top globalistas to cash out, destroying everyone else, just as they did in the fall—literally—of 2008. As always, through the ensuing financial chaos and public desperation, the cabal picks the rest of the winners, deciding which banks and insurance companies would be allowed to fail and then using taxpayer funds to bail out their deep state coconspirators.

Crypto was brought on the scene to capture people's savings that might have moved away from their phony dollar notes. Instead of folks putting their assets into sound, tangible investments that the cabal can't print for nothing and then even earn interest on, they gave the public another one of their fiat-currency options. Real financial security comes from tangible assets like gold and silver that have been used as money for the six thousand years of human history, reliable means of exchange that retain their value against all fiat currencies. Other great investments over time are undervalued property and people who are doing valuable work for societies around the planet.

But everything from the cabal is rigged and falling apart, so they are rushing to reset the entire world into their newest scheme, while President Trump still has not conceded the fraudulent 2020 election. I believe he will soon be back and I could connect those dots for you all day, but just know for now that the bulky lady has not begun bellowing out her ending song yet, and I don't even hear the band warming up, so this game is not over, and patriots like Trump have just gotten started.

With gold approaching $1,900 per ounce and the Fed's dollar notes losing value every month through inflation, for most of us silver is the more affordable option these days. The shiny metal used for tangible money and known as "poor-man's gold" is becoming more and more in demand, while also getting used up in the fast-growing, high-tech industries. Those two aspects have helped it continue to increase in value, especially against the banksters' funny money. Today, an ounce of silver is approaching twenty-five dollars, an amount people readily have available to invest, as opposed to $1,900 per ounce for gold. According to economist Dr. Kirk Elliott, who performed studies with and without an inflation adjustment, under both circumstances silver was the top-performing asset you could have had in your portfolio during the past twenty-one years; next was gold, the Dow, and then real estate. People like to challenge that, but the numbers don't lie. Today, silver demand is intense and supplies are dwindling, but you might find some for a reasonable premium at your local coin shop. Just make sure it's real, and get bullion instead of wasting your money on those "shipwreck" coins. You also have the option of purchasing a partial ounce of gold through something called European fractional gold, but that's hard to come by. But if you haven't already, start building your gold and silver stacks today.

Getting back to the cabal, patriots often wonder how best to wake their own family and friends to the control we have been under with this Satanist group pushing their one-world government. Well, one way to welcome them to this great awaking is by having them search online for George Herbert Walker Bush's New World Order speech. Or send it to them. That will do it—argument finished! In the video, as well as other Bush addresses to the nation, daddy Bush informed us twenty or thirty times that we will have a new world order that follows the dictates from the founding fathers—of the United Nations, not the United States. After eight great years of a people's president with Ronald Reagan, what a shocking face full of ice water that was! It is what woke me up!

As far as helping people see the present anomalies, be brief, keep it simple, and stay calm while asking a few questions like these: Do you find it weird that Biden did not fly Air Force One to his inaugural, may not be doing so even now, and didn't seem to at all during at least the first three months? And isn't it strange that he didn't give a State of the Union speech until way longer than any of the previous presidents? And why wouldn't he have the usual meetings with heads of state from other nations? Did you read that article from the left-wing Politico website that reported how the Pentagon didn't give the nuclear-code keys to Biden? If he's really a full-power US president, aren't those aspects we should have seen? Get people to think. Get them to ask questions. Get them to look. They can't ignore questions, so you've planted some seeds and now you can just walk away. Unless he or she is a crazy, the thoughts will stick in their head as they go home, maybe they will decide to look into it, and they might end up finding the confirmation for what you mentioned.

You might also plant this seed: Whether you like Trump or not, when he was president isn't it weird that the wall was going up on our border and statistically the trouble had all calmed down? But both before and after him with Obama and Biden, our southern border was and is in crisis. Isn't that odd? You could go on with little bits of reality that completely counter the indoctrination from fake news. That's how you do it versus easy and inflammatory statements like "Biden is terrible! Look what he's doing! Trump is the savior of our world." Instead, be subtle and ask questions that will hopefully get them to think, look, and find out more for themselves.

For indoctrinated young people and those few atheists who might still think we are in need of new world order, of course they are fine to believe whatever they'd like as long as they are not harming other humans, but history has shown that the new-world-order people had to scrap that name because we all found out it meant their fascist control of mankind in every sense of the word. So, they just switched to "globalism" and falsely claim its "benevolent" leaders want the best for everyone in the world, as opposed to selfish patriots who only want to help their own nations and just ignore the rest of the world. But it's the same fascist new world order that wants all of us to be good Communists and Socialists so they can be the dictator administrators that own and control everything in those collectivist societies. They deceptively claim we must all come together as one, which is true as far as all being children of God, but the globalista framers of that new world order have no intention of making us their equals. For anyone skeptical of what I am outlining, encourage him or her to search for Klaus Schwab's World Economic Forum and Agenda 2030. They are advocating complete, global, governmental tyranny, exactly as the Bible's book of Revelation warns about with their one-world control of our food and water, currency, military, and justice system.

And these are the same people who want to reduce the world's population from almost eight billion now to less than six hundred million. Almost 94 percent of those living today would need to be eliminated under their plan. Look it up and also check out David Rockefeller's memoirs, as well as his father and grandfather (John Jr. and Sr.), and his great-grandfather (William Avery "Devil Bill" Rockefeller Sr.), who set that family on the path of evil as a con-artist, snake-oil salesman. These people's globalism is not at all what they are presenting to us in the media, but just a bit of research will uncover how they could not help privately bragging about their sinister plans—death and destruction for most of mankind, something their father, the devil, would be very proud of them for.

President Trump is the perfect example of how this deep state sets out to pulverize anyone that comes to power who is for the people instead of the cabal. Around February 2016, my good friend Dr. Sherry Tenpenny gave me a fifty-page, confidential, leaked document from Shareblue Media (renamed The American Independent), one of David Brock's leftist organizations like his Media Matters, both of which are funded by George Soros. The papers were a globalista blueprint full of ways to create false narratives in an effort to delegitimize the entire movement of President Trump and other patriots. It was all very specific and heavily funded, step-by-step instructions for seizing control of the picture surrounding Trump. I then saw the contents of that document become exactly what these despicable liars began putting out immediately into Trump's campaign for president, a deceptive smear campaign that has ramped up more and more over the last four years.

The cabal-supporting Communists and Socialists, who helped orchestrate this dishonest effort to discredit Trump and patriotism, used to hide their politics. Then their true nature became "hidden in plain sight," and now it's no longer even hidden as they clearly push for communism and socialism to take over our country—period. For them, the rule of law is gone. The Constitution no longer exists. That's where we find ourselves.

And that is the near-death experience Juan O Savin describes as our situation right now, just like the precipice General Flynn talks about us being on, and that is why everyone needs to get active. There is also a white hat plan working in addition to our efforts. In fact, according to Michael Lindell and Patrick Byrne, the evidence against fraudulent voting machines like Dominion's involves irrefutable mathematical and scientific proof, which they think will go to the Supreme Court one more time before August or September. Of course, this is the same derelict SCOTUS that has been blackmailed, bribed, and otherwise corrupted to ignore all the previous pleas to at least look at the overwhelming evidence of voter fraud. But when they are challenged to hear the cases this time, if they vote constitutionally and lawfully to take it up and decide on the merits, then we the people have used our constitutional system to its last option for justice. That is what we want. It's what we should do. Follow the rule of law! President Trump talks about that all the time with his staunch position as a law-and-order president.

However, if these corrupt Supreme Court justices, who all took the oath to protect and defend our Constitution, shoot down the obvious election-fraud proof again (while knowing Trump won), I think that is when our military makes its first overt moves. And that will not be through guns on the street, except for a quick crackdown on George-Soros-backed thugs like Antifa and Black Lives Matter, but more of our armed forces grabbing information control through the Emergency Broadcast System, so they can tell Americans why the belligerent occupiers like Biden, 75 percent of politicians in DC offices, and leaders of the complicit main-stench media have all been removed. Those stealthily planned moves will only get one shot at bringing sudden destruction to the widespread network of deep state saboteurs, meaning it has to be precisely timed and executed perfectly. If done before the majority of Americans have woken up to at least understand a little about our cabal controllers, there will be added civil unrest by the duped and indoctrinated slaves of the cabal-complicit media, which could result in the widespread civilian loss of life, a grim consequence that Trump, the Q team, and our military have been patiently working hard to avoid.

While we watch this show and hopefully each do something to help, remember again that timing is everything. Our military and white hats working for US intelligence, brave men and women surrounding President Trump, know far more than any of us. So, if current events make no sense, keep in mind that we don't know what we don't know, and everything will be okay in the end. As I have reassured for a while now, if it's not okay, it's not quite the end. Everyone needs to hold the line, have faith, and pray because we've got this! I hope the Supreme Court does the right thing, but my instincts tell me they just won't, so the good guys will make the right moves when the time comes, and we will take back our country. That's how I see this playing out—our 45th US Service Corp president *may* also become our 19th US Republic leader.

But again, it all goes back to timing, and that will happen on God's divine schedule (see the short, second-to-last chapter, an editor's note titled "Lord Willing, After We Have Helped God Stomp Out Much Evil in Our Time, What Comes Next Biblically?"). Though the outcome will be seen as being from God, for now Satan's forces on this earth are strong, and God wants us to help with their destruction. We will have one shot to do this right without creating some cataclysmic issues across the globe like inciting a nuclear war or collapsing our nation into civil unrest. Those are the possible consequences of a mistake. The enemy is smart, as demonstrated by how they beat us with this last election, although it was fraudulently done. Some rightly counter that the patriots and Trump possibly allowed it to happen as a sting operation to catch those who have long cooked our votes. That stolen election may have needed to be allowed, so that this near-death experience would wake people up. I'm in that camp, but regardless we are in the same situation. Some were disappointed when General Flynn recently informed us that our military is not going to come to save us, so we should go out and run for office. Yes, those were his words, but a little later (at Clay Clark's 2021 conference in Tulsa, Oklahoma), when commenting on whether we would get Trump back in office, Flynn assured the audience of patriots that we already have a president, at which point a photo of President Trump appeared behind him. And what did Flynn add? He said President Trump won in an unprecedented landslide, including taking California, and that all of it will be exposed.

You could claim he is speaking from both sides of his mouth, but this great general knows a thing or two about intelligence, having spent decades in it, including some of that time at the highest-possible levels of our US military and government. Do you think he misspeaks, forgets what he's stated previously, or just vacillates 180 degrees from day to day? Or could it be that he is operating with an intelligent strategy? Looking at the bigger picture presented by Patrick Byrne, Sidney Powell, and Mike Lindell, as well as tip-the-spear truth bombs from Lin Wood (all while Trump is out on golf courses and seemingly unconcerned as we digital warriors watch the show), maybe our former director of defense intelligence and Trump's pick for national security advisor, General Flynn, is just passing along deception nuggets for the deep state to chew on. Folks, there is a plan unfolding, and we don't know what we don't know because the white hats are not going to give their playbook to these globalista criminals.

Getting back to the details of voter fraud, you may remember that little boy in a movie many years ago called *The Sixth Sense*. He whispered, "I see dead people." Today that kid is grown and sees dead people voting by the hundreds of thousands—he's real scared now! The fraudulent practices seen in this past 2020 election included Trump votes ending up in dumpsters, forged Biden ballots trucked across state borders to get to wherever they were needed to falsify a win for him, massive absentee-ballot issues, the same person voting multiple times and even in more than one state, fraudulently marked ballots, the blocking of poll watchers, stopping the vote count in the middle of the night, illegal <u>aliens</u> (yes, that is the correct term) voting by the millions, gerrymandering, and on, and on.

Besides all of that, perhaps the most telling and disturbing form of election theft is the fact that computers now tabulate the vote count. Yet, our founding fathers said the votes ought to be cast in private and always counted publicly. Has anyone ever seen the computer count? In those machines lies evidence of vote theft by the millions. My 2017 book talked about "resident software," which had been installed on virtually all central-server voting machines deployed in the

US, a tool able to easily steal elections with extreme and undetected precision. This was also known as black-box voting, and some evidence suggests this technology was used by Hillary Clinton to steal her primaries from Senator Bernie Sanders.

Thanks to the work of Mary Fanning and others, we have come to learn that this same sort of subversive system we have today is known as the "Hammer and Scorecard," which is the Hammer supercomputer and its Scorecard software. Fraudulent vote flipping is also unseen as it is performed inside Smartmatic and Dominion voting machines. Those leading the effort to uncover the 2020 election fraud, the people providing irrefutable evidence of the theft of our nation, are former New York mayor and federal prosecutor Rudy Giuliani, constitutional attorney Dave Shestokas, US attorney Lin Wood, Overstock.com founder Patrick Byrne, MyPillow.com founder Mike Lindell, Lieutenant Scott Bennett, a team in Washington DC, and, of course, US attorney and federal prosecutor Sidney Powell. Lieutenant General Michael Flynn calls Sidney "the guardian angel of American justice—a warrior for we the people."

The mathematical and scientific evidence is now in. Both foreign adversaries and domestic infiltrators have successfully stolen our election. But does a successful bank robber, one who got outside the building and around the corner with stolen money, then get to keep it because he or she initially got away? No! Because Joe Biden and his cabal backers were successfully able to steal the US presidency, is it his to keep since he got away with it through a complicit US Congress and judiciary? No! The computer-voting system we have now was specifically designed and built to be the perfect election-stealing tool that leaves no evidence. It has been the perfect crime! They've been winning. Until now!

Here at the beginning of May 2021, I think we're close to winning in Arizona and Texas, while the efforts are also ramping up to audit

Georgia. This revealing of the truth will continue to spread, the evidence is there, and the oath that our military took to protect and defend our Constitution, as well as the people, will bring about the bold moves needed at the time that it is best for our country, which will be greatly aided by the Emergency Broadcast System, along with honest and independent patriot shows on platforms that do not censor free speech as big tech companies like Twitter, Facebook, and YouTube do. The public will eventually get honest answers as they move away from watching corrupt media operations full of deep state propaganda, instead relying on news from independent sources like AMP that are at least trying to tell the truth. Much waking of Americans has already happened, but a lot of that is left to be accomplished. We have to get the majority of people to buy in and understand what's really taking place, so that we have little unrest in our streets when the public moves are made that will cause a great shift and the defeat of much evil.

I know we are going to win and that may be helped along by these vote audits in some states, which will set a tone that causes the Supreme Court to hear cases, as well as sway public opinion, even among honorable people who are sane Democrats who may hate Trump but are not lunatics. I'm sure many normal Democrats that severely dislike Trump also don't appreciate Biden. They too have eyes and ears to understand what's happening on our southern border and that liberal leaders want to severely cut back on local police forces. Democrats want to be able to pick up the phone and call 911 when their wife is getting assaulted by a man in their house at three o'clock in the morning. They see what we see. When the election theft is shown to them through a new honest media, they will recognize how their right to an honest vote has been stolen, and next time the fraudulent winner might come from the other side. So the tide may turn from one of these audits in Arizona, Texas, Michigan, Georgia, or wherever else. Remember George Washington's story: History shows that the guy lost almost every battle for quite a while until he began to win, and then we finally got a free America—at least until those European banksters wormed their way back in. US control of our own destiny has come full circle since 1776; here we are again on our way to a second revolution and another victory!

But that process will take place through this information war where CNN (the "Cabal" News Network) had only six hundred thousand to eight hundred thousand total viewers, while Clay Clark got 7.1 million tuning into his Tulsa Health and Freedom Conference. And if CNN were to lose their exclusive contracts to be shown in airports and hotel chains, that would eliminate a substantial chunk of their already-dismal viewership. But this fake news mainstream media still has its clutches in, and control over, a huge portion of our population, the result of just five globalista companies controlling 95 percent of what people hear in a day, propaganda programming of the public through continual spewing of false narratives. In doing so, they are in violation of Section 2384 and 2385 of the US Code, which prohibits aiding and abetting the overthrow of our government, as they have by knowingly reporting false information throughout President Trump's four years, as well as during and since this past treasonous election. The corrupt, complicit media people will also be running for the hills, but the whole process is like turning a massive barge on the ocean: it takes a long time to completely reverse direction.

And maybe the worst of the bunch is Fox News Network because they pretend to be honest and conservative journalists, while their real agenda is to reel in patriots by hanging out limited meat (truth). But their "limited hangout" of what is truly happening never discloses enough to even begin uncovering the foul plans of our cabal captors like themselves, who act as saboteurs while pretending to be part of the patriot movement, ultimately leading good people down the same path as the Democrats—toward a satanic, one-world government. Just look at what they did on election night to spoil the vote for Trump. And how about Chris Wallace, FNN's long-time Sunday political-show anchor? His father was a huge deep state asset—like father, like son? It certainly appears so. Much of Fox's obfuscating the truth used to be through RINOs (Republican In Name Only) doing all the dirty work, but now they are even pretending that "fair and balanced" means feeding us lies from many far-left Democrats.

People are waking up and moving away from the toxic networks to new platforms that tell the truth no matter whom or what it falls on or affects. The new media is being formed, and much credit goes to General Flynn for putting out marching orders to those he calls the digital warriors or soldiers. That's what I am involved with right now, but how do we make the full transition of society? The process will not happen overnight, but the switchover to honest information is progressing as sure as the sun rises each day with more and more honest social media platforms coming online. I believe Facebook and Twitter—along with Google, which owns YouTube—are facing future consequences for their censorship and meddling in the US elections, both serious crimes. Clay Clark's recent patriot conference in Tulsa had all kinds of new independent media that were there to get out the truth, but no fake news networks.

General Flynn spoke at that event but also talked privately to all of us representing the new independent media. His message was one of unity. He acknowledged that it is a business that involves us paying our bills and thanked us for being brave to do patriot work as we take on censorship from the big tech machine, but then challenged us to unite, support each another, and share resources. Today, that's what we're doing. Maybe not all of us. But I am. As is Ann Vandersteel, Scott McKay, Robert David Steele (rest in peace), Charlie Ward, Simon Parkes, and many others. "Where we go one, we go all" is not just a slogan as we can see by these generous patriots with the independent media, who are not only honest but also constantly willing to help other trustworthy outlets. The whole process of moving away from fake news is unfolding nicely.

2

Patrick Byrne: An Unlikely Insider's View of the Stolen 2020 Election and Intriguing History about How America Came to This

As an American businessman, Patrick Byrne was tutored in life by his friend's father—billionaire Warren Buffett. Byrne earned his bachelor's degree from Dartmouth College, master's from Cambridge University, and doctorate from Stanford University. In 1999, he launched Overstock.com, the nation's first major online-shopping platform, and was CEO for twenty years. He is also known as the godfather of blockchain technologies.

In February of 2021, Patrick became the best-selling author of *The Deep Rig: How Election Fraud Cost Donald J. Trump the White House, By A Man Who Did Not Vote for Him*. As creator of America Project (AmericaProject.com), which he founded to advance freedom and preserve the American way of life, today he selflessly represents patriots across this nation and helped fund the election audit in Maricopa County (Phoenix), Arizona.

The following is from information Patrick Byrne presented in April 2021 at Clay Clark's (ThriveTimeShow.com and TimeToFreeAmerica.com) Health and Freedom Conference in Oklahoma, and during an interview with me on American Media Periscope (<u>AmericanMediaPeriscope.
net</u>). For readability and flow, this version is paraphrased, while also retaining the original meaning. In this chapter, Patrick shares pivotal government history lessons, the simple strategy used in voter fraud, the line in the sand that must not be relinquished, and a peek at one week before Christmas 2020 in Trump's White House Oval Office, where friends of the president gathered that night to speak with him about all the evidence of election fraud (see Juan O Savin's chapter with his explanation of this December 18th meeting but from Trump's likely point of view). Here is Patrick:

Many who've heard of me don't know that I had cancer three times during my twenties, and as an invalid I used that convalescent time to earn a PhD in philosophy. During those studies I took a strong interest in the intellectual history of the US Constitution, so I'd like to mention some of that information about our republic, a sort of mini-political and philosophical lesson that I feel is important for these times.

Our tradition starts in Ancient Greece, where Greeks noticed that people of the East like Persians (modern-day Iran) had a different out-look. The Easterners understood themselves to be objects or agents of a ruler. In fact, all those outside Greece were unaccustomed to think-ing of themselves as deserving freedom or being citizens, so where did the western world get those traditions? Well, it was Greece, but the East also came to learn kings were subject to God, which ties back to the Bible's Daniel 5:25–28 where there is a wonderful mo-ment when Daniel interprets this judgment message that God wrote on the wall next to King Belshazzar of Babylon (today's Iraq), in the middle of his banquet:

"MENE, MENE, TEKEL, PARSIN"

Mene: *"God has numbered the days of your reign and brought it to an end."*

Tekel: *"You have been weighed on the scales and found wanting."*

Parsin: *"Your kingdom is divided and given to the Medes and Persians."*

That king lost his kingdom that night, and it is an important moment in history because political power (rulership) had always combined with divine authority in the public's mind—the king was also considered the sun god or some other deity. But that banquet was the first historical time I can find where right and wrong were demonstrated to exist outside political authority, meaning that even a king can be judged and found wanting. So, as far as the East, that tradition is the beginning of their new understanding that became the passion of the Western mind: a free people.

That same shared leadership was found in the Greeks, who started forming governments different from those based on chieftains, or other sorts of tribal systems. They were more inclusive in their rulership with at least every man getting a vote. They had no king. It was not perfect. But it was a start. Greece's Athenians had this idea that a just government can only derive its power through the citizens' consent.

When I was growing up, my friends and I thought we sounded fancy when pretending to be French with our accents and hand gestures. Well, the Romans spent five hundred years trying to act Greek, and any proper Roman family had a Greek professor (some might say "slave") to raise and teach their children. However, an important Greek teacher named Polybius identified that the greatness of their Roman *republic* was something different from Athenian *democracy*, which had all sorts of problems, including much corruption in the power structure. In fact, the period in history when Athenians were most successful is when they stopped voting for their legislators and started using a "sortition" process to select officials—exactly how we select juries today. This change provided the most stable time in Athens' history, so it was Athenians who discovered the main issue with democracy: It can quickly become mob rule like a ship without a ballast that unstably flips and flops from each new wave of the day's majority opinion.

The Roman Republic ended up defeating the Greeks, and Polybius explained that it was because the Romans had invented polycentricity, a government structure with many centers of decision-making in a separation of power. Instead of one absolute decision-maker as the final political authority, it is broken up so that decisions are split between the courts and a senate, or other separated areas of government. As a way to provide checks and balances, this idea breaks up power, pitting the pieces of government against each other—and it came from the Romans' greatly improved Greek system.

My main reason to mention this is because of the recent discussion about Biden and the Democrats looking to pack the Supreme Court, which means creating more seats so their president can appointment all the new judges and thereby gain the court's majority opinion. This ultimately eliminates the dissenting power of the previous court that might have disagreed with the current president.

As mentioned, during my bouts with cancer, I spent years researching every part of our Constitution, an instrument that breaks up power just as Rome's Polybius taught us. Unfortunately, our time has seen all kinds of rights built into our form of government that have been eroded away. Those in power today are trying to consolidate authority, instead of allowing our founding documents to work at keeping it separated into three areas. One of the most fundamental ways America avoids absolutist government is by breaking up its powers, a tradition that goes back two thousand years. But our present leaders are working diligently to defeat those checks and balances, hoping to pack the

Supreme Court with four more positions, expanding the judges from nine to thirteen, which would leave the US with a Democrat executive branch rubber-stamped by the judicial branch, and a legislative branch also controlled by the Democrat Party right now—all three Democrat dominated to give them whatever they'd like.

There were two other traditions from which we derived our government: One taught a lot involves the 1215 British Magna Carta, where English King John promised his barons church rights, no illegal imprisonment, access to swift justice, and limitations on feudal payments to the Crown. But the other amazing example is the Dutch, an important group not given sufficient credit. They were a bunch of Germanic people who did not want to live under anyone's rule, so they moved out to an unused swampy area of northwestern Europe, where they proceeded to create new farmland by draining the water. When they first got there, this society needed to work out a governing solution, so they went through a conscious decision-making process for farmers tasked with draining swamps to make land that they would use to grow stuff. Like any group starting out on a great task, they needed a single leader to organize the work, but not an overachieving demi-god figure; their concept of that person was a "first among many," just someone like a hired mayor to organize them, and not in any way a ruler they would bow to.

That Dutch influence on our founding does not get taught in our American school system because our and our kids' history books give all the credit to "the Pilgrims from England," who came to this land supposedly bringing their British free speech and religious toleration. However, England's policy of religious persecution was what those Brits were escaping when they went to Holland, where they spent twenty years developing this new governing system that they used to flourish before coming to America as Dutch pilgrims.

In fact, John Locke was a great philosopher who taught about our political science, one rightly described as English, and someone whose work our Founding Fathers all read. *Two Treatises of Government* is his amazing writing, but Locke left England during that country's 1688 Glorious Revolution because he was going to be hung! He went to Amsterdam, Holland, where he spent three years absorbing all the Dutch ideas of government, such as religious tolerance, free speech, and how it should be by and for the people. Locke learned that a society is better when they don't follow the example of England, making one person an absolute ruler. Instead, the Dutch would only surrender the little bit of rights that were needed to achieve government having only enough power to get certain needs of society accomplished. John Locke went back to England and wrote that book, but it was after studying Holland's system of government. Yet, somehow the Dutch are mostly left out of our education on the founding of US freedom traditions. Dutch intellectual history ended up becoming the foundation of our US Constitution.

In 1798, Thomas Jefferson wrote the *Kentucky Resolutions,* a book contending that free government is founded in jealousy (meaning mistrust) and not through confidence because skepticism causes us to bind down governments with constitutions. In other words, as James Madison pointed out, "If men were angels, we wouldn't need constitutions." So, a fundamental foundation of freedom must be a constitutional republic that binds government because man's normal nature is to make it grow, and grow, and grow. Do we see that today? Yes!

Our system, constitutional republicanism, is characterized by breaking up government as opposed to a direct democracy that is mob rule, where a country of three people would mean each person in a group of three is always at the mercy of the other two who could team up against the third at any moment. Likewise, 151 million could vote to take everything from the other 150 million. Instead, a constitutional republic separates powers so government can't get too big for its britches.

The fundamental deal early Americans made was that we would give up some rights and powers to have needed government, agreeing to live under the consent of the governed, but that handshake included us getting free, fair, and transparent elections. By now, probably few reading this believe we got that on November 3, 2020—someone welched on the deal and it was not an accidental! If we allow them to get away with elections that are not free, fair, and transparent, they have successfully dissolved the fundamental idea of America's government deriving its power from the consent of the governed—from us! Again, this whole tradition goes back 2,500 years to Athens, but our leaders have gradually taken away many of our rights during the past many decades, and now if they get away with an election that was so obviously crooked, we're headed toward a severely compromised freedom that none in US history has experienced.

In fact, here in America today, all our government institutions have failed us because everyone is corrupt—from the Department of "Justice" to the mass media, investigative journalists, the FBI, the rest of our intelligence community, the Office of the Inspector General, the Government Accountability Office, and every other institution you might think of. All those are in on the scam, so these people are pushing in all their chips. Today's *Washington Post, New York Times,* and other prominent, mainstream media follow no traditional standard of journalistic ethics, only pretending to give both sides. Though this past election was replete with fraud, the media's only blind, deaf, and dumb position has been that Trump is making false and baseless claims about the vote being rigged. They have slid all their chips on the table's center, throwing whatever bit of credibility they may still have into the pot, and it's going to be hilarious when the poker hands are finally shown.

Along with Mike Lindell, retired general Michael Flynn, Sidney Powell, and others, I've been deeply involved in efforts to unscramble this past election, and Lindell is not bluffing when he says we have computer-forensic-file proof—the truth that will come out in the weeks ahead. That is why these people who stole the vote are going to all the trouble they are right now to try snuffing out our foundational freedom traditions, the last vestiges of our constitutional society. We all know how much religious toleration has been eroded in recent decades, a direct frontal attack on our communities. And many reading this know personally about how our free speech has been eroded in recent decades. That's just two from a long list of recently compromised rights that Americans have much more fully enjoyed in the past, traditions that go back for centuries. And honest elections are the final right they need to remove from us permanently, the taking away of our ability to conduct free, fair, and transparent elections.

Knowing that, here is what happened with the rigged 2020 election that involved 3,006 counties in the United States, of which six are unique for having the state's population overwhelmingly concentrated in just one county: Clark County in Nevada has Las Vegas with two-thirds of the state's population, Maricopa County in Arizona contains Phoenix with a large percentage of their state's entire population, Milwaukee County is the most populated in Wisconsin, Wayne County in Michigan has Detroit, Philadelphia County has the most people of any county in Pennsylvania, and Fulton County in Georgia is home to Atlanta. Are those not the prominent *swing* states from this past election, where those counties paused voting, and then all came up with enough votes to make Biden president? Can you see why their unique population feature made them so important in stealing those state's elections? They are the anchor counties of six swing states, which means bad people need not steal 3,006 counties because it only takes a concentration of their cheating in those six, which was how they flipped all the crucial swing states, thus turning over the Electoral College, giving the election to Biden—while over 80 percent of US counties voted for Trump.

In the months leading up to the 2020 election, I became involved with a group of cyber-forensics experts who had been studying election fraud. They mentioned countries where certain election systems led to scandals like Serbia, Ghana, other African countries, and the Philippines. From their experience and before our elections, they warned that these nations' vote scandals were generally (but not always) associated with a window of time where vote counting would be paused, so that would be a strong indication of monkey business happening with our November 2020 vote in America—which is exactly what happened! Some places stopped the count for three hours and others took up to six, but whoever heard of that happening in America? You already knew or have probably guessed that the six places where the US vote was halted on election night were in those swing states, and specifically the counties in them that make up a high percentage of those states' populations: Las Vegas, Phoenix, Milwaukee, Detroit, Philadelphia, and Atlanta.

To me the fraudulent pattern leaps off the page, so it's funny to hear our media and others claim we have no evidence—at least that right there is some proof, and Socialists are behind it! Unfortunately though, our enemies have what's called "information dominance." They own the media so they can spin reality to this ridiculous point we're at now. The magnitude is hard to even comprehend, but their goal is to cover up any lie that is uncovered with another lie to cover that one, and in that way confuse as many Americans as possible, so no one can completely pin them down on the real truth, or their lies.

That's the bad news, but the counter to it (here in April 2021) is that more than half of American adults now believe the election of Joe Biden happened because of significant or very significant vote fraud, and if that's the number that actually admitted it to pollsters, the percentage is probably much higher! In fact, the number here in the spring of 2021 is somewhere between 51 percent and 64 percent, and probably closer to the latter.

And we have something else going for us that probably will take an-other history lesson to explain: During the US abolitionist movement leading up the 1860s American Civil War, there were two ways to be antislavery. Of course, neither was being a Democrat because they were the proud pro-slavery party—all for maintaining slavery and killing the Indians (Native Americans). Before 1954, when Abraham Lincoln became the first leader of a new Republican Party, the only alternate to the Dems was the Whig Party, and during this time those two ways people chose to be antislavery were either "contain and slow it until the peculiar institution eventually dies out" or "just abol-ish it right now!"

Well, the Whigs were the ones to adopt the more moderate approach to antislavery, thinking they could contain it until the practice would hopefully die out. In an attempt at finding middle ground on slave versus free states, the Whigs and Democrats signed the 1920 Missouri Compromise, with which our US Congress tried to equalize the num-ber of free and slave states that could join the union going forward, in part by outlawing slavery in the northern part of the Louisiana terri-tory, only above latitude 36°30′ north. That law ended in 1854 when Southern legislators would not allow creation of Kansas and Nebraska territories (both above latitude 36°30′ north) unless the ban on slav-ery there was removed. The Kansas-Nebraska Act of 1854 allowed for the expansion of slavery in those western territories, repealing the 1920 Missouri Compromise, and collapsing the Whig Party because they no longer possessed an intellectually honest way to continue working toward a soft approach at abolishing slavery. Their attempt to just contain slavery became impossible with this loss of the major mechanism to do so.

In 1953, before the Kansas-Nebraska Act passed in 1954, on the oth-er side of the country in New Hampshire, four fellows in opposition to that law gathered at a tavern in hopes of creating a new political party based on eliminating slavery. Founded by Amos Tuck, that effort became the Republican Party, and his good friend Abraham Lincoln later became their first candidate for US president. We know that the Lincoln-led Republicans went on to eliminate slavery with the Civil War, and then the Republicans were against the Democrats' Jim Crow laws of the late 1800s and early 1900s, legislation that mandated racial segregation, even up to 1965. In fact, Democrat president Woodrow Wilson (1913–1921) resegregated the US federal government that the Republicans had pushed to desegregate—and Wilson even brought back and bolstered the efforts of the racist, murderous Ku Klux Klan.

All along, true history shows that Democrats have been the constant oppressors, though Republicans have lost their way on occasion. I'm a lifelong small "l" libertarian, so I've never really associated myself with a party, and it's a good thing because Republican leadership today has fallen away from the honorable path, while the Republican Party remains our only vehicle able to fix this current mess. Starting a third party now makes no sense because the problem is mainly the leadership and infrastructure of the Republican Party, which stands right now as a terribly corrupt crowd, possibly only able to look down on a somewhat-worse Democrat Party.

Today, the greatest threat facing humanity is America getting snuffed out, the nation with a 2,500-year tradition riding on our shoulders. Will we survive and maybe even thrive in our continuation of individualism or be the last great power that falls to authoritarianism? The whole world is watching us after our opponents pulled a jujitsu move on us with this past election, but if we go down, the entire planet could see a long period of darkness. Keep in mind that the Roman civilization was the last time a just and world-dominating government fell. It led to a thousand years of darkness. The lefty elites, Chinese Communists, and tech giants all have the same vision for the planet: a small group of them who will make decisions for the masses, allowing those few to own and run everything, as they control every aspect in the lives of the many.

If the earth becomes ruled by a relatively tiny group of fascist elites because they ended up with America as their prize, the lights go out everywhere. I'll put a twist on part of President Lincoln's Gettysburg address from 1863 when he talked about how "government of the people, by the people, and for the people shall not perish from this earth": If we don't get the present threat to humanity corrected soon, our planet will see a thousand years under a government of the goons, by the goons, and for the goons.

A week before Christmas, on the night of December 18, 2020, I and few others met with President Trump in the Oval Office. He was a tired fellow, but I don't think he wanted to lose the election, and he didn't seem to fully realize how bad some of the people around him were—how they really were *not* fighting for him in the least. I would estimate that most of the White House staff just wanted the president to concede. Their goal was to have him accept the Biden transition and leave office—horrible advice, especially considering the stolen election! Here is a man putting everything he has into leading America the right way, while many around him keep reflexively chanting, "No, no, no, no; you can't do that, you can't do that, you can't do that." And when that prompting is not enough, they come up with reason, after reason, after reason why he must comply, though their recommendations were all terrible.

Sidney Powell, retired general Michael Flynn, I, and a few others were there to present an opposite side from Trump's own staff, who looked like idiots and were later revealed as such; they were just terrible, keeping important options and opportunities from him! That's when my heart really went out to Donald Trump because it had to be incredibly painful working through this terrible event, and then your own people pile on, selling you out in so many different ways. Again, I don't think Donald Trump wanted to lose. He wanted to fight. But he was frustrated. And defeated. The problem was all the negative behavior around him, leaving the man with no idea of who he could

25

trust. In fact, I'd say most of the White House senior leadership, especially under the general counsel, were bad.

Unfortunately, others in attendance that night had staff members who were equally bad. For instance, Trump's personal attorney Rudy Giuliani had a senior "brain trust" that was so unpleasant, difficult, and obstructionist, we considered the possibility they might actually be working for the opposition—that's how bad they were! Through the fall of 2020, I got exposure to all of those people, many I hope not to see again and some who detest President Trump. I'd say at least 40 percent of the trouble he faced was them. I saw it firsthand! We all saw it. It was unreal! At one point I even spoke up to tell folks in the room that the conversation that night had been the most surreal I had ever witnessed! Seeing goofball lawyers yelling at the president was astonishing! And as I describe in my book, General Flynn…well, I'll leave that for you to read in my book, *The Deep Rig: How Election Fraud Cost Donald J. Trump the White House, By a Man Who Did Not Vote for Him*.

As you see from that title, I did not vote for President Trump—in either of his elections—but I have since become a big admirer of this man who reminds me of the hedgehog in a parable by ancient Greek poet Archilochus, "The Fox and the Hedgehog: A Story of Triumphs and Tragedy". He writes, "The fox knows many things, but the hedgehog knows one big thing." As an example of that hedgehog, Trump's one big thing is his understanding of the many ways elites have sold out our country over the last thirty, forty, or possibly even eighty to ninety years. They bargained with China for this country and the bill came due, so they tried to pay it by presenting the Chinese Communist Party) with America, on a silver platter. But Trump did not let that happen, instead standing up for this country by dismantling the elites' deal. I would say that has been his most important work on behalf of all Americans, and the rest of the world.

But right now, the Democrats are doing all they can to completely change the US, working at efforts like admitting new states and packing the Supreme Court by adding more judges that would be chosen by Biden. Let's not kid ourselves, at most our nation has only a couple years to come out of this fight unscathed; otherwise, we will become the victims of a complete, socialist coup. And there is no way to establish a whole new political organization to stop it, so we must take over the Republican Party from the inside. We all need to get involved, and a few immediate ways would be to join with my AmericaProject. com, Sidney's DefendingTheRepublic.org, or Flynn's AmericasFuture. net groups. Each has its own focus, but we are all patriot driven. And we must keep waking up folks to join honest platforms like Mike Lindell's FrankSpeech.com while also getting off Facebook, Twitter, and Google, which want to help snuff out our traditions.

Another way you can and should help involves assistance with election integrity through the voting process, and by that I do not mean only taking the four hours of training to become an election observer; I'm talking about taking the full two days so you can actually work at a precinct, especially in swing states that were used to not only stealing the US presidency, but also congressional seats like the four they stole in Virginia, two in Nevada, and half a dozen in Texas. This has been going on for decades, though they really went for broke in 2020!

The US tradition of government could have only come from the Judeo-Christian philosophy of natural rights, and especially ideas out of the Protestant revolution. Governments of the world can be divided into two basic forms: One is a just and morally upright system that derives power from consent of its citizens, and the other is an authoritarian model that cares nothing for its people. As part of our transition steps between the two, recent generations of Americans have seen an erosion of so many rights that we all grew up with in the past thirty or forty years. And when we crossed the line to corrupt elections, honest government was completely given over to the successful authoritarians who have controlled our vote—at that point there is no more morally consenting citizenry.

During 1983 and '84, I lived in the kind of world these people are trying to create in America. When China was first opened up to receiving students from the West, I went there for studies, so I recognize many developments happening in our society today that ring a bell from my time studying Mao Zedong, or Chairman Mao. He started the People's Republic of China and ruled as head of their Chinese Communist Party (CCP) from 1949 until his death in 1976. That time gave me the background to see that a Maoist revolution is what we are presently facing here, a slow snuffing out of the conditions that have allowed Americans to live free. And I think the whole ball of wax that will decide whether they solidify authoritarianism over the US—or we defeat them and regain the freedom enjoyed by our ancestors—hinges on them possibly getting away with the massive 2020 election fraud. If so, it will continue, and they will be able to maintain vote corruption, grinding us toward something we've only read and seen in science fiction, up until now: the dystopian future of a society full of great suffering and injustice, brought about by the combined desires of the hard left, the CCP, and tech giants, all of which think they will escape the hardship by helping direct that oppressive society—but like us, most will end up either dead or slaves. But it won't happen! In fact, the possibility is not even close at this point because we have gathered all the proof and data needed to win this.

What we are now experiencing is an attempted fascist coup, and to properly explain that contention, I'll start with the socialism branch of the political spectrum, and 110 years ago in Italy where a man edited the Italian *Avanti* newspaper. He and his writing were extreme lefty, hardcore socialist. His ideas for organizing society differed from those of Russian revolutionary and Communist Vladimir Lenin, in that this Italian wanted something called "syndicalism," which is a labor movement that establishes local, worker-based organizations (like unions) to advance the rights and demands of laborers through strikes. This diehard Socialist briefly left his newspaper to fight in World War I and managed to retain his fundamental ideas for organizing a socialist society throughout the fighting, but after helping wage war for Italy, he added this prideful wrinkle:

> *"Only we who have been bloodied in battles should set the course of the nation in the future."*

Here's where most of us have been taught a bunch of fake history: That hardcore lefty, Italian Socialist was Benito Mussolini, the fascist-socialist leader of Italy from 1922 to 1943, which shows that fascism is just another type of socialism. Mussolini was loved by the left for being the proverbial dictator who made trains run on time. But since World War II, we all were taught a crazy history that claims fascism comes from the right, even though our conservative principles are derived from the American Constitution that favors the individual over the collective, and collectivism like socialism, communism, and fascism come from the left, through the ideas of people like Mussolini, the famous Italian Fascist-Socialist—just the sort of people now coming for us!

Though I don't mean to scare anyone, we should all know who is behind today's collectivist agenda, an enemy that includes the past fifteen years of Chinese-military literature referencing how their "shashouijan," or "assassin's mace," has been coming for the United States. Instead of fighting according to established rules of war, 2,500 years ago mace was something used by Chinese kingdoms that would send an assassin to sneak into the other king's bedroom and effectively sucker-punch him, an attempted one-hit knockout of the other side to take over without a fight. The Chinese war mentality dictates that the greatest way to win is without actually firing a shot or arrow. Much of America's national security literature of the past fifteen years has seen a discussion about what China's upcoming shashoujian for the United States might be, maybe some amazing new aircraft carrier, hard-to-defend hypersonic missiles, or an extremely effective, newly created anti-ship missile. We've wondered what it will be, but I think we're living through their assassin's mace right now, with part of it being this Chinese psychological operation involving COVID. Where did the China virus start, and who showed us endless videos of Chinese people walking along and then suddenly falling flat on their faces—supposedly instantly dead?

About the supposed Washington, DC, Capitol Hill insurrection on January 6, 2021, I want to relay a quick story told to me by a bartender during my travels through the Republic of Moldova, a country bordered on each side by Romania and Ukraine. Leading up to an election in 2009, the most popular candidate of the Moldovans was an anti-Russian guy. When he lost, the whole country knew that the vote had been rigged. The pro-Putin person was fraudulently put into office, which caused public protests at government buildings. Putin's response was to send disguised goons into the country by trains, busses, and even hitchhiking with backpacks, sleeping under bridges and trees. Once Putin had some of his saboteurs in place, whenever the public held another election protest or rally, the goons would infiltrate the group and attempt to incite and lead them into violence and breaching government buildings. These sorts of tactics by henchmen having gotten them labeled as "agent provocateurs," people who provoke certain actions by others.

For some reason, America is mostly unfamiliar with the concept, but much of the rest of the world has seen plenty of it. But why are these sorts of goons used? Well, like others who launch provocateur campaigns similar to those during many of the color (or colour) revolutions of the 21st century, Putin knew he needed to play for the backing of Moldova's middle class, and that large portion of the population would never support protests where people charge into government buildings, break things, and commit violence. He was attempting to discredit those rallying against the stolen election.

Fortunately, 2009 Moldovan society was smart enough to understand the tactic, so every goon that showed up to incite nefarious actions against the police or government buildings was quickly seized and turned over to the authorities by patriotic Moldovans. So, let that be a lesson for us relatively naive Americans. Whenever anyone tries moving you toward those kinds of harmful actions, be smart like the Moldovans and understand that's the surest way to lose.

I think the truth about what happened at our Capitol in early January of this year has yet to be seen, but one day before January 6th when Congress convened its joint session to count the electoral votes by state and confirm the results of the presidential election for Joe Biden, I and others presented election-fraud information to a number of senators and their staff. We gave them everything they needed to be able to ask the exact right questions in challenging the electoral vote of certain states. So, that is what we anticipated happening—senators would stand and dispute votes because they had all the intellectual ammunition they would need. But that January 6th breach of the Capitol, most likely by agent provocateurs, something that probably happened even before Trump finished his speech, changed the course of events and pointed our nation in an entirely different direction.

All that said, the goons won that day because good, patriotic Americans were not as seasoned in these sorts of infiltration tactics as the Moldovans, who could have easily spotted the instigators and grabbed those infiltrating provokers, letting them know we would be keeping the rally peaceful. That morning it looked like we were probably going to win the whole thing through challenged votes. In fact, there were almost a dozen US senators and their aides who were ready to use what we had been teaching them—to be prepared to stand and dispute the electoral votes from half a dozen states.

Unfortunately, after the "insurrection" of that day, none in our Senate had the stomach for challenging the vote, so everyone showed up the next day to rubber-stamp the process—it was over! Please remember that Moldovan lesson because we can't afford to make the same mistake again. I hope everybody reading this understands we lost because that happened; we would have won. Of course, some help from Vice President Pence would have been nice, but even though that didn't happen, we had prepared to get the job done until we lost that opportunity when our side ended up in the Capitol building. Who knows for sure what would have happened without the "insurrection" because the level at which our government has been sold out to traitors is somewhat unknown, but the right thing to do with all the patriot muscle we had that day at the Capitol would have been to grab the agitators, hold them in the grass, and just keep the peace. Someday we will learn what happened.

The main message to get across here is that you and I are not alone! They want us to think so. They want to divide. But we're together. They constantly strive to atomize each of us, making patriots think and work in separate units. But combined we are the majority, so get involved with like-minded groups such as my American Project and uncensored (free speech) social media platforms.

Remember, though, to keep a sharp eye out because, probably sooner than you think, someone is going to ask you to start taking part in public expressions of disbelief and discontent. They will push and prod you and your friends, stoking your outrage to violence so they have reason to throw patriots into FEMA (Federal Emergency Management Agency) camps, where they can take all kinds of other unconstitutional actions against us. Yes, we've been sucker-punched. But we're in this together. You are not alone! And already, we are working together, which is exactly what will get America back on track!

3

Graham Ledger: Calling Out the COVID Scam from Its Inception

Through decades of tireless research and expert broadcasting, Graham Ledger earned two Golden Microphone awards, two Emmy awards for newswriting, and spent many years as the national television host of *The Ledger Report* on One America News Network (OANN).

For more than thirty years, he has remained at the forefront of disseminating the latest crucial information needed by anyone seeking the truth. Fortunately for this country and everyone online, Graham recently agreed to join our family at American Media Periscope (AMP), where he will continue his honorable service to Americans as a rare, trustworthy news anchor, as well as AMP's vice president of operations.

To give you an idea of his reporting at the tip of God's patriot spear, the following are somewhat paraphrased (for consistency and flow in this book format) video transcripts and articles put out by Graham at the onset of the COVID-19 outbreak in the spring of 2020. Here is one man making sense in the midst of much nonsense:

Dr. Fauci's America

Compliments of Dr. Anthony Fauci, what is life in America like today? Well, thanks to Mr. Fauci, "Don't expect anything like normal anytime soon." US business enterprises like professional sports are attempting to do both the impossible and the contradictory: They are now working to maintain league operations, while simultaneously adhering to Fauci's guidelines.

Though the two goals are mutually exclusive, today's National Basketball Association is poised to try salvaging its season through the NBA commissioner's grand plan that brings all team personnel and players to the Disney basketball complex in Orlando, Florida. The NBA has come up with about one hundred pages of new rules for the Wuhan-coronavirus sports bubble they are creating, and they read more like a decree from Hitler's Germany or the "Big Brother" book, *1984*, by George Orwell, rather than any roadmap to pull off a somewhat normal basketball season.

For example, the players must socially distance when they're *off* the court, but what's the point if they are knocking shoulders, arms, legs, and heads *on* the court? Players must wear a mask when they're near one another *off* the court, but again, they are swapping sweat *on* the court, face-to-face, just inches apart as they play.

The NBA has been going on and on with their creation of new rules like league directives on levels of access to areas of facilities, and tiers of operations based on whether people are coaches, players, or support staff. League management requires that any violation of these mandated restrictions should be reported, just as any big brother would dictate. And those who might decide to leave this protective bubble where they must endlessly live and work—maybe venturing out for a burger, taco, or beer—will be subject to a ten-day quarantine. For ten days, they can't play.

That's the new, impossible NBA. Humans cannot operate that way. The restrictions will not work. Their hundred pages of COVID-19 requirements are impossible, contradictory, and lack the common sense of a human touch. The average age of an NBA player is twenty-six, so besides playing basketball, these young athletes need to live their lives. But they will not be allowed to. And for what? This age group is showing virtually no deaths from the Wuhan coronavirus, but thanks to our dear medical leader, Dr. Anthony Fauci, the NBA is stomping on the lives of these exceptional young men.

Surely, if Fauci had his way, Donald Trump would not only be forced to wear a mask 24/7, but the president of the United States would also be holed up in some basement, just like old, sloppy Joe Biden. I'm through with Anthony Fauci and tired of being careful. We can't live life in a bubble—right, John Travolta? The unenjoyable existence of an overly careful life is one not lived. We don't have to be reckless, but neither must we be excessively cautious.

The total global deaths from the Wuhan coronavirus were 450,000 over the first six months of record keeping. As our planet approaches 8 billion people, 500,000 is not a lot. In fact, back when the Black Death (bubonic plague) hit our planet in the middle of the fourteenth century, 75 to 200 million people died—at a time when the population of the entire world was only around 400 million. No matter what the true number of deaths was, those years saw a huge percentage of the global population wiped out. With the world back then at 400 million, compare the deaths of 75 to 200 million with today's 450,000 out of almost 8 billion.

The Power Trip of Illinois Governor Pritzker

What is Mr. Pritzker actually saying with this statement:

"Lifting all of our [COVID-precaution] mitigations at the end of May would likely lead to a second wave of outbreak…"

The truth is he will not curtail his economy-killing COVID restrictions because it would help President Trump's reelected efforts. Pritzker is concerned about allowing his state to attend Windy City sports like the Cubs, White Sox, and Chicago Bulls since Americans freely living their lives—at sporting events, working out in public gyms, eating at restaurants, or even going to their jobs—might help the economy recover, even quickly.

If governors like Pritzker, Cuomo (NY), and Newsom (CA) cave to opening their states, those economies and the US financial situation could recover in time for the election, which may cause people to be encouraged. Should the stock markets continue up to new records, allowing retirement accounts to keep growing, they may decide Donald Trump did the right thing six months prior to the election, and that he'll probably continue doing so; thus, Americans may be more likely to pull the election lever for Trump.

That is what you mean, Pritzker. You will not reopen Illinois until you have helped put the nails in the coffin of President Trump's chances for four more years. You don't care about your residents, defeating this virus, or stopping the spread—as if you even could. There is not a shred of evidence that anything you're doing has slowed COVID-19. Yet, you sit there telling Illinoisans to forget about summer because they are only going to get hot months of discontent, a grueling lockdown.

Pritzker is not confessing to any of this; instead, he just vaguely claims Illinois must continue restrictions until *maybe* June, but as that time rolls around, he'll likely let his state continue under lockdown through the next month—happy homebound Fourth of July; you are still locked down! Then he'll decide the state must extend it into August, "just in case." He will promise to start releasing the stranglehold by that time, but he also understands it will be too late for the economy by then. He knows it. You know it. I know it.

So, Pritzker is sitting fat, and what choice does that leave Land of Lincoln residents? You can give in and follow orders, leave the state, or defy the lockdown directives. Hey, take a look at your northern neighbors in Wisconsin. Their courts set them free. So, it's now up to you folks: In order to live free, it seems your only option is to defy.

Numbers That Don't Lie

California Governor Newsom is mostly punishing younger people by shutting down drinking establishments, but he allows restaurants serving alcohol. So, every California bar with a liquor license ought to also apply for a restaurant license and begin selling food. That way, they can bypass this nonsense. And the other aspect of Newsom hammering business owners is how hard those kinds of closures hit the state's economy, at a time when California already has a tax shortfall of $60 billion. The governor is shooting himself in the foot.

The other numbers this guy is upset about is that California hasn't flattened the virus curve. Remember March and April when Newsom railed about the urgent need to flatten the curve? Well, the curve is up. In fact, California claims its COVID cases are spiking, which backs up the warning I gave three months ago about lockdowns: When you lock people up, especially young ones, you're only delaying the inevitable case spread, and in California it is mostly among young people, his focus for punishment.

This is the natural process of a society gaining herd immunity from viruses. And these young people Newsom abuses—ages one to thirty–have almost a zero mortality rate from COVID. Many are running around asymptomatic, even contracting the virus, but developing no antibodies because their flourishing immune systems fight it off so quickly and effectively that antibodies don't even register in their blood work. Isn't that amazing?

37

Newsom continues targeting his own foot as he extends the lockdowns that strangle California's economy. He knows his large, struggling piece of US finances will harm the reelection chances of President Trump, so he's still pushing the closures, most likely through November, choking his state's commerce as much as possible in order to help doom Trump. Here is Governor Newsom:

> "It hasn't gone away. I know a lot of us thought, 'It's gonna get warm. Once it gets hot, it all goes away.'"

And Gavin even denies the increasing help from hotter weather, but my current reporting effort means examining the daily data, and as expected, those numbers show that warm-weather countries like El Salvador, the Philippines, Thailand, and Vietnam have been experiencing their higher temperatures and humidity as the reported death tolls are only in the *hundreds*. Look it up for yourself. Spring 2020 showed El Salvador in the hundreds, the Philippines just reached over a thousand, and the entire country of Vietnam claims zero.

Now, I don't know how accurate their accounting is in these countries, and they are certainly not doing the widespread testing we are, but the bottom line is that warming weather and rising humidity help beat back transmission of viruses. It curtails the spread, which is something Newsom will not admit. Here's that from him:

> "Look at what's happening in some of those states that are experiencing triple-digit weather, consistently, and are experiencing record numbers as well. We have to sober up to this reality. We're still in the first wave. We're not in a second wave. We're still in the first wave."

Yes, we are still in the first wave that Newsom barely slowed down—only to mightily unleash it when he opened up again. And he had to end the lockdown, though his desire was to keep the California economy shut down straight through November, just to hurt Trump's reelection chances.

Newsom was forced to open because tax revenues began dropping, and California already faced a $60 billion hole in the state budget that he has to make up at some point. So, you California residents are warned. Where do you think he's going to make up the shortfall? Newsom will place it on the backs of all you state residents, and he'll especially come hard after you "evil" landowners.

Americans in all states have a choice. You can keep listening to the mainstream media breathlessly misreport the spread of COVID-19, or do your homework like I do—day in and day out. The truth about the virus lies in the data. Corona is not a lethal threat to the vast majority of the American population.

No More Lockdowns

Here in March of 2020, more than ever why is it every American's fundamental duty to question authority? Because it is crucial that we the people hold temporarily elected politicians accountable for their response to the Wuhan coronavirus. This entire lockdown of our society and shutdown of the US economy is 100 percent government induced. The virus did not cause the market crash or toilet-paper shortage. With help from their mainstream-media accomplices, government caused society to cease functioning normally, which is nothing new from politicians.

But why would many millions of Americans go along with their governors suspending our constitutional rights? Why is this acceptable? Why suddenly trust the government and their operatives in the mainstream media with something monumentally life-changing like control over our liberty? Because people have been needlessly and purposely frightened by those same entities, resulting in governors from places like California, New York, Illinois, and Virginia being able to issue draconian, anti-constitutional edicts, without concern for legal or political backlash because they've so scared the citizenry. The government and media collaborate to create a panic, and then the politicians impose their heavy-handed, preplanned solutions—for our own good.

And they will not allow us to assemble for worship on Easter Sunday, the year's most important celebration for all denominations of Christianity. We are banned from practicing our religion in mass, while the majority of blue state residents are fine with that—annihilating the First Amendment—poof, gone! There go fundamental constitutional rights, unilaterally suspended by governors. Can you see how these actions are fitting from authoritarian leaders who wish to permanently walk away from this crisis having gained more centralized governmental power?

Their dictatorial recipe includes frightening the daylights out of people and then disingenuously making a public statement like "Oh look, people are scared. We better do something." And, boy, do they. Their solution is for you "nonessentials" to be fined or even tossed into prison for picking the wrong time to go out gazing at the night sky, or maybe you just forgot *your papers*.

Ladies and gentlemen, this is a problem I have been warning of for weeks, and no matter what they say, these people are not allowed to decree that you must place yourself under house arrest or face their consequences. America has this "crazy" Declaration of Independence with a core theme of liberty, freedom, and God-given rights. The government's cure is more dangerous than the Wuhan virus, so I say this to you people in California: It's time to revolt. Resist these unlawful edicts that attempt to negate the US Constitution. When enough of you deny the whims of these radical governors and mayors, you will have your rights back.

Don't get me wrong; this virus is serious. It should be taken that way, but we must also guard our constitutionally protected rights, including what used to be prominent in an American's DNA: our fundamental duty to question authority.

Repeated Failures on Wuhan Coronavirus Reporting

What unreported COVID-19 facts do we know here in April 2020? Since even before the draconian government response to the outbreak, I have been crunching the numbers, and, quite frankly, the data has never warranted shutting down of our government, our economy, our livelihoods, and much of the rest of our lives. It hasn't made sense from either a statistical or rational perspective. We've been reporting the fact that a vast majority of those contracting COVID recover, at least 98 percent. This means only 2 percent die and the rest are fine, with or without taking hydroxychloroquine. This is encouraging and should greatly reduce worry among Americans, but those numbers are not something widely known because the fearmongering mainstream media won't share that sort of reassuring information.

News organizations also ignore estimates showing that around 50 percent of the US may have already been exposed to the virus and recovered, meaning they have natural immunity, which leads toward societal herd immunity. This process happens rapidly across our highly social young people with strong immune systems, thus helping insulate the older and sickly from the pathogen. Again, why is this not being reported?

The media reports that the Wuhan coronavirus strikes the aged and infirm with lethal force, which is true, but to what degree? New York City disclosed that 70 percent of those who have died from COVID were over age sixty-five. But whether young or old, virtually all deaths involve people with underlying health conditions. Those are eye-popping, overwhelming statistics—and not being reported.

Only 8 percent to 10 percent of tests on symptomatic Americans are coming back positive for Wuhan coronavirus, which means 90 percent of those with flu-like symptoms have the flu. Now, think about those numbers in relation to the state-level, mainstream-media-fueled, panic-inducing government response to COVID-19. Is it commensurate with the numbers? The obvious facts are not being reported about the Wuhan coronavirus.

Clarity from an Early Analysis of the Data

The deaths from COVID-19 tell a story of survival: As we learn more about the virus, it's become clear that this bug is not very lethal. You who've been led astray by government and the mainstream media have been in self-imposed hiding since late February or early March, but you can come out now. It's safe. In fact, when the actual numbers are studied, it will be fairly obvious that these politicians needlessly tanked our once-robust economy, acting politically on impulse and raw emotion.

The National Vital Statistics System (NVSS), which is under the sprawling, bureaucratic umbrella of the Centers for Disease Control (CDC), keeps a daily death count on its website, something called the Provisional Death Counts for Coronavirus Disease. This is morbid data listing COVID deaths versus those caused by flu or pneumonia. The NVSS began tracking coronavirus deaths from the first week of February 2020.

I want to give you some curious data from the many columns, the first of which is the number dead from COVID-19 in the United States. The column to its right has the total dead from all causes, next are those who died of pneumonia, and then flu deaths. So, for the three-month reporting period (February through April 2020), these columns show US deaths from COVID, all causes, pneumonia, and then flu.

The second column reports 740,000 total US deaths, including those from COVID, murder, car crashes, lightning, or whatever. Americans killed by the Wuhan coronavirus were 38,500, which is about half what the mainstream media has been claiming. Residing in a final column—that I have not mentioned yet—we will find the explanation for their doubling of that number. But before I mention that fifth column, know that the number dead from pneumonia was 66,000, and a curiously low stat are the 5,800 who died of the flu because the 2019–2020 flu season was looking fairly severe through January 2020, at the outbreak of COVID.

In fact, before February 2020 rolled around, about forty thousand Americans had already died during the influenza (flu) season. Then, supposedly at COVID's outbreak in February 2020, the reported number of flu deaths plummeted. Now, what about that fifth column? Well, it claims seventeen thousand died from a combination of pneumonia and COVID. Here is the entire list, so you can better visualize the data:

<u>2020 US Deaths from February through April (except the 40,000 prior to February)</u>

38,500	Wuhan coronavirus
740,000	All causes
66,000	Pneumonia
40,000	Flu during the same flu season, but *prior to February*
5,800	Flu for the entire three months from *February through April*

What can we conclude from the CDC data? First, it answers my question from two months ago: How many said to be dying from COVID would have also succumbed to the seasonal flu? Well, American flu deaths were at a clip of about *7,500 per month*—that is, until the government began tracking COVID-19; suddenly at the height of the flu season, for the entire month of February 2020, flu deaths supposedly plunged to *only 1,500*. Those new thousands in February who "died from COVID" would have also—or did—die from the flu.

We can also conclude that pneumonia is a much more lethal threat than the Wuhan coronavirus. And as mentioned, deaths by COVID alone are fewer than forty thousand. On top of that, the forty thousand is an inflated number because of the liberal diagnoses of the cause of death being from COVID-19, an overcount compliments of the CDC.

And here is something else to take away from the data: Thirty-eight thousand are said to be dead from COVID. If we divide that by 330 million Americans, it tells us that your and my odds of dying from it are .0001 percent, same as the flu. So, despite the fatalistic rhetoric surrounding this virus, the actual numbers dying from COVID-19 tell a story of survival.

COVID, Lockdowns, and Liberty

I would rather be a free person dying of coronavirus than live like a government slave engulfed in fear and panic. I guarantee that radical, anti-constitutional politicians like Bernie Sanders (Socialist Democrat), Gavin Newsom, and Bill de Blasio (NYC mayor) are loving this Wuhan coronavirus lockdown—shutdown—shakedown. These sorts of moments in time are when leftists shine. Through this entire episode of house arrest—whether warranted or not—what will be the net result? Is it leading toward *more* freedom? Not likely. Without a doubt, it is going to mean less liberty. This massive, government-mandated, stay-at-home order and the resulting economic downturn are the perfect opportunity for more government control.

If you don't believe me, just listen to the Marxist governor of California. Each day, Gavin Newsom gets on camera and scares the living daylights out of millions of Californians. This guy methodically goes through the Wuhan coronavirus death numbers as if they are some kind of gruesome lottery that everyone is playing but no one wants to win. It is sick, tortured, and demented. After that, he chastises people who are not following his explicit orders, those who are so criminal they would walk on the beach in defiance of this man's directives.

Newsom never speaks about the Bill of Rights with its First Amendment that guarantees the birthright of Americans to gather on a beach. Instead, he makes threatening decrees from a dictatorial attitude of "let them eat cake" and "long live big brother." The California governor informs his audience that he will allow a limited number of people to spend a minimal amount of time outside—but only for food. And after his put-upon population is granted the right to forage for nonexistent toilet paper through empty shelves, they better immediately return to "house arrest," or they'll face his penalty. Hey, what a benevolent guy to allow folks food and even let them step outside. Gee, thank you, Mr. Newsom; you are as wise as you are kind.

So, as Stockholm syndrome takes hold of the inhabitants of our nation's most populous state, we can bet the framers of our Constitution would have harsh words for Californians, something like:

> "What the hell are you people doing!? Have you lost your minds? Why would you allow a temporary politician to suspend your God-given constitutional rights, which will most likely result in forever losing many of your freedoms—as well as those of future generations."

All this is extremely disturbing, not as much about the virus but more the government and mainstream media response to it, which is why I would rather be a free person dying of coronavirus than live like a government slave engulfed in fear and panic.

Collapsing the Economy to Destroy a Reelection

In all of American history, our time has just seen the greatest political conspiracy to defeat a sitting president, while also destroying our God-given liberty. Orchestrated by blue state governors and mayors who are working with fellow radicals at the federal level in Washington, DC, through use of the Wuhan coronavirus, this cabal has launched a political nuclear bomb. Their attempts at impeaching President Trump did not resonate with the American people.

Not nearly enough of us paid attention when Adam Schiff, Democrat US representative from California and chair of the House Intelligence Committee, weaponized that body in his attack on Trump, abusing the US Constitution for political gain. And most Americans were tuned out when Jerry Nadler, Democrat US representative from New York and chair of the House Judiciary Committee, made his presentation on the Senate floor, misleading the public by claiming President Trump had committed an impeachable offense.

So, guaranteeing that they would finally get our attention, their plan B was to convince us that a bug was coming to kill us; the Wuhan coronavirus would sweep through neighborhoods like the black plague. That worked. Suddenly folks paid attention, and seizing the moment have been blue state governors like Cuomo, Newsom, Pritzker, Wolf (PA), Whitmer (MI), Northam (VA), Murphy (NJ), Cooper (NC), and Inslee (WA). These people did with the virus what Nancy Pelosi (Democrat US House Speaker) and Chuck Schumer (Democrat US Senate leader) could not do to the United States Constitution. They manipulated reality for the purpose of harming President Trump and in doing so trashed a once-vibrant economy. The virus was their excuse to hammer their states' economies, transforming America's lowest unemployment rate in history into the type of job losses we last saw during the Depression.

In a partisan scheme to defeat President Trump, blue state governors know their combined forces control about a third of the US gross domestic product, with California and New York serving as ideological and political bookends. Does that sound fantastic? Is it too far-fetched to think politicians would purposely trigger a recession or depression—negatively affecting millions of American lives—just for political gain? Doesn't that seem outlandish and even impossible in freedom-loving America?

Well, it's not. There is no coincidence in Newsom sounding like Pritzker, who says the same things as Northam, who mirrors the statements from Cuomo. They are all working together, using the same playbook to scare the tar out of people until average Americans hand over more of their constitutional rights. These governors demand President Trump supply everything from personal protective equipment (PPEs) and ventilators to a federal bailout of their state economies. But no matter his response, when people die, those same state leaders blame Trump and make it stick by enlisting lies from their coconspirators in the mainstream media. These phony blue state governors never take responsibility for any of their own mismanagement of the COVID-19 response; instead, their consistent game is to hit Trump with the blame, pushing their political scheme as far and as long as possible. They have too much invested, they have too many Americans capitulating, and they have tasted too much power to simply relinquish it.

With even a glance at the true numbers and facts surrounding the Wuhan coronavirus, their entire partisan, state-level response screams "unwarranted." Yet, these radical governors keep moving the goal posts. Whenever their claimed criteria for reopening are met, they simply set new requirements. For example, California's Newsom vowed to relinquish his stranglehold on the state when hospitals were cleared from the coming surge of COVID patients. But when the surge never came, he changed to requiring the impossible: Newsom demanded two weeks completely free of COVID deaths—in the most populous US state—before any of the fifty-eight counties could re-open for business, even on a limited basis.

Again echoing the larger plan, similar requirements came from governors in blue states like Illinois, New York, and New Jersey. But of course they did so because these fellow conspirators in blue state seats of power are working together, collaborating for the gain of their club members, rather than any desire to protect the public by stopping the spread of the Wuhan coronavirus. Their one focus is to alter the course of political history, crashing the economy and keeping it that way through summer, all with the single goal of harming President Trump's reelection efforts. Again, this has been blue state governors helping to perpetuate the greatest political conspiracy in US history to defeat a sitting president, while also destroying many of our American freedoms.

Live Your Life

The irrational politically motivated response to China's Wuhan coronavirus—here in March 2020–smells wrong; the numbers don't add up. Massive, coast-to-coast, corona craziness simply does not align with the empirical data. Right now, Americans have a one in 55,000 chance of even contracting the virus, let alone the *1 in 3 million* possibility of dying from it. Those are excellent odds. In fact, in some states you are more likely to win the lottery. So go buy a ticket. Better yet, go ahead and live your life.

The numbers don't make sense. During the 2018–2019 influenza season, the average American had a one in five thousand chance of dying from the flu. In 2009, even though the swine flu—also called H1N1, or what Joe Biden calls N1H1—numbers were not widely publicized, there was a one in twenty-seven thousand chance it would kill a US citizen. That is exponentially less than one in 3 million, yet Americans saw no irrational panic instigated by politicians and their media, no shuttered cities, no stock market crash, and no government stimulus.

So, something is not right with the response. Even China's Wuhan residents have only a one in 500,000 chance of death. Again, media-induced hysteria here in America does not add up. We US citizens are more likely to die from heart disease or cancer than COVID. In fact, even dying of heatstroke is a one in 8,000 chance. And weighing oranges to oranges, using the age-old chance of being struck by lightning, you have a one in 200,000 chance of that putting you in the ground pushing up daisies, while you have a relatively tiny one in 3 million chance of the same from COVID.

Knowing all that, do any of these monumentally extreme restrictions against liberty make sense in a rational way? Is the reaction from our stock market, blue state governors, or the mainstream media commensurate with this Chinese contagion? No. So why the apoplectic, disproportionate response? There's simply no other explanation than political gain.

Moral Responsibility

Through his constitutionally based axiom that has long helped lead our American republic's move away from laws and leaders that inhibit liberty, freedom, equal protection, and God-given rights, Martin Luther King Jr. urged us to exercise our moral responsibility to defy unjust, unfair, and unconstitutional edicts from government. Risking his life, MLK defied radical politicians, standing his ground against prejudicial decrees that trampled on the constitutional rights of American citizens.

If he were alive today, what would he say about 2020 Americans being forced to abandon our First Amendment rights? How would King react to us being denied the right to assemble? Would he act like today's spineless Catholic priests and bishops, simply ignoring our right to practice religion? I don't think so. How would he feel about our religious leaders of many stripes capitulating to dictatorial edicts from men and women with the temporary title of state governor?

MLK would be publicly speaking against this loss of liberty, and even acting out through civil disobedience in open defiance of these unconstitutional decrees. Look at the nut-case health officer in Los Angeles who just delivered a bombshell for the city's residents, letting them know to expect the continued suspension of constitutional rights until *at least* July. Imagine the next Independence Day when we will celebrate that deadly break from England's authoritarian rule and freedom for millions of Americans: In our nation's second largest city, Los Angeles, US citizens will be stuck in their homes under *house arrest*. Happy Fourth of July! Your liberty is now dependent on some health bureaucrat, an out-of-control mayor named Garcetti, and California Governor Gavin.

During this year's July 4th celebrations in the City of Angels, 244 years after our founders spilled their blood to form this union with its constitutionally guaranteed freedom under God, ten million LA Americans will not be allowed to exercise their First Amendment rights, losing their due process and equal protection. This is a full-blown, five-alarm, constitutional nightmare. Where is the hope? Where's our resistance? We must resist. But there is already hope residing deep in every patriotic American who understands the constitutional picture. Thinking people who get what Martin Luther King bravely executed over fifty years ago must replicate his efforts—right here and right now.

And you will not be alone—one patriotic American we all know, a blonde guy from New York City, has been politically overwhelmed by a bunch of blue state, partisan, hack governors who are slow-walking any form of reopening their states. Why? Because of a virus? Please. No. As the outbreak panic got rolling in early March 2020, some of you doubters pushed back against my blasting this entire virus episode, but now even you folks know the truth of this sham. The entire US government response to the Wuhan coronavirus has not been about health; it's meant for defeating the probable November reelection of our New Yorker president. If these governors succeed in keeping their states' businesses closed through the summer, I really hate to say this, but they will succeed in beating President Trump.

So, what does he have to lose? Donald Trump should immediately and radically enforce the Commerce Clause of the US Constitution, the one that state governors like Cuomo, Newsom, Pritzker, Northam, and company are in violation of. Trump must issue them cease-and-desist orders, demanding they allow their residents to get back to pursuing all the life, liberty, and happiness they are due as Americans—we must reopen. And if they do not comply, the US Department of Justice needs to issue arrest warrants for these governors, while federalizing local sheriffs and sending in the National Guard. If that sounds outrageous, would you use the same description for this denial of liberties to more than a third of the US population?

That leads me to an appeal for all patriotic, informed, thinking Americans. We must act right now—with or without President Trump's enforcement of the Commerce Clause. Los Angeles, Pittsburgh, and Buffalo, it is time! Virginia Beach and Rockford, it is time. Lansing, it is time. Now is the moment this country needs resistance and defiance. Open up California. Open up Pennsylvania. Open up Illinois. Our forefathers risked it all for us. Now it's our moment to risk everything for future Americans.

Just as Martin Luther King challenged our parents and grandparents, today you and I have a moral responsibility to defy unjust, unfair, and unconstitutional edicts from government.

4

James Grundvig: Scenario A—America Restored (1871 to 2021)

With over 140,000 views on the American Media Periscope website, the following is an updated version of a January 2021 article by the "Great Grundvig," a nickname given him by AMP viewers.

At 12 noon on January 20, 2021, it was checkmate.

The United States of America Service Corporation (USA Inc.)—owned by the British Crown—ceased to exist. Number 45, President Donald J. Trump, was the last president of USA Inc. As part of this likely scenario, Joe Biden is of no consequence—since the US military will neither recognize the election theft nor the service corporation that Biden was sworn into. Biden is not president.

How did we arrive at this moment in history?

Up Periscope.

After the Civil War, the US was in deep debt, having borrowed money from England to finance the war's supplies, food, factories, machinery, munitions, etc. Seeing an opportunity to put Americans on a 150-year path toward enslavement, the global cabal—modern "money changers" operating out of Venice, Italy (the same type that Jesus Christ warned about)—used their agents to assassinate a powerful man who would have opposed the deal: Abraham Lincoln, our sixteenth president. With Honest Abe eliminated, Vice President Andrew Johnson took over for a few years as our seventeenth president, and then the eighteenth came along to occupy the White House in 1869: President Ulysses S. Grant.

During Grant's term, on February 21, 1871, the forty-first Congress convened—and made a deal with the devil. How would those politicians pay back all that debt owed to Great Britain, Ireland, and other financing entities? Congress enacted the following:

"The territory of Washington, DC, created into a government by the name of the District of Columbia, which by name it is hereby constituted a body corporate for municipal purposes..."

In essence, Washington, DC, became a wholly owned "port" city under the authority of the British Crown. That allowed for the subversion of common-law rights and installation of the Venice, Vatican, and British Crown "admiralty laws" of the seas, which—in perpetuity—put America in *service* bondage.

With the Republic of the United States of America replaced by USA Inc., new laws were enacted, such as taxation, creation of the IRS, phantom property rights, and the straw man that is bonded birth certificates (our full names written on those documents in capital letters). Again, that was the forty-second Congress in 1871. Fittingly, forty-one years later, the US Congress sitting in 1913 enacted the Federal Reserve Act that allowed a private banking cartel to create a new form of American money—out of thin air—and it included a fractional reserve system that would further enslave America with massive debt obligations. By the 1930s, the Rockefeller dynasty had taken over US academia and medical institutions, using the latter to establish their Big Pharma cartel that converted millennia-old, nutrition-based medical education into schools that produced doctors focused on pharmaceutical sales.

After two world wars that the banking cabal dragged America into—the first by sinking the Lusitania in 1915 and the second with the 1941 attack on Pearl Harbor—any challenges to the admiralty laws and the central-bank, money-printing system were met with ferocious attacks.

Here is a short list of events surrounding those challenges:

- The 1963 assassination of President John F. Kennedy because he challenged the CIA and the banking cabal with his plan for a new monetary system

- President Richard Nixon ending the dollar's convertibility to gold in 1971, which was one hundred years after establishment of USA Inc. in 1871

- Keeping President Ronald Reagan in line by threatening his life with a 1981 assassination attempt

- Orchestrating the 2001 World Trade Center attacks (9/11) to prevent GESARA/NESARA from being rolled out, a planned replacement of the private banking cartel's Federal Reserve notes

What has been the good guys' latest and greatest challenge for the cabal? As a way to rescue the Republic of America after President Kennedy's assassination, a half-century plan has been carried forward by two hundred honorable American generals, "white hats" in the US military, some of which recruited billionaire businessman Donald Trump to become our cabal-crushing president.

On Christmas Eve of 2016, US military Special Forces removed the cabal's thirteen black (has nothing to do with skin color) families, and they did so during satanic rituals being held by those people under their palaces in Venice. You will notice that the operation occurred during the presidency of Barrack Hussein Obama.

From there, President Trump and his military-planner generals launched their plan's final phase that involves cleaning out corrupt US agencies and removing the banking cartel's Federal Reserve system. By the way, the latter pays the pensions of our federal judges and attorneys. The final phase also aims at breaking the yoke of the British admiralty law system—imposed upon us long ago—including their American Bar Association that sets curriculum in US law schools.

Change is coming, and it is going to be seismic!

Direct Hit:

Again, in Washington, DC, at noon on January, 20, 2021, the US Service Corporation died on the vine. It automatically devolved. Joe Biden was not legally inaugurated. He was not sworn into a living entity. Thus, he has not become the president of the United States.

Instead, Scenario A:

The US military has taken control, including both houses of Congress, which provides for a "continuity of government" whenever replacements become necessary. They will be sworn in temporarily to replace any senators and representatives who might be removed. From there, the military will run a cleanup operation against the remnants and proxies of the cabal, and then either inaugurate President Donald J Trump for a second term—as only the *nineteenth* president of the newly restored Republic of the United States—or call for new elections to be controlled and monitored by the military.

A new dawn for the Republic of the United States actually began at noon, January 20, 2021. Welcome to the new America, same as the old America!

5

Sean Morgan: Trump, Devolution, and the Vax

What if President Trump knew the deep state's plans? What if he knew they would steal the election? What if he knew they meant to release a biological attack that the cabal would use as an excuse for medical tyranny? Is Trump honorable? If those suppositions are true, what would he do?

I assume he is a trustworthy leader in our struggle against the cabal, based on him consistently advocating for the American people, our military, and the rule of law; his promises in the 2015 campaign that were followed by four years of policies and actions that backed up his words; his record of calling out and punishing evildoers like Jeffery Epstein, other child traffickers, the lying media, corrupt politicians, and ill-intentioned countries around the world; and his continued support for freedom since leaving office.

That said, you too must perform the due diligence to determine if Trump has integrity. I would suggest you look into his executive orders. Also keep in mind that, before Trump was president, he was a volunteer informant against organized crime (the Mafia) and the deep state's international pedophile-ringleader, Jeffrey Epstein.

Besides the question of President Trump's character and intentions, how about his competence? Is he an effective strategist? The mainstream news would tell you otherwise, but I suggest we again look at his extensive track record of success.

So, working from the premise that Trump is an honorable and competent man, what would he do upon learning that malevolent actors were planning to attack our people biologically and steal the US election? Understanding the kind of man he has shown himself to be, and knowing that the American presidency afforded him vast capabilities, we can assume he would have done all he could to prevent as much harm as possible from the upcoming election fraud and medical tyranny.

Further backing up this scenario, and even on top of the entire Q operation and Q team (who have told us much of the above), Patel Patriot (Devolution.link) has independently confirmed the same through his substantial use of open-source information that also proves how Trump knew the deep state's plans to steal the election. You can find all Patel's work at Devolution.link. It is not hard to learn these facts, even with a brief look at his extensive research.

While running for reelection in 2020, countless times President Trump publicly warned that massive vote fraud was coming. Besides that, his executive orders addressing stolen elections and his creation of organizations to secure elections—like Space Force—show how a compromised 2020 vote was at the forefront of Trump's mind.

And as far as President Trump knowing about the deep state's plans to release a virus, after which they would subject innocent people around the world to medical tyranny and base it on vaccines, we don't need that assurance from some source close to Trump. We know he knew because of openly available information, such as his executive orders and legislation, as well as by examining those he hired and fired, the key players he either removed or put into significant roles.

Here at the beginning of 2022, what does all that mean for American? Well, if Trump knew the deep state would do these things, and he also understood that a sleeping, media-indoctrinated US citizenry would not go along with him outwardly taking down the country's deep state controllers—without a civil war that our enemies like China could exploit (using that time to attempt a takeover of the US)—what countermove would the president of the United State have left to utilize?

The answer is one word: *Devolution*

Trump's plan was to allow the election to be stolen, something the cabal didn't expect, which is why they made DC a militarized zone. The cabal was ready to go kinetic, primed for physical warfare to defend its election coup. But why would Trump allow America and the Americans he loves to lose a world leader like him who is on their side? Well, without the theft of the presidency, US citizens who have unknowingly spent decades under that control of the deep state would never wake up enough to understand what has been happening to them. And in their continued ignorance of the cabal's activities, duped Americans would not allow Trump's fix to the putrid election system, which has been rigged to steal their voices through vote corruption like vulnerable machines, dirty voter rolls, and lack of identity verification.

Devolution is a process of decentralizing US power, while ensuring "continuity of government."

Through Patel Patriot's *Devolution* blog series and the many Friday-afternoon interviews I have done with him on American Media Periscope, Patel has laid out the key players to whom Trump devolved his presidential-cabinet powers. Patel's site also lists the key combatant commanders who were tasked with retaining military power for the white hats—despite the swearing in of an illegitimate US commander in chief and secretary of defense in early 2021. There is a reason why the twelve people in charge of our nuclear weapons have not been making noise about the fraudulent Biden presidency. Those military men were and are key to Trump's plan carried out to devolve power away from him—before he left office.

But how about those jabs? Why would Trump allow the deep state (with its corrupt FDA and soulless Big Pharma) to roll out harmful vaccines? Well, we must consider the alternative. Like the usual maneuvering of high-fatality warfare, Trump faced not being able to stop the China-virus biological attack. He could not even go against the pharmaceutical companies because they and their cabal media would have effectively labeled him an "anti-vaxxer." Disparaging vaccines, as he had many times before becoming president, would have brought on a 24/7 media blitz with disingenuous cabal reporters ranting on and on about how "deranged" and "dangerous" Trump had become—not that they hadn't attempted that already for half a decade.

But this time they would have convinced the majority of vaccine-taking Americans—who have been allowing the vaxxing of their kids all through childhood—that Trump is a "deadly threat to the world." This would most likely end with our most valuable white hat player—Donald Trump—being forced off the field by his wrongly destroyed public opinion, removing him from office, and handing the most powerful position in the world back to the cabal. Then they would have kept our country locked down for years, stealing what was left of our freedom and prosperity. Our fall would have come through the ensuing economic warfare that would lead to their ideal "great reset," the ending of any remaining freedom around the world.

Instead, Trump introduced the Warp Speed vaccine-development program, forcing a rapid vaccine rollout that ended lockdowns years before the deep state had planned to let us have our outdoor lives back. This strategy saved us from the massive number of premature deaths that would have been caused by years of lockdown, something else potentially catastrophic to people around the entire planet. Warp Speed also forced Big Pharma into rolling out dangerous vaccines without proper studies and transparency, which removed their US-Congress-granted legal protection, leaving them vulnerable to being financially taken down.

As I am writing this, we are not yet at the "reveal stage" of the operation. At some point the American people need to know, beyond a shadow of a doubt, that the election was stolen and these COVID vaccines were designed to hurt us. Daily now, the polls move in our favor on those two points. However, after decades—even hundreds of years—living under deep state control, the numbers have yet to reach the required critical mass necessary to avoid civil war.

When public awareness is optimal, Trump and his team will reveal this plan and do so at a time that avoids honorable Americans fighting each other. Until then, you can review the unimpeachable—like Trump—evidence that proves this plan is truly in place. Prepare yourself for the coming upheaval and ultimate liberation; you can do so by reading the *Devolution* series at Patel's website, Devolution.link, and by watching the interviews I have conducted with him on AMP.

Please follow me at *Making Sense of the Madness* on American Media Periscope and at SeanMorganReport.com.

6

Lt. Scott Bennett: Notice of Unlawful Orders of Biden Administration and Treason

Lieutenant Scott Bennett is an American patriot, former US Army special operations officer and analyst of global, psychological warfare, counterterrorism. He is the author of *Shell Game: A Military Whistleblowing Report to Congress* and now hosts two weekly shows on American Media Periscope: *Shells Games* and *Great Awakenings*.

With over three hundred thousand views on AMP's website, the following is a somewhat paraphrased (for consistency and flow in this book format) version of Lt. Bennett's crucially important article from January 2021, something every freedom-protecting US citizen can use today to help in this battle against the deep state. Here is Lt. Scott Bennett:

Joe Biden is not the president of the United States of America, despite what we hear from the propaganda machine that includes the mainstream media, Democrats, fake Republicans, etc. Daily, these deceivers bully and brainwash Americans into believing he is. I know because I was in Washington, DC, not long ago, working with General Michael Flynn's team and others, examining the evidence and affidavits from technical experts who provided the proof of election fraud, treason, espionage, and cyberwarfare attacks.

Without disclosing too much or identifying people who might be put in danger, I can say with absolute authority that the materials provided by military personnel, cryptologists, attorneys, and analysts prove beyond any doubt that the US presidential election on November 3, 2020, was a corrupt fraud, high treason, and an act of war by China.

For several weeks, I sat with experts presenting amazing documents, videos, and other materials that had me enraged and nauseated. I interviewed technical geniuses who provided testimony and evidence clearly showing that Barak Obama, John McCain, Mitt Romney, John Brennan, and others committed high treason. For their crimes, those still alive should be prosecuted—and promptly executed.

As testimony to the severity of this damaging material presented to us, the CIA—and most likely, Mossad—hacked into our phones and computers, planted microphones, set up honey traps, and broke into our hotel rooms to search for our evidence. As a result, our location was changed every few days while also being surrounded by gun-carrying Navy SEALs, US marshals, and Special Forces soldiers.

Essentially, Joe Biden's presidential election resulted from these aspects of a multidimensional fraud:

1. The use of mail-in ballots was justified because of COVID-19, the Chinese virus.

2. The Chinese Communist Party (CCP) had purchased Dominion voting machines with software that manipulated the election numbers to their predetermined percentages for each candidate.

3. Fake ballots were transported into vote-counting polls to reflect the manipulated computer numbers.

4. Others contributing to the fraud were delusional Democrats, fake Republicans, and a hysterical mainstream media, most all obsessed with removing President Donald Trump by any means necessary.

5. The Supreme Court also seemed to play a passive-aggressive role by abandoning its constitutional duty to rule on controversies between the states—nothing is more controversial than evidence of a corrupted election where one candidate had been shown to be controlled and bribed by foreign nations.

The implications of this stolen election are that those nations and people supporting Joe Biden have since attempted to control, dominate, brainwash, imprison, or destroy anyone who supports Donald Trump, while also working to erase each of his presidency's official political actions. We see this already with Biden's executive orders to stop US border-wall construction, assist foreign people with an illegal border invasion of America and grant them citizenship to vote, subjugate the US to the Paris Climate Treaty, and morally destroy Americans through indoctrination of the population into a fascist, transgender-homosexual agenda. Any of these efforts could ignite civil war in America.

From overwhelming evidence, we can clearly see that Joe Biden's election was a fraud. As a result, he has no lawful power or legitimacy; therefore, no word, order, policy, or instruction from Joe Biden (or his representatives) have authority, power, or legitimacy. Being unlawful, no Biden administration directive should be accepted or obeyed in *any* way—to do so would be treason.

Knowing this, our strategy to counter false and dangerous Biden orders is as follows:

1. Use this document as a *notice of legal service* that, due to the overwhelming evidence of fraud and corruption, all orders, policies, and instructions from the Joe Biden administration are unlawful and unconstitutional.

2. Collect the legal filings and exhibits provided by attorneys Sidney Powell, Rudy Giuliani, Patrick Byrne, and Joseph Kline as evidence of this fraud and corruption.

3. Demand that it not only be acknowledged as factual and accurate by government agencies, as well as state and federal courts, but that this fraud mandates those bodies reject all Biden administration claims to US presidential authority.

4. Declare that every political and governmental person or agency (like mayors, town councils, supervisors, members of Congress, police, judges, etc.), who do not reject—as unlawful—all claims and orders from the Biden administration, are violating the US Constitution, have abdicated their authority, and are complicit in treason against the Constitution of the United States, as well as the constitutions of US states.

Send this notice by certified mail to all members of Congress, military leaders, state and local government officials, churches, and media. Truth is the best psychological operation and the natural antiseptic for lies. Rejection of tyrants and their orders is a duty all free people have to God and their fellow countrymen.

7

Maria Zack: Prominent Italians Helped Steal the 2020 US Election for Biden, and Average Brave Citizens from Italy Came Forward to Expose It!

Maria Zack is a business and political strategist, top global-governmental affairs expert, inventor, public speaker, and the entrepreneurial founder and CEO of numerous successful companies in many industries, including her current Quantum Solutions Software, which is working to develop integrated, project-management tools with social media applications. Maria is most proud of her 2017-founded Nations in Action (NationsInAction.org/Home), a nonprofit promoting transparency and accountability in governments, as well as advocating for the success of families. Nations in Action boasts many valuable efforts completed through their advocacy work and has recently been focused on exposing the greatest election theft in history, the fraudulent tabulation of November 2020 American vote.

The following is from a June 2021 interview of Maria Zack by Sean Morgan and me. For better readability and flow in a print format, this is a paraphrase that retains the original meanings. Here is Maria Zack:

I never suspected that the morning of November 4, 2020, would be America waking up to the nightmare we saw with Biden successfully stealing the election, but the shocking reality immediately caused our team at Nations in Action to spring into familiar operations. We were not new to election fraud, having already involved ourselves in helping uncover 2018 election fraud in Broward County, Florida, where officials actually held people's ballots while they voted, along with other crazy criminalities going on there. I am happy to report that Broward County Supervisor of Elections Brenda Snipes was removed by Florida Governor Ron DeSantis, and we were happy to be part of those supplying important information to help make that happen.

Because of that background, in mid- to late November 2020, we were contacted to see if we might be able to help with a situation that arose in Italy that involved Arturo D'Elia, <u>head</u> of the information technology (IT) department at Leonardo, a multinational Italian defense contractor (eighth largest in the world) specializing in aerospace, defense, general security, and cybersecurity. A seemly sincere and honest man, Arturo was in the room during the 2020 US election when Americans' votes were being flipped online by Italians—from Trump to Biden! D'Elia and his family were reaching out for help because they did not want to participate in that fraudulent attack on the US. We discovered this company with a checkered past is 34 percent owned by the Italian government and used to be called Finmeccanica until a corruption scandal took them down, after which they rebranded themselves. So, by any measure, Leonardo is not new to corporate malfeasance.

After learning all this in the immediate days after November 3rd, we took the buckshot approach in sounding the alarm, sending out pleas for help from most everyone in my Rolodex, trying to notify President Trump that something was wrong with this Italian involvement in US elections, and it needed a thorough investigation. Luckily, on Christmas Eve of 2020 (during dinner at President Trump's Mar-a-Lago home in Palm Beach, Florida), I was able to personally hand President Trump a letter, which informed him that the election theft took place in Italy at the US Embassy in Rome, and it was facilitated by a man named Stefano Serafini, a US State Department foreign service officer, a man working in conjunction with General Claudio Graziano, an Italian commander and chairman of the European Union military committee. Graziano is also a former chief of staff for the Italian army. These two were involved with flipping American votes and coordinated that effort through Leonardo's company man, Igzanio Moncado, who worked for a subsidiary of Leonardo while also serving as the Italian liaison to Iran, Qatar, and China—surprise, surprise.

We had been trying to help keep Arturo D'Elia safe and were thrilled when our communication capabilities allowed us to learn that he had been taken into custody, a helpful situation where the bad guys would have a harder time getting to him. D'Elia also supplied whistle-blowing information to intel services, which later passed us photos of characters mentioned in the previous paragraph, allowing Nations in Action to create a "wanted poster" of those involved.

Other related disclosures we received besides Arturo's were about a man I recognized from his nefarious efforts during the 2016 US election. England's Alexander Nix is an MI6 operative (British intelligence) and the former CEO of Cambridge Analytica, a guy who admitted (before Britain's Parliament in June 2018) that his company had extracted personal data from up to 50 million Facebook accounts, an illegal operation that was *alleged* to help President Trump.

So affidavits concerning election fraud committed against our 2020 American election were created by people in Italy who had firsthand experience, and I'm happy to report that there are many Italian vote-corruption investigations presently going forward—which is something all of America needs to know about! However, because of the corrupt US mainstream media, only new, honest, media reporters like those at American Media Periscope—and a young Italian one named Daniele Capezzone—were willing to break the story, and they will always be known as truth-telling heroes for providing that brave help. Because of John and Daniele, our information quickly spread through others in today's new honest press, causing the rats involved to begin scurrying for cover, all from those two sources of truth that helped Nations in Action have a voice to call this international fraud on the carpet.

Another Italian aspect to all this involves their "financial police" institution called Finanza Guardia, an agency that has uncovered many infractions at Leonardo and has exposed how the Barack Obama administration stole fourteen pallets of cash through Obama's 2015 Iran "nuclear" deal. Those dollars were flown through Dubai, before getting transferred by way of Italy to Merrill Lynch at a bank in Switzerland. And it is imperative for people to understand how those piles of US cash began Barack Obama's 2017 engagement in US election efforts. Like Finanza Guardia in Italy, the trail of that money is something else we at Nations in Action are investigating right now.

Again, this is all hugely important information that America needs to know because many sources are contending that all those 2015 US taxpayer dollars ended up being given to American saboteur black hats and their partners in foreign countries, who may have used it to finance the whole Russia collusion narrative against Trump, a deceptive intelligence communities' effort involving much information that originated in Italy, as well as through Maltese academic Joseph Mifsud, who helps train British spies. Mifsud was at the center of the

Russian collusion story because he introduced George Papadopoulos (a dual-citizenship US and Greek individual who was a foreign policy advisor to Trump's 2016 campaign) to a Russian spy that Mifsud represented as being Vladimir Putin's niece. Mifsud also told Papadopoulos that the Russians had incriminating emails on Hillary Clinton, and that same academic was actually escorted out of Italy by Stefano Serafini, the man mentioned earlier who was the go-between for the US State Department at our US Embassy in Rome and those like the CIA, Italian General Graziano, and Leonardo, all of whom helped with the theft of our 2020 American election. Right after November third, Serafini escorted Mifsud to London where Mifsud was able to quickly retire, conveniently eliminating any chance he could lose his pension for being caught helping with the theft of our US election.

We are excited to know that Italians continue to unravel this 2020 US election fraud, a current effort that involves way more people than I could have hoped for. And I certainly didn't anticipate we'd be part of exposing information about the scandal involving the false Russia-collusion narrative, which turns out to also be closely tied to Italy. This Nations in Action effort to find the truth has been quite a journey that was obviously orchestrated by God, as evidenced by so many people who have given us important information for which we are extremely grateful.

As far as how this ongoing US investigation of 2020 vote fraud might play out going forward, from my unique perspective that includes extensive experience with information technology (IT) involving computer algorithms, I think every state should recall their Electoral College electors, after which they should each complete a forensic, cyber examination involving true experts, and not yahoos with no IT experience. As the CEO of an IT company, I have been appalled at what some states are representing as an audit, and I challenged several in the Georgia General Assembly about the way their contract was written with Dominion Voting Systems. That document denies tax-paying users any right to examine their computer code, which is something my IT staff would shoot me for if I had ever suggested something like that being included as part of a contract with the American people. It is wrong! America deserves transparency—which comes first.

Second, it is incumbent upon each state to conduct a forensic cyber audit. Third, it is imperative that we recall the electors. I have been an alternate elector, so I understand the process, including what we need to do—find out who did this, where they did it, and when they pulled it off, piecing together the facts little by little. In fact, after the election, while everyone was talking about the machines changing our votes, I was speaking with people in Italy about how they must come clean. The perpetrators were former Italian Prime Ministers Matteo Renzi and Giuseppe Conte, who both coordinated their efforts with Italian General Claudio Graziano. Conte's government fell in January 2021, followed by much scrambling, turmoil, arrests, and the murder of five top Italians in March 2021. Italy's troubles have been many and are far from over. With Finanza Guardia conducting financial investigations, I think you will see Italy eventually needing to speak up about their role in America's stolen 2020 election.

And when they do, Mr. Biden will find himself facing the fact that his fraud has been discovered by the American people and the rest of the world. Already, foreign leaders know Biden did not win because they have intelligence communities that have also acquired intercepts of Italian communications, which prove Italy helped orchestrate the theft. All this shows how compromised—and probably blackmailed—Biden truly is, and many governments around the planet already know, so it's up to the new Italian government to step up and come clean. If not through any other disclosures coming up soon with US election audits, at least we know that Italy can act any day now to set the record straight. That would change everything going on in America today.

Humanity's great divide that is presently happening in nations all over the world involves an honorable old guard of public officials working with citizens who are also trying to keep honest, constitutional government for their countries. But a deceiving and infiltrating new guard, who only represents an elite and small fraction of the population around the earth, is disrupting all they can in their traitorous efforts to take over. And just like America, Italy is seeing that fight involving its intel services, politicians, and parts of the financial apparatus that includes multinationals like Finanza Guardia.

Someone I know, who is closely helping with the fight against police corruption in government, recently mentioned how they used to only keep an eye on a few bad guys, but lately the nefarious activity is getting so pervasive that some areas of leadership involve corruption by more than 50 percent of the players. Luckily though, these rampant corruption issues are causing a massive number of average local citizens to stand up for honor and justice, just like some good people in Italy who had the courage to make a difference in the American election investigation. Italians are going to help bring the US back, which will eventually also greatly benefit their nation.

8

Jaco Booyens: An Honest and Urgent Plea for *Your* Intercession with *Our* Children and Grandchildren

Jaco Booyens's mission is promoting life by transformation of our culture through a new uplifting media. He is president and CEO of the film production company After Eden Pictures (AfterEdenPictures.com), and as the older brother of a sister who is a sex-trafficking survivor, he took on the effort to direct the 2014 feature film *8 Days,* a project made to raise awareness about the reality of sex trafficking in the United States and worldwide. Jaco is also the founder of SHAREtogether (ShareTogetherNow.org), a nonprofit organization fighting against the global crisis of sex trafficking. Originally from South Africa, Jaco is now proud to be a United States citizen, and you can visit his ministry online at JacoBooyensMinistries.org.

The following September 2020 presentation was given by Mr. Jaco Booyens to Sarasota (Florida) Patriots executive director, James Bauman, at the online Sarasota Patriots Sixth Annual America Truth Conference, and in conjunction with me at American Media

Periscope. For better readability and flow, this is a paraphrase that retains the original meanings. Here is Jaco:

Here in America we have a nation where the evilest aspects of society have always been hidden in plain sight, yet we have not known that because the abuse has been normalized over time. And evil works its long-term game plan, being patient to attack America bit by bit over decades. Unfortunately though, the people of our country look out to the future only as far as four years, hoping that possibly a new president will make needed changes while countries like China, Russia, and the Middle East build legacies, laying out and running long games that stay on course, not pivoting like we are prone to every four years. Many countries pass rule and reign down within the family from generation to generation, staying on point, whether for evil or good.

I would argue that Satan works the same way, coming at us to steal, kill, and destroy, especially targeting his ultimate foe—Christian America, which is also a friend and helper to God's Israel, and probably that nation's last-standing ally. We seem to be the Jewish people's only remaining light on the hill. In fact, America is the lamp to the whole world, demonstrating how a free and Judeo-Christian society should operate.

However, over time we have been trading freedom for safety and not realizing how much the most important and vulnerable in our society need securing, saving, and protecting. The book I believe in, the word I follow that has come from God himself, declares this about our responsibility as adults to protect all children:

> "It would be better for him to have a millstone hung around his neck and to be thrown into the sea than to cause one of these little ones to stumble" (Luke 17:2).

Today, our children continue to be under attack as they have been for a long time! However, the world's societies are awakening to what has been happening to our innocent little ones. In fact, I would characterize this period as the "Great Reveal," a time when God is revealing who in the church is actually walking the walk—and who is not. And the Lord is uncovering much evil that has been happening without the knowledge of so many good people around the planet. This may be the biblical time spoken about in Luke:

"For there is nothing hidden that will not be disclosed, and nothing concealed that will not be made known and brought to light" (Luke 8:17).

I was born and raised in South Africa, where most know we lived through some perilous racial struggles that were one-sided one way and flipped to being one-sided the other way. I also saw my sister overcome the evils of child sex trafficking, becoming a survivor, an amazing woman, and a massive victor. I witnessed all that firsthand before arriving here in the United States, where I have learned how America leads our planet in the commercialization of sex with children. That may be a bitter pill to swallow, but it's one we have to understand because those turning a blind eye for decades are the reason it is true: Americans have looked the other way, not wanting to acknowledge or believe the evil exists in our nation.

We love sending missionaries around the world, and I'm all about that, but while we fight human trafficking in places like Cambodia, the Philippines, the Dominican Republic, and Haiti, no one wants to shine a light on the evil crawling around the crevices of our society. We readily admit it exists outside our borders, but the truth is that a massive operation is happening inside the US every day! Why? Because we have allowed it. We normalized it over time. And the church ignores it. For decades, the American church has abdicated its position in the public conversation about child sex trafficking, forfeiting US spiritual territory. In the 1960s, we embraced the sexual revolution, a movement that began with the fall of Adolf Hitler. The Nazis were set to win Europe, then eradicate Israel, and finally attack America, which Hitler considered to be his greatest future foe. When they lost, a new battle strategy was launched to infiltrate our entertainment through Hollywood, turning it into a Trojan horse that would corrupt America, so they could more easily go after our children.

And along came Alfred Kinsey to add fuel to that evil fire. Not that we should trust Wikipedia very far, but they list Kinsey as an American biologist, professor of entomology and zoology, and sexologist who, in 1947, founded the Institute for Sex Research at Indiana University, now known as the Kinsey Institute for Research in Sex, Gender, and Reproduction. Kinsey was all about sexual-experiment studies on children—twenty-four hours a day and with many as young as four and five years old. Yet, the guy is celebrated in Hollywood, we give him peace prizes, and he's made out to be the greatest scientist of a decade, all combining to present him as an American hero. But the guy abused children and desensitized our culture to the idea of adults having sex with our kids. His long-term goal (which we've almost already reached) was to normalize pedophilia—child sex abuse!

Decade after decade their corrupting game plan has continued to check off the boxes, regardless of who's in the White House. They have worked steadily to eliminate America's moral fiber and the family unit. How have they managed it? Well, first they convinced the US that prayer should not be practiced in school. Then they came after the nuclear family, questioning how a "family" should be defined because the way you move a culture is by changing the language, and then society follows. So, they "refined" our communication away from only characterizing family as a marriage involving a husband and wife, causing us to question the traditional definition of family. They applied peer pressure and subliminal messaging supplied by the extremely powerful entertainment establishment, a formidable force they have constantly wielded for nefarious purposes. Our God is creative and gave us the same skill to be used for good, but in the wrong hands, it's an effective corrupter.

Just as their father, Satan, has for millennia, they got us questioning our truth and reality, the corruption of man that began with the devil in the Garden of Eden when he deceptively asked Eve, "Did God really say…?" They redefined the nuclear family away from the common, hardworking father who loves and takes care of those in the home while the mother helps, and both work through life's trials together, standing as one strong family, the backbone of society. Over time they discounted the existence of that picture and incentivized fathers to leave the home, replacing Dad with the self-serving and cold government.

Recently, it has gotten to the point that our generation has to deal with the language infiltration of a "gender" question that has moved our culture away from the foundational reality of male and female. They are challenging everyone: Maybe you're not a man. Should you be a woman? Once they found great acceptance pushing family fluidity, the absurdity of gender questioning became less far-fetched to a corrupted view that had already embraced sexual immorality. They were told, "Love is love," which came to mean most any "love" is good, including sexual love, fetishes, perversions, or just lust.

In the 1960s, a movement started for men who (sexually) "love" boys, which by the 1970s established the North American Man/Boy [sexual] Love Association. However, love is supposed to be sacrificial, yet they created a lustfully sexual form of "love" that makes no sacrifices, only taking into account the involved adult's feelings, just a fulfillment of the pedophile's desires. But it hurts to love. Love is not easy. Ask any wife. In every marriage it becomes tough to love your spouse, so God teaches us His agape love that is sacrificial, unconditional, and not always comfortable or easy. And that process teaches us discipline, so we can more easily be loved back. Contrary to a mutually loving relationship, those corrupting the idea of love work at removing the necessary discipline involved, which makes relationships that miss out on the marriage-caused corrections we gain from truly loving another. As they have purposely redefined love to remove that discipline, it turns into just some desire for self-satisfaction—"*my* agenda, *my* needs, *my* motives!"

Again, they have hypersexualized our culture through the entertainment industry that many of our kids get addicted to, or at least are influenced by. They have also heavily infiltrated the colleges our children choose, meaning the corrupters descend on them to indoctrinate young people through a full-court press that normalizes promiscuous sex, and that is at their most vulnerable time when they first leave home to figure out the world on their own. In fact, I would argue that sex is the most powerful—and dangerous—weapon on earth because God created that formidable force to bond two people together. Couples are given an overwhelming God glue:

> "For this reason, a man will leave his father and mother and be united to his wife, and the two will become one flesh" (Ephesians 5:31).

Sex is not meant for just some feeling we get when procreating; instead, we consummate marriage as a synergistic tripling of two peoples' power, an upgraded weapon supplied by God to fend off and push away evil forces like pornography and other darkness. The rightful place for sex is between a husband and wife uniting together, a godly union that punishes evil!

And by its nature, when that act from God becomes distorted, when sex is contorted into something just for self-satisfaction and pleasure, bonding still occurs! If fifteen-year-old and sixteen-year-old boys have sex with each other, the bonding still happens because, again, sex is a glue; but afterward, there is a ripping apart and shredding of those involved as they end the relationship, which is why there has never been a clean divorce. There is no such thing. As a child from a broken home, I'm not judging, but I do understand there is harsh residue from lives having massive pieces torn apart when those two people separate, especially when both are young.

Anytime sex occurs during the formative years, pieces of those involved are gone forever because the experience becomes imprinted on the brain. And when the porn culture is pushed so much as it is in America, predominantly corrupting the moral fiber of the nation's men, it helps normalize sex with children while also convincing men that women are here for their pleasure, and it's because the guys think they somehow deserve it. In fact, when that goes on long enough, even women come to embrace the notion that they are objects, self-identifying as things, and only secondarily valuing themselves as people. This is why we see "role-model" women like Beyoncé displaying herself as a sex goddess, sometimes as a very pregnant and naked woman, massively self-objectifying, just as the long list of influential celebrities like Nicki Minaj also do. And when the culture builds these women up in the eyes of young ladies, we are telling those teens and other singles that this is their way to get attention, affirmation, and "love."

That powerful force is leading women down a dark path, while society is breaking up the nuclear family, removing the father from the home, taking prayer from schools, and separating marriage by encouraging relationships that do not involve the pairing of one heterosexual man and woman. Then they challenge gender by constantly posing questions like "Are you really a man?" or "Maybe you're not a girl." And they even give names to the movement like LGBTQ (Lesbian, Gay, Bisexual, Transgender, and Queer/Questioning), Transgender Equity Fund, Transgender Health Care Society, Man/Boy Love Association, and you name it! And today, they want the world's oldest profession, prostitution, to be relabeled as "sex work," so they can defend adulation and harlotry by claiming "people have a right to work." Hey, states like Texas and Tennessee are right-to-work areas, so would that also include the right to employ someone in sex work? And this means that sex involving force, fraud, and coercion can suddenly be defended in the culture.

Our college students have been completely infiltrated with Marxism and Darwinism to the point of defending prostitution and, even worse, supporting a movie like *Cuties*, the April 2020 production by Netflix that shows preteen-dancer competitions where the little girls wear skimpy costumes and perform provocative dance moves. This sort of push on the culture is why we're seeing more and more Americans defending pedophilia; they are literally blinded and deceived! From a moral standpoint, the spirit of deception has fallen upon our nation.

We have become a country that embraces sexual immorality because that was part of the plan to break America, a nation that cannot be defeated militarily. Instead of taking us on by brute force, they have attacked our nuclear family and broken the nation morally by corrupting American youth. When a five- to fifteen-year-old child is sexually abused, that previously fully functioning person is gone for at least a decade—if they return at all! We see women wait thirty years to finally report publicly that they were raped. Why so long? Most of us can't understand the level of trauma that occurs when a person's dignity is stripped sexually. Again, sex is a powerful weapon that can easily destroy. Used in the established manner God outlined, that act between a married man and woman was originally designed to build societies, but by using the same wrongly, nations can be destroyed. No culture in history has survived sexual immorality, and most fell within just three generations. In fact, the world's strongest empire ever went away because of it. That was Rome.

As a nation created *by* God and *for* Him, America was founded to serve the Lord through practice of godly principles like the acknowledgment that all men are created equal, having an inherent claim to life, liberty, and justice. So, the US is a place where children should be safe, not sexualized, profiled, and attacked—even in kindergarten! But it's happening anyway! But how? The church neglected its watch, allowing evil to exist even though good men are available but doing nothing. Born-again heroes for God have always risen out of the church, and others too can be good, but the biblical church has reliably supplied good men that stand to meet the world's challenges. I absolutely hold myself and the rest of the church accountable because this mess has been created on our watch and in a massive way, including how we let prayer and God be removed from schools and elsewhere in public. We also allowed family and marriage to be redefined, and we have even watched as the crazy questioning of gender has found some initial success. Again, how have we gotten to where we are today? As the church has looked the other way, those breaking America down morally have patiently played the long game, slowly but surely checking off the boxes of their evil plans.

I want to talk a bit about how predators profile their future victims, as well as the state of our country today, in relation to the heinous practice of sex with children. To do that, I'll first give some history to show that this didn't happen through random, individual pedophiles roaming the streets in red-light districts. Quite contrary to that notion, it's an industry that is somewhat unorganized while also having aspects well-planned in the bigger picture. The reality of how it has been right in front of you the whole time, hidden in plain sight, should rattle you to the bone, sending shivers down your spine. The despicable, perverted practice has infiltrated every sphere of society in all age groups, most likely including your own child's classroom, and all the way up to the battles we have been fighting on university campuses, part of which involved me speaking at thirty-five colleges this past year. There are other organizations I proudly walk with, such as Charlie Kirk's incredible Turning Point USA, a group that provides conservative voices for college campuses.

That is about adult students, but who is fighting for today's high schoolers and middle schoolers, as well as the need that came along in 2019 when we even had to start stopping the damage being inflicted on our elementary schoolers and kindergarteners, which is how infiltrated our culture has become; they are attacking and sexualizing the youngest now! Why do they do it? Because whenever you break a child, that same person as a young adult is much easier to indoctrinate, as evidenced by how simple it has been for the Black Lives Matter movement to sweep into high schools and college campuses all across the country. When the child becomes sexually compromised, pedophiles have broken vessels that can't fight; instead, these injured little people become long-term, subordinate adults because that sort of injury often takes decades to heal. When they hurt major percentages of society in this way, they get a dependent population. Sex is a secret and the compromised carry that hidden shame, so they are literally not up to opposing these controlling people. From there, the Fascists continue to expand government, more and more tightly ruling the citizenry.

Another aspect of the problem is how a large number of Americans have been taught that we are a democracy run by the majority's ever-changing opinions—which are shaped by the dishonest media! But the US is a republic, so we must recapture that perversion of our language, resolving to always talk about ourselves as a republic. In a democracy with majority rule, an Electoral College has no power, so the majority decides for the minority. But republics protect minorities, especially children, while the world's democracies have often forgotten them, sexualized them, and left them behind. It's a subtle difference, but powerful.

Here in the US, our elections have been compromised and taken over, while a vast number of good people don't even show up to vote.

I know this is so because prayer was allowed to be taken out of our schools and we are still trying to overturn Roe v. Wade, something it seems we now have a shot at doing, thank God! We must reclaim territory given up by the neglectful church that used to act as watchmen on the wall, until so many climbed down and handed America to the enemy.

The mass epidemic in our country today is not COVID-19. It is children being sexualized, as well as the commercialization of sex with children—both in epic proportions. My sister was trafficked in 1994, so I've been in this fight a long time, being blessed to help rescue kids in places like Haiti and the Dominican Republic. That said, our focus has been the United States, working alongside honorable nongovernmental organizations (NGOs) that fight tirelessly to restore lives, day in and day out. Do you know that an enslaved victim who is being child sex trafficked has an average life span of only seven years? The abuse is intense, including broken bones, so we're not talking about lovemaking that involves some romantic, gentle, Romeo and Juliet scenario—this is constant child rape. I'm not detailing everything to fearmonger but because these are the realities. Child sex trafficking is mostly not what you think. Sure, some of it is "snatch and grab" by white vans that stop quickly and then speed off, stealing kids away from their unsuspecting parents. And we have rescued children from tunnels, cages, and closets.

But the actual standard practice and real picture you should have in your head will make you vomit because it's a friend, extended family member, or neighbor! The fastest-rising trend with children sold for sex in America is a process called familial trafficking, where someone related to you or an acquaintance is selling their own children, who are normal, high-functioning kids that go to school and may even play on the softball team, while also performing as a sex slave for help or gain—like protection (maybe safety from family members), goods, services, or money. But it is sex that is being facilitated by sick individuals who have embraced darkness, monsters allowed to continue roaming the streets of our society today like the thousands of pedophiles New York City Mayor Bill de Blasio let out prison to prowl the streets. Ask the former mayor why his city is now often ranked as the second-highest child sex trafficking place in the world.

Our massive problem is a lack of common sense and an agenda that puts pedophiles into society without even requiring them to register as sex offenders, normalizes sex, and uses sex to sell almost everything. This is hugely compounded by a revered upper class in the entertainment industry who are often broken and insecure because many of them have been compromised sexually, causing these stars to perpetuate the cycle. Our country constantly sexualizes women and girls through the images put in front of young men and boys; the average age of a US boy's introduction to porn is eight. But an elementary school brain is not equipped to deal with that; they can't comprehend it! Even adult married couples are not able to deal with pornography. It only destroys, while also acting as an entry drug to child sex trafficking. It is a fact. Know it's true. It's undeniable.

That may hit home and challenge some readers, but I am not here to judge you because my goal is to love you into the kingdom of God, especially you perpetrators. I want to see your heart turned, a redefining of your life as one touched by God to a point where you are able to enter the fight on the right side this time. But know this: if you are on the wrong side, we are coming for you! And those on the track of just viewing and watching porn right now, understand it is the same road that leads to children being sold for sex.

By US law, an act with children is separated from the kind of sex labor trafficking that might include a fifty-two-year-old woman. For sex to be illegal with someone who is eighteen or older, there has to be force, fraud, or coercion, while all fifty states say sex with children up to seventeen years old is illegal, so the child is always a victim of a sex crime. That protection for our kids is fantastic, and it includes the Los Angeles area, but it is also a place where those excellent laws are not enforced, which means there is no actual protection, so the legalities might as well have been written on toilet paper! Yet, that doesn't stop American politicians from hoodwinking the public with those kinds of wonderful laws that may even carry a thirty-year prison sentence while showing no prosecutions! Because there are none. Zero jury trials! District attorneys won't pick up these cases and judges won't bring them into their courtrooms, so these guys who are having sex with minors are not made to face the thirty years. A pimp might get some time, but what about the guy paying for sex with a child? That is where we stem the tide and stop demand in this country. We need an all-out effort to take back sexual morality in this country. Instead of just pointing to figures, we must look inward, analyzing ourselves to see if you and I are contributing to the crime of sex trafficking. Yes, watching porn is contributing because you are creating demand and someone always supplies what is needed to meet demand. Am I saying every person who watches porn will someday pay for sex with a child? No, but you are on that track.

COVID has only exacerbated the porn issue for men, and even some women, who maybe had looked a little until losing their job caused them to spiral deeper into the habit. During COVID, we have seen an epic spike in online child sex trafficking, and even before that, children have long been sexually groomed on most every social media platform and in online chat rooms, even those through video gaming systems like Xbox and PlayStation. Predators play a long game. They're good at it. And very patient. At times they even run circles around law enforcement because our police force does not normally receive this kind of training. And these days society wants to put everything on law enforcement, but then not sufficiently fund them. In the fight against sex trafficking that I am involved with, we cannot survive without law enforcement that can break down doors to rescue children, something that cannot be done without a warrant. And how do we arrest someone without police, who also have to be available to help us build a strong court case so justice can be served?

It is preposterous to think this fight can be fought while we defund the police, yet that foolish effort is being pursued in places like Los Angeles County, today's top US city for child sex trafficking. They even want to take money from special task forces and other units that deal with sex trafficking, those experts that always suffer most from lack of funding. But these people are all about defunding, and it seems to make no sense to many, but maybe it does fit when you know the long game is to sexualize our children.

And how are they accomplishing the hypersexualizing of our innocent little ones? These people enter our children's classrooms through the World Health Organization (WHO); the United Nations Educational, Scientific, and Cultural Organization (UNESCO); Sex Ed for Social Change (which is the shortened version of their previous name, Sexual Information and Education Council of the United States, or SIECUS); and the International Planned Parenthood Foundation (abortion clinics). These entities make up the overarching governing body for US curriculum, and together they are the ones writing the prospectus on children's sexual health, which has become America's horrible "comprehensive sex-education curriculum"!

In fact, these corrupted curriculum suppliers first tested their newest material on Africans—who completely rejected it!—but since no one stands up for those poor people with no organized governments (living in villages), the WHO and Planned Parenthood falsely reported that the program worked well there. After that, in 2019 they mandated it for Europe, with no way of opting out, and then finally turned their eyes on finding an initial American suitor that would allow it to gain a foothold in our country. And who do you suppose proudly stepped up to allow this sick, twisted, vile, pornographic curriculum in American schools? None other than the California governor who is in the middle of being recalled for other nefarious deeds: Gavin Newsom. Not even chancing the measure in front of the state's school board, by executive order he just signed to have it cancerously seeded into every California child's classroom.

Now, let's talk about what is in that sex curriculum that goes from *kindergarten!* through twelfth grade: Sex education at five years old! Kindergarteners are taught masturbation! Do you hear me? And all ages are taught to claim sexual "agency" over their bodies, which means tiny kids are taught to decide for themselves what is good for their bodies, even though we all know those little ones do not have the capacity to make the important decisions about their bodily functions. These curriculum writers want to take that role away from the parents—the God-given custodians who feel the love needed to protect their own children, not allowing them to be abused. But if these people can convince kids to rule their own body choices, and then somehow remove a child from their parents, they can open the kid up to despicable pedophilia. And even while the child is still with their parents, this promotion of a child taking agency over his or her body choices is meant to drive a wedge, splitting the parent and child relationship so the grade schooler or secondary student is at least open to making sexual decisions that might differ from the parent's sound judgment.

And it gets worse: From there this same curriculum pushes gender fluidity, encouraging transgender-testing exercises like one involving their "Gender-Bread Person," a cartoon stick figure that has a little kindergarten kid decide on the spot whether he or she is a boy or girl; they are told to either pin a male or female sexual organ on their cartoon person, after which the kids learn some sexual slang and then the exercise laughs it all off. The next day the same child can play this game again and choose differently, so in this way the predatory curriculum normalizes gender fluidity.

Over 144 times from kindergarten to twelfth grade, abortion-giant Planned Parenthood chimes into the coursework, endearing our children to their organization, even telling them at one point that their religion does not frown upon what the abortion mill teaches, and that any mental conflict with the child's upbringing should be discussed with their local "priest." Why not ask their parents? Why not a Baptist pastor? Why specifically a priest? Well, as many of us already know, these days sexual immorality has also invaded every sector of Christian "religions." All denominations are dealing with sex issues. In fact, it is laughable to think the world could be so overrun with this sexual perversion, and it not similarly invades the church. But we Christians are living *in* the world while we are no longer supposed to be *of* it. We must not support worldly ways. Instead, God asks us to produce biblical outcomes that often run contrary to the world's desires.

Part of this curriculum is a book called *Perfectly Normal* that was written for ten-year-olds (fifth graders), a completely non-normal text that asks our grade school kids whether they have had anal sex yet! If not, it acts as a handbook for how these preteens can perform it safely! Another issue is with popular online magazines like *Teen Vogue* that write articles on perverted topics like how teen girls can "sext" (text their nude body parts) their best selfies by using recommended lighting, poses, and positioning.

After learning all this, an obvious question you probably have is "What other people are facilitating this sexual corruption of our children?" Well, look at Reed Hastings, the cofounder and CEO of Netflix that put out that *Cuties* movie with its child pornography, a guy who also sits on the board of Facebook and used to be part of California's state board of education—the very group that is allowing our California children to be taught all this sickness! And by the way, after California signed on to the perversion of our kids, it was then welcomed into Washington State by Governor Jay Inslee, after which it spread like wildfire to twenty-seven American states—including Texas! Austin embraced it in their independent school district, and the first vote of the Texas state school board also said "yes!" Luckily though, through God, sheer force, and pressure, the next time it was brought forward, we were able to help strike down their attempt to implement the curriculum statewide. Including our entire nation, that was finally the first victory we had against this comprehensive sex-ed indoctrination.

The curriculum also involves fully illustrated puberty books like *What's Happening to My Body for Boys* and *What's Happening to My Body for Girls*—which are 100 percent pornography! Yes, they are animated, but still porn, and a five-year-old brain certainly cannot handle all that—even a fifteen-year-old can't properly deal with the images and concepts they are being shown and taught. Now, layer that trauma to our kids on top of their heads being filled with the Black Lives Matter movement, Darwinism, socialism, and Marxism. Our children simply cannot survive all that intact! And when that child is sexually compromised the first time, from then on, the guilt, shame, blame, and self-loathing set in, being held closely, hidden in secrecy as a festering issue clouding their minds. Before getting set upon by the pedophile curriculum, these same young human beings are endowed with unlimited potential, having been born in America with the environment to dream, thrive, and lead others to great outcomes, a potential future full of joy and accomplishment.

Instead of allowing our kids to flourish, the abuse and its resulting guilt create adults who want to just blend in and stay out of the moral fight; internally, they feel like compromised people who should not be allowed on the good side of that struggle. So, they're already fighting themselves, blaming themselves for being abused. But it's not their fault! They are real victims! And it was all purposely done to them by our despicable leaders, while society's good people—the massive majority of the world's population—are not coming to their rescue, not willing to find out what is happening and fight for these defenseless little people. In fact, by sending the kids to learn this stuff at public schools, a child's mind tends to believe his or her parents approve of the material taught. On top of all that abandonment of our children, the one group that is always supposed to be in the fight—we Christians in the church who are told to enter the struggle representing good—have left the children to be gutted by these sadistic villains of history. This is serious stuff!

Societies of the world have been tragically spiraling deeper into sexually corruption, but there has recently been an amazing and wonderful development. The first leader in the history *of any nation* actually used his power and office to strongly proclaim, "Child sex trafficking is not okay!" That was in the United States, and it was President Donald J. Trump. Why hasn't every past president and prime minister on the whole planet done that? And trust me, my organization has fought this cancer under three presidents, so I can tell you that President George W. Bush did not do it, and President Obama's administration would not even acknowledge that any tiny bit of this widespread US scourge is happening in our country. These same men actually incentivized organizations to fight it offshore—but not here! They have not wanted Americans to learn that the problem even exists in our nation.

Contrary to that neglect, I stood only five feet away from President Donald Trump in the Oval Office when he signed an executive order to combat and attempt to end child sex trafficking. This was only three weeks after President Trump became the first US president to even attend, let alone speak at, the forty-eight-year-old annual March for Life event during January 2020 in Washington, DC. Later, while I stood in that Oval Office, using no uncertain terms he instructed the FBI. "You *will* hunt these people down." He also appropriated funding for surviving victims to get much-needed rehabilitation and restoration. We have never seen that! This is a massive victory. Trump prioritized protecting children!

As an immigrant, I can tell you that America has been and still is the greatest nation in the history of the earth; just talk to others like me who left their homes to come here. Ask them why they came. Probably for a better life. I bleed red, white, and blue. But a great future has been guaranteed to no nation, and ours will depend on today's American children, so we cannot allow these things to happen to them.

Knowing all that, the devastating destruction Newsom had already dealt to that state was not enough for the California governor and the state's general-assembly leadership, who took only forty-five seconds to pass a bill called Assembly Bill 2218 (AB-2218), the Transgender Wellness and Equity Fund, which got no media coverage! By the way, do you wonder why these bills are always presented under LGBTQ or transgender? It's because politicians are deathly afraid to vote against anything LGBTQ, considering it political suicide. So, these sorts of bills fly through the California legislature, especially if it's something brought forward as a supposed "health" measure.

But getting back to AB-2218, the new law sets aside God-given biological gender and declares that every California child has "sexual agency," which means a three-, five-, or seven-year-old child (it has predominately been girls) can be influenced by any nefarious adult to wake up one morning and claim they presently consider themselves the opposite sex—giving them the right to puberty blockers! This is today, folks. Go take a look at California AB-2218 and see what it says for yourself! Against the parents' wishes, an elementary-age child is legally allowed to be supplied with Lupron, a powerful pharmaceutical typically given against prostate cancer, which mostly hits elderly men. This prescription-only pharmaceutical prevents and stops the natural puberty cycle of girls, so any future menstrual cycle will not happen; she won't have one! And this medical procedure can essentially be "self-prescribed" by a preschooler, now that this bill has become California law. Of course, it was signed against the counsel and advice of doctors, who warned that this would create personality disorders and prevent these future adults from being able to biologically bear children, even though a consistent 95 percent of adults end up *wanting* at least one child. But California says, "Hey, tough luck; you will be permanently sterilized." This is happening in California! We must do something! Contrary to any rational thought, that same legislation has now spread throughout our nation, so, on top of Roe v. Wade, we will now need to fight the permanent sterilization of American children.

Unfortunately, it gets worse! Just judging the man from his work, what Gavin Newsom votes into power reveals him as an agent for pedophilia. California took it a step further when the assembly and senate passed SB-145 (Senate Bill 145), after which Newsom approved it on September 11, 2020. This bill amended sex-offender laws in the state so that when a man or women decides to have sex with a child—who is within ten years of the adult's age—the case will be left up to the judge to "determine" if there was sexual abuse. This means anyone like a twenty-three-year-old teacher, clergy, or sports coach can sexually abuse your thirteen-year-old California middle schooler son or daughter, and the "potential" prosecution would be left up to the discretion of some random judge—even as to whether the twenty-three-year-old should be registered as a sex offender! In that state, judges will interpret the law on statutory rape, age of consent, and sex trafficking. But those laws were put in place with the help of many good California NGOs (nongovernmental organizations), and that long-settled legislation will still say that sex trafficking a little boy or girl makes them a victim. So, the perpetrator would normally be facing thirty years in prison, but SB-145 nullifies that, leaving it up to a judge to decide if the abuser should even be registered as a sex offender.

Getting back to the school curriculum I'm exposing, if you publicly showed this obscene coursework in your town square, you would be put in jail. So, why has the filth been allowed in our children's classrooms? Well, in 1970, an obscenity-exemption statute was signed, with the honorable intention to allow helpful law enforcement and medical personnel to observe obscene material that would otherwise be illegal. But then it was expanded to the scientific community, which was the excuse used to later include educators because of anatomy teachers and other science subjects. Eventually, it has become okay to desensitize and sexually exploit children, grooming and coercing them in a sexual direction—all under the law, which is now as difficult to change as Roe v. Wade.

Then when we want to help that harmed child, bringing him or her back from abuse is such a difficult rehabilitation that it may take decades to repair the damage from being exposed to things they shouldn't see, if it works at all. The reality for today is that this is legally in the classroom and being used to attack your children, all because we didn't show up and vote when it mattered or have allowed stolen elections. This is serious! So, I am asking what your child or grandchild is worth: If you have him or her in a Christian school at a church where these curriculums are not allowed, then you are one of the few. But most Americans do not have that opportunity, so I highly encourage you to defend what your child and other kids see because it has long-term consequences.

So far, we have not crossed the terminal threshold of a nation's third generation being completely corrupted by our schools, but we have definitely passed the second generation, and these monsters are working on this one. I am sorry to say it, but our public school system is toast and needs radical reform, while our foster-care programs have been infiltrated by pedophiles. However, we can still turn the tide on sexual immorality, and it begins from the ground up with your own family taking ownership of this issue, including your votes against candidates who are pro-abortion or don't care about school choice. I believe God can redeem every human heart, but public education is fatally broken, so it needs to be demolished and rebuilt before we finalize a sexually immoral education for the third generation. History shows that no society has survived after embracing sexual immorality past three generations, so it is nowhere near fearmongering to say we are on a clock here! Just look at our society that allows shows like *Cuties* on Netflix, a program rated for mature audiences while having children on the cover picture. And all this desensitizing of society to sexual perversion includes some Americans defending the actions of people who exploit children. It is preposterous!

Because we're all free in the US, Americans are not taught to be situationally aware as opposed to a kid in South Sudan who understands death could come any day. We need to educate ourselves on identifying children in distress, so we must learn what sex trafficking looks like. You can access that education at JacoBooyensMinistries.org, where you will find our feature film *8 Days*, a movie that gives you and your teenager a clear understanding of what sex trafficking looks like.

Once you understand the massive problem, talk about it with friends and those in your community, asking and answering questions which will lead to protecting local children. Go to your school PTA meetings, see your principals, and meet with or get in front of the boards of education, where you can raise the questions about what is being done to our kids, as well as the fact that we must use education time to warn children about the dangers of possibly being sex trafficked, and help high school freshmen understand the potential perils always present online, which includes what to watch out for and how their behavior can diminish or increase sex trafficking. Are we letting them know how predators profile them, so they won't overshare their personal information online?

All this demonstrates how sick our society has become. Normalizing sex with children cannot be allowed in any way, shape, or form, and there is certainly no place for embracing a movement that wants to classify pedophilia as a sexual orientation. Anything that morally erodes our children and culture can never be defended, or America will be driven to its knees! We must band together and restructure the family. You fathers need to look at your own hearts, and you moms, who do your husbands no favor when you hide his or your sexually immoral acts and habits, get help! Seriously, get help!

And speaking directly to you in the church, we need to support each other, so when a guy among us admits to struggles with porn, we do not ostracize the man. Instead, out of Jesus's love, we wrap our arms around him and rally to his side. Get him help. Build him back. We need fathers! We must have more watchmen on the wall who will scripturally defend the least and most helpless of us, standing in to be that voice for the voiceless. That's what we need in our nation, people pulling together again to support what is right! And God will join us in that effort!

This past election was about whether we as a nation will embrace the spirit of death or the spirit of life. Those who follow the spirit of death harm law and order, rape and abort children, and burn down cities. You must embrace, vote, and fight for life because you were fearfully and wonderfully made by God for this purpose and time. So, be a watchman or watchwoman on the wall, challenging your leaders and school principals. Educate yourself by going to ShareTogetherNow. org, and connect with us because there are many ways we can inform and empower you. Get into the word of God and build family in this country! The Bible tells us this in 2 Chronicles 7:14:

> *"Then if my people who are called by my name will humble themselves, pray, seek my face, and turn from their wicked ways, I will hear from heaven, forgive their sins, and restore their land."*

This is the hour we are in, and America is not just some ethereal land. Many of us take seriously that we are made in God's image, godly families experiencing life together and looking out for each other. The flag, Oval Office, and the president are symbols of that, but it boils down to individuals and their choices, so we have to fight for our homes and communities, educating ourselves on these issues to understand why handing our kids over to just any classroom or online experience is dangerous!

Even with help from that highest level of our nation's leadership—like President Donald Trump displaying urgently needed moral courage—as long as there is the worst sort of evil in this world, we cannot defeat it by working from the top down. Jesus built the church from the bottom up, meaning we serve a bottom-up God, which is lucky because a top-down God would have already judged you and me as having failed, disqualifying us. Instead, our God, who is the definition of love, looks at you and me each morning, and revives our lives by proclaiming this sort of sentiment and reality for every one of us:

> *My grace and mercy for you are again renewed; come son or daughter, let's charge the hill in defense of those among us least able and most vulnerable. Before the sun sets today, stand for godly, righteous justice. However, if you don't, tomorrow morning I will repeat my love for you and urge that you return it through our little ones, setting aside some of your day's entertainment or other less urgent activities, just long enough to reach your hand down to an abused child, at least using part of your day to try relieving some of an innocent little boy or girl's suffering.*

9

Sam Sorbo: Why You Too Should Home Educate Your Child [or Grandchild]

Mrs. Sam Sorbo studied biomedical engineering at Duke University before pursuing a career in entertainment. She is an award-winning actress, author, radio host, international model, and homeschooling mom to three children, and she is married to actor Kevin Sorbo (*Hercules* television series and movies such as *God's Not Dead* and *Let There Be Light*). Mrs. Sorbo seeks to inspire parents to home educate and has written two books on the subject, *They're Your Kids: An Inspirational Journey from Self-Doubter to Home School Advocate*, and *Teach from Love: A School Year Devotional for Families*. Both books are available at www.SamSorbo.com.

Mrs. Sorbo cowrote, produced, and starred in the feature film *Let There Be Light*. To correspond with the film, Sam and husband Kevin wrote a devotional titled *Share the Light*. Learn more about their latest film, *Miracle in East Texas*, (MiracleInEastTexas.com), and for Sam's other work, please visit her social media platforms at Facebook.com/SamSorbo and Twitter.com/TheSamSorbo.

For flow and readability in a book format, the following has been paraphrased from a September 2020 presentation given by Sam Sorbo at the Sarasota (Florida) Patriots Sixth Annual America Truth Conference. Her meanings remain unchanged. Here is Sam:

Keeping with the theme of *They're Your Kids,* I want to talk about home education in the age of COVID, and that starts with a quick story. I've been counseling a lot of parents new to home education, and one was a gal recently sitting at my kitchen counter. Of course, schools closed by COVID caused much trepidation with parents suddenly asked to home-educate their kids, a position they never guessed they'd be put in. So I asked this mom in my kitchen, "What is it that you are you really afraid of?" She looked at me with tears in her eyes, started sobbing, and replied, "I'm worried I'll fail my son." Honestly, I was that person! My kids were still very young, so I was maybe not on the verge of tears.

My approach to home education was as something interesting to try out, and the needed change for my family came when the school did not seem to be serving my child well with the instruction, other things happening in the classroom, and maybe most importantly, they were putting me in the role of a substitute teacher—the unglamorous taskmaster who gets all the scorn and none of the fulfilling feeling of a mentoring relationship. So, I decided to try home education for a semester and see what happens. Unlike COVID forcing the issue as it has for some families recently, my transition was probably easier because I chose it, and I felt like I could do no worse than the school had; at least I'd maybe improve on that.

A similar situation faces parents everywhere in this time of a virus panic, moms and dads dealing with school policies on vaccines, masks, and social distancing, all of which has caused us to keep our kids at home, though most kids still take online lessons from the same school system. Why would anyone consider that computer-screen option, especially when the real problem is that those institutions are not doing well at the supremely important mission of educating our children? Why continue with what they're doing and just bring it into the home when most any parent can do a better job on his or her own?

Forgive me for not couching it better, but let's speak bluntly about why public education does such a poor job, something our parents are finally waking up to. You may not know this, but schools tend to teach two weeks or less on our American Constitution because many have instead made room for instruction on the United Nation's Universal Declaration of Human Rights, which maintains that everyone must be *given* lodging, food, clothing, and a job. But how do we provide those to everyone, once they all understand it will be granted simply by virtue of existing? Children are not stupid; that scenario sets up a conundrum in the child's mind, seeing how certain items are granted to everyone by a governing authority. Internalizing that thinking, a kid sees a world of other stuff that should be granted to them. Maybe a little boy doesn't have fancy sneakers like his friend, or a seven-year-old girl sees that her backyard is not as nice as the girl who invited her over, so they compare what they have to their little buddies running around in cool shoes, fancy jeans, with a backyard full of swings, toys, and an elaborate jungle gym. Here is how they might think about and process that situation:

"Why didn't I get those things? According to the United Nations, because that other kid has it, I too should be given those! So, what happened? Either my mom and dad are idiots because they aren't working the system well, or the program did not give our family what we deserve, meaning there is obviously nothing my parents can do. Whatever the reason, I want what is coming to me and I am just going to go take it!"

Besides that reason of a twisted unfairness, why else might a child feel justified to take someone else's stuff? Well, the schools have also taught them "survival of the fittest," which is bullying, something schools are having a real problem with, right?

Again, speaking bluntly, our teenagers have people like the self-proclaimed anarchist/Socialist Howard Zinn filling their heads full of falsehoods through books like his *People's History of the United States*, which is today's standard high school history text—that is, if it has not yet been supplanted by *The 1619 Project* (from the *New York Times*), a book that has been widely discredited because of its lies. Just a few of the disingenuous claims are that the US did not start as a sovereign nation set up for the freedom of the people; its founding principles were not life, liberty, and the pursuit of happiness; and we did not begin as a nation in 1776; instead, it was 1619 with the first slave ship. The book's main lesson for our children's mind to latch on to wrongly teaches that there is no redemption possible for the United States.

So, Mom and Dad, buyer beware!

The real focus of schools is anti-child, with lessons the skip over the fact the Darwinism is only a theory, instead having our kids think it's fact. And when we teach high-energy children that they are a mutation, an accident of nature, the idea establishes survival of the fittest as the law of the land. With that mindset instilled in every child, how do we have any authority left to criticize a bullied kid who takes the animalistic solution of grabbing a gun and shooting up the school? We are all just animals trying to dominate other animals, right? Wrong!

Another issue away from a home education is how children at public school cannot question the information in their lessons because government does not invite criticism as schools used long ago when our ancestors were taught lessons in logic, critical thinking, debate, rhetoric, and problem-solving. Today, kids are not allowed to question anything fed to them.

Probably the worst issue is how schools have removed Judeo-Christian instruction, replacing it with a completely contrary, anti-God religion—atheistic, secular humanism.

Schools also train children to identify authority and then obey it, the perfect indoctrination to facilitate a future citizenry that will follow every whim of politicians, governments, and their health agencies. And what have they learned about how to make obedient little robots? Throughout the day, schools instill behavior modification by ringing that bell to change classrooms, and when kids get in the room, make sure they do nothing unless formally instructed by a teacher at a blackboard. In other words, any action or request out of the ordinary should be met with "You can't!" And if "bad" little boys and girls don't completely comply with the day's orders, he or she will certainly not receive a gold star on their forehead. Hey, if you don't have the required piece of paper, *you can't* pass. And if you don't want to use the approved pencil, *you can't* move on—the class will shun you—*you can't* participate!

Another life lesson taught in school is that children can stop learning. How strange is a paradigm were graduates are excited that they "never have to crack a book again"?! That's certainly how I felt. But an education that produces that attitude has to be a perversion of the learning process.

Besides the harm to our children, why do I mention all that? Because so many parents, many of whom are college graduates and most being at least high school grads, claim they cannot teach their child. But the product of worthwhile education ought to be having the ability to teach what you've learned to someone else. Think about that for a moment. What good is knowledge if you can't impart it to somebody else? It's providing you little value by keeping knowledge to yourself, not sharing what you know with someone else.

That is the beauty of the exchange, whether it's wealth created through a commercial exchange or humans creating knowledge in another person, through exchange of information. Without the laws of physics discovered by Newton and Boyle, we would not get far, so the ability to impart facts should not be reserved only for those who have gone to some kind of educator's college, especially when we're talking about grade school stuff.

The other significant issue your children get for "free" from public schools is oversexualization built into the curriculum. The fact is that our schools have become grooming grounds for young children to be sexually trafficked, as demonstrated by today's second graders being taught adult topics like intercourse lubrication. And that sort of sexualizing kids is also why we have this huge push toward transgenderism. Those setting the lessons understand how hooking the children with that mentality at an early age makes it easier to own them for life.

And what is the main reason we send our kids to school? To get a good education, right? Well, that's not happening! Solid fundamental education has been virtually removed from the public school system at this point, which is why most young people don't get civics (the study of the rights and duties of citizenship). This is why so many Americans in our time think the Supreme Court is a legislative body that creates and passes laws, when the truth is that they only provide opinion about laws already on the books. We've all seen man-on-the-street interviews where a large percentage of Americans can't tell the questioner who our vice president is, how many branches are in the US government, or even what the names of those are. People today can't answer even the easiest components of American civics. Schools today won't teach the importance of a citizen's role in our representative government, so many don't understand the value of their vote and how the Electoral College process works to put politicians into office.

And it is not because they're stupid. This result was done to them on purpose. But why would schools do that? Why little or no civics? It's for the same reason there is a big push now to eliminate the Electoral College, and the people setting the public school curriculum are the ones wanting to "rid" us of the Electoral College. Why would these government people want to do that? Well, let's think this through: our government is of the *people*, by the *people*, and for the *people*, which means complete power resides with the *people*! Yet, for years, and years, and years, we send our children to learn from a place run by the corrupt, power-hungry government that—by its nature—would not want to teach people to keep their power and certainly not hand it over to the self-interested government!

And from that lack of civics, we get misguided actions like what happened after one particularly terrible school shooting, where the uproar resulted in our youth marching on Washington, DC, to get guns taken away from all honorable American gun owners. And that's not even a federal issue, just as most political issues aren't, so why would they be marching in the District of Columbia? It's because they have not been schooled on the people's rights versus the state's rights, and how our federal government only picks up the scraps. Completely contrary to those facts, these kids think all power resides in DC, and to a certain extent it does today, the result of decades where federal government has usurped power, while federal schools teach our people how powerful DC is, a despicable perversion implanted in our children through the daily indoctrination.

Government schools teach little or no civics because it conflicts with their interests and goals for society, which are focused on us turning more and more power over to them as the central authority. The fact that our federal government is at all involved in education is a complete conflict of interest. And who gets the brunt of the harm? It is we who instituted federal government rule over education, and surprisingly allow it to continue year, after year, after year—we the people must unyoke from that self-serving institution.

How bad is it? What is at stake? It is our freedom! And once we lose that, the rest goes out the window. We talk about how the Second Amendment allows citizens to be armed against a possible out-of-control federal government, and how that amendment protects all our other rights, but the more willing we are to sacrifice the other rights, as we have been more and more in recent decades, the more likely there won't be much left for the Second Amendment to protect. Just look at the first and simplest amendment about free speech. From getting constantly bombarded for decades now with political correctness (stopping free speech), today's average American is easily cowed away from speaking the truth. The Second Amendment is there to prevent a power struggle against a tyrannical government, but without free speech we're already impotent.

So, let's talk about a solution, which is home education. Luckily, Americans are losing their blinders since parents have recently been looking over their children's shoulder at the public school lessons coming across the home computer screen. The scales are falling from parents' eyes through exposure to exactly what has been happening during class time. A teacher recently went on social media to lament the fact that parents are able to hear his "lessons," which are an indoctrination into his worldview that claims humans have no gender roles and no defined gender—no differences between men and women. He was concerned that parents might find out and disapprove of his hypersexual lessons, especially the conservative parents who still have a traditional, moral foundation that would undermine what he was trying to do to their children.

Parents are learning how public schools undermine the values and morals that Mom, Dad, Grandma, and Grandpa work at instilling into their children or grandkids. Also, cause and effect are backward in our public schools, which is why children always ask whether the current information being taught will "be on the test." But the object of an education is not to pass exams. And this method of teaching to the test is a reason why parents who went to public school feel incapable of schooling their own child—teaching ability was never on one of their tests. So, since they didn't pass that exam, they think they don't know how to do it. But as a child, you never sat for an exam on using the bathroom, tying your shoes, or dressing and feeding yourself. Yet, you taught that to your children. Why stop there? Why is age six when we bring on the "experts" to take over? And even if you question your ability to teach reading, there are books that instruct adults on that. What about teaching math—too hard, right? There are books to help you with that too! In fact, home-educator textbooks show you exactly how to teach each lesson, and if one does not do it well enough, today there are many, many others to choose from. And those wonderful learning tools have mostly been reviewed by a bunch of parents like you, so they will collectively let you know which worked well.

The beautiful development these days is how homeschoolers have such easy access to excellent online and printed materials. Knowledge and the ability to teach it are no longer restricted commodities. Does that frighten teachers' unions? You bet! There's a well-kept secret that public education doesn't want you to know: through today's internet, finding an excellent education is easy, whether ordering the best books and supplies or just locating an online teaching program. But the government wants to trap you in this misnomer that you need a teacher—you don't!

A teacher is not necessary to homeschool kids. Parents need only engage their children in the art of learning, stoking the fires of curiosity that God granted every one of them. Then just watch them prosper! If your child asks, "Why are frogs green, Daddy?" A great answer would be "Gee, I don't know. Let's go look it up." Show them how to learn. Every one of us should always by learning, which is a beautiful part of life that schools contradict, having us believe our education either ends after twelfth grade, or we can go on to specialize in a narrow subject. Instead of tests, homeschooling focuses on knowledge, ability, and opening the entire world to the child. Schools often close them off to exploration, creativity, and imagination, much like the four-walled institutional classrooms they sit in all day. Again, the solution to what we're seeing today is home education.

Looking at the mass destruction on our streets these days, with all the rioting, looting, and building burning, sadly, I guarantee much of it stems from students' lessons learned in public schools: looting is survival of the fittest. In fact, I heard a Black Lives Matter protester excuse her behavior by claiming, "Hey, if you want a TV, you take that TV. The businesses are covered by insurance. It will be paid for." Of course, if she were really out to bring fairness to society, the insurance would not matter; she would acknowledge that you never take what is not yours. Though misguided, at least this looter felt some level of moral code, knowing she was doing wrong. But people have been so stoked with anger and fear that they've given in to the devil's bait and acted on it.

Much of the destruction can be blamed on the anger they've been instilled with, this idea that the United States is an inherently racist country. A comment on my riot-criticizing video suggested I look at "all the atrocities the Allies committed after World War II," as if that makes today's America just as evil. And not only are we not our ancestors, the US was even kind enough to rebuild our enemies' lands after World War II, unlike other victors throughout history who claimed the defeated territory. So, don't tell me we're somehow as bad as the people we fought against. Unfortunately, we did not vanquish communism in World War II, so it moved here to America and found a home in the Democrat Party—that's our fight today!

A main reason parents give for not home educating is a concern for the social aspect, kids spending time with a lot of other children. But if schools continue to mask and distance the students, that argument has been taken off the table because of COVID. Recently, they've basically been chained to desks, with no lunch hall or outdoor time. It's absurd what they're doing and planning to do with kids at the schools. And their plan for a public education at home is about sitting on Zoom all day, the last place you'd want your child—unsupervised screen time for five to eight hours per day. Even the simplest of educations, sitting them down at home with some classic literature, would be much better! And that way, girls would not be taught that they are not necessarily girls, or boys not boys.

Where can you go for information if you're considering a home education? I suggest you look at our website, SamSorbo.com, where I've posted many short videos to empower parents, helping educate them on how to get it done, which is certainly not rocket science. It is easier than you think, more rewarding than you can ever imagine, and keeps the family together instead of the wedge school puts between parents and their children. Home education completely eliminates that sort of barrier to having the closer relationship we want with our kids, and that they want. Some videos talk about how you can become the hero for your child, while others acknowledge that parenting is hard and home education is much easier by comparison. Again, parenting today is facing a crisis from schools that undermine Mom and Dad's authority; it's the way public education is set up while we feed right into it when we send kids off to school with the idea that we can't educate them. Instead, we toss our kids in schools that we are endorsing as the place and people they should spend every day with. This undermines our authority, which is part of the reason our children won't listen and roll their eyes at us. After spending all day with the school authority we've endorsed, parents find it hard to reassert their role as the authority in the home.

On top of that, children in schools learn to question parental authority because the humanistic, anti-God education they are sent to—for an atheistic indoctrination—is completely counter to Americans trying to teach their kids the truth about eternity-altering faith in Christ. And some teachers purposely slam our children with the sort of philosophy you would not want them anywhere near, the kind of ideas from politicians you may work hard against; yet there your child sits, taking it all in from the person who sets aside hours per day to build a trusting mentorship with your kid. A perfect example is the teacher I mentioned earlier who was lamenting the fact that parents might be able to listen in on his classroom, uncovering the lies he has been putting in our kids' brains. And just how badly do they want to keep us from learning what they've been teaching our children? You may have heard how some schools insisted parents sign a form agreeing not to monitor on-line classes, a request that should raise all kinds of red flags.

Another issue in these modern times is how we've infantilized children of all ages. During the time of our founding fathers, by age twelve or thirteen, an eighth grade graduate would be fluent in Greek and Latin, as they headed off to the best universities at the time, such as Harvard and Yale. That is not happening today. Actually, don't send them there! Those are now indoctrination schools.

Please use the resources I have created and made available to help parents easily transition to a wonderful home education. The greatest love story you will ever know is between a parent and child, the God-given mentoring relationship you are sacrificing by sending your child away to be "educated" by the government for *forty hours per week*! I urge you to make the sacrifice, instead of sacrificing your child to the schools. I want to give you an important quote from my book, which is by Kevin Williamson at the National Review Institute:

"There is exactly one authentically radical social movement of any real significance in the United States, and it's not Occupy, the Tea Party, or the Ron Paul faction. It is homeschoolers, who, by the simple act of instructing their children at home, pose an intellectual, moral, and political challenge to the government-monopoly schools, which are one of our most fundamental institutions and one of our most dysfunctional. Like all radical movements, homeschoolers drive the establishment [batty.]"

So, if we parents have a chance to drive the establishment institutionalists crazy, we all ought to jump on that opportunity.

I've been asked about the effects of groups in school like the LGBTQ clubs and their recruiting efforts, as well as if there's some way to remedy the problem under the law. I think it's too late to be resolved legally, and once you've exposed your child prematurely to anything inappropriately sexual, that is also too late, which is why I urge parents not to sacrifice your child to the beast that can easily devour him or her. A hungry, foul lion roams school halls, eager to indulge its appetite for young children, or kids of any age.

Here's a tragic issue in our schools that can have devastating effects on an immature teenage girl: Dr. Lisa Littman researched something called rapid-onset gender dysphoria, which is a modern issue in schools where young girls are being exposed to LGBTQ clubs, after which there is normally a cluster outbreak of girls identifying with one of the sexual orientations represented in the club. It becomes fashionable! At a time when these young minds are trying to figure out their place in the world and just want to belong (while at the same time they are also looking to exert a sense of individuality), they are easily seduced into the idea of being different, even though they are actually striving to fit in with the group of peers they've chosen. It's a race to see who can be the quirkiest, funniest, and in other ways show they're the best at being different, so they get seduced into something involving sexuality, which is already an extremely seductive force.

And this sort of hypersexuality is facilitated by effective Planned Parenthood outreach to schools, convincing girls it's fine and normal to prematurely have sex. And those nonvirgins often shame any holdouts to the point where the rest want to have sex just to avoid being the only ones left. Also, knowing girls have a built-in excuse to abstain because they might end up with a baby, Planned Parenthood and others hand them birth control, something they're often not responsible with at such a young age, so it often leads to unprotected sex and pregnancy—the perfect opportunity for adults in the business of abortion to convince the young girl to have her first abortion, after which they own her! They just do. They own your child through the shame involved, and it is so difficult to win them back from that life-altering state of mind.

Why role the dice, offering your child on the altar, and then hoping the little boy or girl you love so much will come through this massively influential public school experience intact.

I'm heartened to have convinced many of the fact that taking their kids out of the public school system is only eliminating a lot of real harm from coming their way. Do schools do some good? Not enough to warrant subjecting your innocent child to that environment. We must rethink how we look at education because most of us are products of public schools, so we've been indoctrinated into wrong thinking about education. Step outside of that paradigm where you had not thought to free your child from the institutional indoctrination; instead, take a journey with them to explore the world, and in that processing see him or her have a genuinely fulfilling life.

We have put together a lot of tools that can help in many ways. Please follow me on Facebook, Twitter, and Instagram; sign up for my newsletters at SamSorbo.com; and get helpful books like *They're Your Kids* and *Teach from Love*, the latter of which is a school-year devotional that walks you through how to teach godly virtues and moral principles, another aspect sorely lacking and even countered in a public education. For information on all the films Kevin and I have made, and those we are working on, you can go to SorboFamilyFilmStudios.com. Lastly, LeadersForLifeFilm.com is a movie I've just finished helping with; it makes the case that a nation like ours, which no longer values life, will understandably see more and more violence in the streets.

Again, home education opportunities are amazingly abundant today, especially now that you can take advantage of unlimited information about it on the internet. You are able to give and teach your child anything they or you desire. Once you begin, like anything, the newness can be bumpy, but you will soon grasp the tremendous opportunity this COVID virus has afforded you. This challenging situation may be an opportunity the Creator is using to introduce a different way of thinking. I can imagine His great work happening in the United States right now because the author of America and freedom is God the Father, who seems to be offering all parents a reprieve from the school madness; and an awesome opportunity for ourselves, our families, our nation, and, most importantly, our irreplaceable children. Do a quick search to find some of the many homeschool communities around you, and then connect with other parents on the life-altering, home education path. *You can do it!*

10

Simon Parkes: Unique Insights on Patriot Intelligence

England's Simon Parkes has an extensive worldwide following at SimonParkes.org, where he provides high-level intelligence on topics like the political landscape and deep state corruption. He has become a trusted source of intel, in part because of his upbringing in a family with links to British and American intelligence, including a mother who worked for MI5 (the UK's *domestic* counterintelligence and security agency). However, while Simon's mother was being managed by MI5, she was really working for the United States' NSA (National Security Agency). Likewise, Simon's grandfather was employed by MI6 (Britain's *foreign* intelligence service), while actually reporting to America's CIA (Central Intelligence Agency).

As a single parent, Simon's mother raised him from 1965 until her death in 1979, and during this time she worked on secret German-language documents that came from the British and American quarters of a divided Berlin, Germany. Some of these documents related to American-recovered, crashed UFOs, which the US had ex-Nazi German scientists analyze and attempt to back-engineer. This was made possible because sixteen hundred German scientists, engineers, and technicians were relocated to America after World War II, in a US program called Operation Paperclip. Simon's mother died under suspicious circumstances in 1979 when she asked to be released from the work, after which Simon received an envelope with 2,000 euros that was pushed under his door, along with a note that read:

"Don't look back, Dick Whittington."

Whittington was a medieval-period merchant and politician. So, Simon relocated to London. His grandfather was also a British diplomat who held the position of vice consul and consul at the British Embassy in Pondicherry (now known as Puducherry), India. While in India he was awarded the OBE (Order of the British Empire) and CBE (Most Excellent Order of the British Empire) medals, as well as knighthood, which he turned down. In 1936 Simon's grandfather was one of the "Wise Men of Twelve" or "Jury of Twelve," who voted on a question regarding King Edward VIII, which was whether the king should be removed after the special branches (national security **and** intelligence) uncovered a Nazi plot to infiltrate the king. This attempted ouster had nothing to do with the king wanting to marry a divorcee, as history tells it. Over a secure teleprinter link and in code, his grandfather was asked:

"Should the king go?" or *"Should he stay?"* Simon's grandfather voted *"Go."*

In 2010, Simon went public with his experiences, causing predictable ridicule from the mainstream media. During 2013, with a serving and retired group of twenty military personal, he was invited to tour a space-radar base in North Yorkshire. Simon was the only civilian that day and ended up being the sole individual handed a commemorative medallion coin, which was number eight-six out of only five hundred worldwide. This was a limited edition made to celebrate fifty years of the USAF being based in North Yorkshire. This visit was a game changer, suddenly ending the British media's hounding of

Simon, who went on to establish a worldwide organization that he will talk more about later.

The following is from my April 2021 interview of Simon. For better readability and flow, this is a paraphrase that retains the original meanings. Here is Simon Parkes:

In summing up the current psyops (psychological operations) our planet is experiencing, the major efforts break down to two: We have the cabal deep state (what we used to call the Illuminati) still engaged with their long-running, nefarious psyop that includes the fake news media everywhere. This group seeks world domination. That evil is being countered by the good guys, or white hats, who have a psyop running to awaken people to the other cabal's psyop, while foiling the bad guys' attempts at predicting and circumventing the white hat plan. Both sides are playing a very difficult game at the moment.

Some of the recent activity has involved Mossad (Israel's intelligence service) satellites, which have the capability to interfere with worldwide communications and the new quantum financial system that is about to roll out for the planet. The Mossad satellites have the ability to prevent a white hat like President Trump from addressing the nation, if he were to do so from a nonterrestrial (space) position. Fortunately for America, hunter-killer satellites designed to incapacitate or destroy other satellites took out the problematic Mossad satellites, so space now belongs to America.

As a crucial part of the deep state's past efforts to counter the good guys' satellite surveillance, they had a sixty-mile tunnel running beneath the cabal's Vatican and extending toward their stronghold in Switzerland. This had allowed Roman Catholic leadership to secretly move its gold and other resources, without American NRO (National Reconnaissance Office) spy satellites being able to view and record the movements. When American teams made it into those tunnels, they found thirty-foot-deep assortments of stolen items on either side of the tunnel. Some of it dated back to ancient Egypt's Great Library of Alexandria, which was established over 2,200 years ago. When the items were recovered and collated, the estimated worth was something like $34 quintillion US dollars ($34,000,000,000,000,000,000).

The white hats needed a large number of crates and airplanes to remove it all. Much ended up in the US through a deal that helped the Italian government save face, while also remaining intact, partly because they worked with the white hats to expose all this, getting them somewhat off the hook. Items that could be identified, such as a painting that has a known painter or an understanding of where it came from, were returned. As an example, some valuables were returned that belonged to the czar and czarina of Russia. But the vast majority of the wealth is going to be used by the white hats to reset the world's financial system.

As far as Joe Biden's presidency, it's important to understand that any television politician is not very important when compared to those we do not get to see on a screen. Capturing, charging, and releasing a bad public figure back into circulation is not a relatively sizable issue because people like Joe Biden aren't the core problem, as are those who purposely don't appear in public. The latter are those involved in child trafficking, those who control the international money laundering, and the ones calling for hits on people. So, it's relatively easy for the white hat operation (psyop) to maintain a public status quo, while the real battle is being fought behind the scenes.

The real Joe Biden passed on months ago, which can be corroborated by video like the one of Biden stumbling up the stairs of Air Force One, but instead of focusing on the three or four times he stumbles, notice how the actor reaches the top of the steps, after which he stands tall like a young man when he turns to salute. However, once he turns to go into the plane, he hunches over again, seeming to remember his role as an old man. In that instance we saw an actor, where as other times the supposed on-screen Biden has just been a computer-generated image (CGI), and still others closer up might just be another person wearing a Biden mask. Like Castle Rock studio in California, there are several replica White Houses around the US, the locations where actors portray Biden for the cameras. It's all happening through the good guys who are ensuring that comments, mistakes, and bits of information are dropped, all designed to help wake up as many people as possible.

Joe Biden is no longer with us, and I won't go into details about how that occurred because words like "execution" are difficult for the general public to accept, especially if it is said that some white hats did away with him. But this is war, and most people aren't aware of who is orchestrating certain events, such as how that Nashville bombing in December 2020, which was detonated in a recreational vehicle, was actually done by the white hats—no one died.

People have asked me to talk about the fencing around the White House, which had to do with National Guard-loving President Trump, in large part because he respects the armed forces and its veterans. So, they were not protecting the bad guys from the white hats; instead, they were sealing off a location that normally can't be and doing so as cover for the work that needed to get done there.

Speaking of our military, when my YouTube channel was at about three million viewers, I took a huge hit in losing it after being one of the first to explain that every US vote is part of a quantum system that allows the US armed forces to follow every ballot. Talk of a watermark on the ballots was a bit of a smokescreen because each one was traceable from space. On January 20, when Biden was supposedly inaugurated, there had been no plan to arrest him though they did pick up some of the smaller fish. On the cabal side, about an hour before Biden's inauguration, Spain had an explosion in Madrid, which was part of a bad guy message to the white hats, warning that they better not arrest anyone that day, or explosives would be detonated in every European city. That is part of the reason the white hats held off from any action on Inauguration Day.

Three year ago, somebody came to visit me who had just been on Air Force One with President Trump, and then two weeks later, a person from President Putin spent hours explaining Putin's plans and how they fit the worldwide picture. I've always supported the good side, so I decided to involve more people by creating a group called Connecting Consciousness (ConnectingConsciousness.org). We now have about seventy thousand people worldwide, including throughout every state in the US, each with its own coordinator who looks after and manages a group of members. Particularly in the English-speaking world, I have sought to build a strong, spiritual, patriot group who can support each other. I'm certainly not a millionaire, so I just created it out of love, belief, and a search for truth, which has led to my belief in God, who I think wanted this group to form. Some of my information comes through these members who are confident that I won't reveal sources, which is especially important because the group includes people with military intel.

Those now awake are upset that voter corruption hasn't been dealt with yet, whether that is militarily or however, but they don't understand why this white hat psyop is being played. Solutions just seem to be progressing too slowly for them. Unfortunately, though, here in April 2021, 75 percent of the entire English-speaking world is still asleep. Had President Trump and the armed forces intervened on day one of the stolen election, it would have been sold as a coup against the US Constitution. So, the whole plan for the US has been to wake that three quarters of the American population to accept the truth when it is finally able to be released, creating less-shocked people and enough already informed to help the others who will be wondering how they missed all this. It's a difficult game, but always remember how the US military cares about the people and the Constitution, so the last thing they want is to cause a societal breakdown in America.

The 2020 support for President Trump's reelection was so big that he flipped California to the Republican side. In fact, the only state Trump didn't win was New York. But the difficulty in overturning the fraud is because of the US courts. Good Americans believe their judiciary is honest. And of course, those enforcers of the Constitution should rise above politics. The courts must remain independent from outside influences, but the majority of today's US judges are not independent—they've been compromised. And that means the US armed forces could not count on the courts backing their actions against a stolen election. So, any move the military might have made earlier would probably not have worked out well.

With the finances, what will unfold is a new system that will starve the bad people of their lifeblood—their money—which will facilitate a conversation with those like mainstream media who will either need to change to honest news or be replaced. Along with a new means of exchange and compensation for labor, I expect President Trump to return. There will be a whole new breed of lawmakers, judges will be retrained, and public education will get revamped. We need to pull the old system out, root and branch, and then make a new creation that gets America back to God and human-first values, instead of today's focus on profits.

To spread this idea of a more honorable way, we are lucky to have new platforms coming online like Mike Lindell's FrankSpeech.com. However, that alone won't bring Trump back, so we need overt action to help wake a huge percent of the English-speaking world, those who believe the mainstream news narrative. From my own conversations, I know the white hats are disappointed at the number of people still stuck in the old paradigm. We have a British saying:

"Sometimes a person has to be slapped around the face with a wet fish."

Sometimes the truth has to be pushed into people's faces, which I think is coming because we've gone as far as we can with the soft and gentle approach. I believe this awakening is going to take a bit more, whether that's an act of God or whatever; it's probably got to be more physical—and that's just around the corner.

As far as the timing of Trump getting back in office, I think any date that has attention forming around it is probably not right, though I am thinking it will happen sooner rather than later. We are in a long-term war with the deep state, something President John F. Kennedy was also a part of when he was murdered in 1963, not because he was mentioning US sighting of UFOs, but from his efforts back then to do exactly what we are now—rooting out the cabal! He was stopped because he wanted to give power back to the people.

Going forward from Kennedy to the attacks of 9/11, most would say the latter was part of an effort to get the US into another world war. It did lead to conflicts in Afghanistan and Iraq. Many think 9/11 was used to help Congress pass draconian laws. But the reason that is not under-stood—at least for taking down World Trade Center Building Seven—is that it contained all the gold the good guys were planning to use for a second attempt at eliminating the cabal (Kennedy being the first). But just like the murder of Kennedy, that threat to the deep state was foiled by the cabal stealing all the gold. So, the good guys learned they had to play it differently going forward, which brings us to this third attempt right now to move America and the rest of the planet to a system that treats humans as humans, instead of slaves. That is the history where President Kennedy in 1963 and thousands of Americans during 9/11 lost their lives in the cabal's attempt to prevent humanity from breaking free. But today, we are taking them down without soldiers and tanks on the streets, a military that would somehow force freedom.

The cabal is all about the money, which I call their "spell gem" because it always controls people in a negative way. Used properly, money is an important commodity for ease of trade, but it has also been what man has enslaved people with. In regard to debt forgiveness being a possible part of the financial reset, I do believe most all debt will be forgiven, and as one of his first acts, I'm hoping President Trump's return will include doing away with income tax. I'd also like to see credit cards, car loans, and mortgage interest down to 1 percent, and I think that is where we're headed.

In regard to humanitarian projects connected to NESARA and GESARA (National and Global Economic Security and Reformation Act), which are programs that do away with the Federal Reserve Bank, the Internal Revenue System, and the rest of the deep state's shadow government, the only people who will receive any reward out of it will be those who are spiritually good and want to do something honorable for their neighbors, communities, families, and friends—no one evil will get the funds.

The new currency will be the United States "note" with no dollar sign on its physical form, and it will be different from previous gold-backed notes in that it will be gold supported as the new *standard*. The US note will be tradable on a one-to-one basis with many other nations' notes, and the whole system will have levels, or tiers, with one being the "sovereign," or highest, followed by descending values of two through five. Five will be the tier of an ordinary person in public, and they will have the opportunity to go to certain participating banks and show their potential plans for humanitarian projects. If he or she is proven to be spiritually honorable, to have good intentions, why wouldn't they be supported and empowered?

Those expecting to get rich from holding suitcases of Iraqi dinar currency will be disappointed, though some with stacks of dinar, who are holding it because they believed in the system and want to do good work with the money, will be supported. And I think that time is close. The Iraqis set their budget and an exchange rate but have thus far held back from publicly advertising it, so we are not yet able to know what the exchange rate is for the dinar.

On March 11, 2021, President Trump was duly elected as the commanding officer of a US military, having 80 percent support from our armed forces, which means the deep state's control within the military is now quite small. My hope is that President Trump soon returns as the nineteenth president of the United States (Ulysses S. Grant was eighteenth), picking up where he left off, but this time with a restored US Constitutional Republic (as it was during Grant's time). Both Flynn brothers (retired Army Lieutenant General Michael Flynn, former National Security advisor for Trump, and active-duty army general Charles Flynn, commander of the US Army Pacific Fleet) had a recent meeting with President Trump, one at Trump's Florida residence at Mar-a-Lago and the other in the Pentagon or Capitol building. So, the Flynns have their marching orders, two brothers playing very different roles in the areas of military and humanitarianism. Both have proven themselves to be above corruption.

One important area Trump has concentrated on fixing since he was first elected in 2016 is the problem of human trafficking. The white hats have been securing, taking out, and filling many tunnels that had been used for that purpose, and their weapon of choice has been the neutron bomb because it creates no radiation fallout. Shockingly, some tunnels are at a depth of twenty to sixty miles underground. In 1974, part of my mother's work was on a nuclear-powered boring machine, a device we know about today but it was in the prototype stage then. The front of it had a nuclear reactor made to melt rock, and the bad guys have been using those sorts of advanced technologies to create an underground tunnel system, something we learned from the clever German Nazis.

Keep in mind that sex trafficking is not only about the money but also a way of life for satanically evil, deprived people, who have formed their own religious club that worships the devil. To them, Satan is all that matters, but the financial rewards also motivate them. This intricately involved, insane group of people is totally separate from the rest of us who have a semblance of decency, so they need places like their secret tunnels where they can meet, hide, and undertake unspeakable acts, ceremonies for their witch and wizard covens.

Part of my work over the past ten years has been to help adults and children coming out of that horrifying, captured life, an existence where children are sexually abused for the fun of it, and also because that sort of torture prepares them for future cabal work. With that in mind, if you are part of the deep state and want to control the world, how would you prepare a potential future president, someone like maybe Barack Obama? Well, you want to begin controlling them early in life, so you still have that "asset" when you've helped put him into high office. I've worked with a number of survivors like children who've been tortured, some from Hollywood and others with impoverished backgrounds. Having seen all that, I can assure you that this is a war against evil, and good is going to win!

We've all seen videos of George Herbert Walker Bush's funeral, where former US presidents, their families, and other prominent folks found a surprise envelope in their folded programs. There has been much speculation about what was written inside those, so let me tell you the two simple sentences given to the cabal members that day:

"We know everything. You're going to be arrested when you come outside of the church."

The only one not receiving the message was the younger Bush, who'd already had an interesting and helpful chat with President Trump. Many wonder why Trump would surround himself with people he knows to be untrustworthy, but when you've lived a life in espionage (working with spies), it is easier to see that he was giving these people a chance to denounce their past and turn good, a repentance that former Vice President Mike Pence failed to take advantage of: Trump gave him a second chance. He did not come clean. That was his choice.

One of the few crimes I have a hard time forgiving is anyone who purposely hurts a child, for which I've been accused of not "evolving" enough. But sexually abusing a child is something truly evil people do, and in this battle between good and satanic, the latter needs to be dealt with, which includes the legacy of a few wrongly revered people. H. G. Wells was an author employed by British intelligence and also a member of the Illuminati, while Orson Welles (no relation) performed a wonderful radio broadcast of H. G.'s *War of the Worlds*. What people don't understand is that Orson Welles was tasked with the experiment to see what fear his broadcast would cause, which turned out to be vast numbers of people getting crazy with panic and arming themselves to protect against what they thought was surely Martians coming to get them.

Having learned from Orson, today's white hats have realized they are responsible for the narrative that will develop from every action they take against the cabal, so they wisely understand they can't just plow through the situation where they have a chance to take down some bad guys; they must consider whether the public's response will remain peaceful.

I am often asked if Jeffrey Epstein's life is still intact, and what I can tell you is the cabal was out to kill him, so the good guys removed him and that possibility. Epstein's girlfriend, Ghislaine Maxwell, has been the more important of the two, mostly because she'd had the greater interest and involvement with planning. He was adept at meeting the personalities and doing the deals, while she took the organizational side, so her capture supplied information like that which liberated some tunnels. This is why the white hats are not letting her out on bail—not because she would run away, but for her safety from the deep state who would kill her within a half hour of release.

Maxwell also supplied information about the Evergreen Marine Corporation and its Ever Given container ship, which is one of the largest in the world, and is the vessel that the good guys intercepted in the Suez Canal for six days in March 2021. It was on a nefarious mission involving the setup for one of the deep state's last-resort plays, or final cards, which included the nuclear weapons that were on board. There was also a ton of other material like nerve gas that could be used by terrorist organizations. We've known for a long time that the air-conditioned containers on those kinds of ships have been used to move children around, so some military that got on board had body cameras, taking footage to be shown at upcoming military tribunals. Most is not for public consumption, but some may be used to help wake people.

That enormous vessel had HRC as its call sign (identification through unique numbers and letters written on the side), which is also interesting because Hillary Rodham Clinton's secret service name was Evergreen—like that shipping company. The boat's autopilot was taken over through a command signal relayed from space, and once in the Suez Canal, the Russian and American navies blocked each end of the Suez; neither navy could enter the canal since it is a demilitarized area. So, this was the Russians working with the Americans to block the ship's exit of the canal, after which the ship was overtaken by white hats, moved, and then thoroughly searched. Its two Egyptian pilots and the captain were arrested because they must have known what was going on. Except for the dreadful loss of life found on board, it was a wonderful operation with many rescued.

Some have asked about John F. Kennedy, Jr., and I'd rather not give my perspective on that one, but if he is alive, his role in the future would certainly involve his help with healing. I can envision him and possibly one of the Flynn brothers traveling state to state, holding conferences to bring people back together again. John Jr. would also make a very good president.

Some people may not be aware of this, but about two and a half years ago, there was another attempt by the deep state to drop a pandemic-type virus into America. That substance was intercepted and captured from what we call a Chinese-English school. From that success, the white hats had already been working on an antidote back then, and they also became aware that the Chinese Wuhan Institute of Virology was about to transport another batch of this virus, sneaking it out to let loose in America. However, their planned operation was foiled when the guy carrying the virus was shot in a marketplace. Unfortunately, though, the shopping area had a stone floor, causing the culprit to drop his four-inch-long vial, which broke, releasing the virus. Of course, the Chinese were not expecting that, but it gave the Americans time to prepare by Trump putting together military doctors and medical suppliers to create a vaccine. However, since it is illegal for the military to sell a vaccine to the people, the good guys employed a private company that was paid a large sum to say they created it. Of course, other companies joined in manufacture of their own vaccines, resulting in a range of them: some that do nothing, others which are pretty good, and substances I would not want to be in the same room with.

Unity exists among a group of major world leaders: US President Donald Trump, Russia's Vladimir Putin, China's Xi Jinping, and Vietnam's Nguyen Xuan Phuc. They are all working together behind the scenes, but the issue to be worked out is whether the Chinese military will try to remove their own leader (Xi) because many elements are the bad guys. I've talked with the Chinese elders, who used to be called the Red or White Dragons, and I can tell you they just want a better world, so they will support Xi Jinping and other good people—the military is who we're not sure of.

Some high-ranking people who've done bad things have already faced justice, but the United States seems to hold a magic aura around ex-presidents, which means the white hats are reluctant to make immediate moves that would harm America's image, even if the reveal is about events that happened decades ago. There have been some high-ranking, totally evil people in America who have been removed, with a lot more to come, though I've not agreed with the notion that thousands of bad people have already been executed. It's true that a lot of charges have been handed down against cabal individuals, who've been allowed to continue roaming free as long as they don't leave the continental United States.

I respect the American people and think they deserve the whole truth, instead of the white hats' possible plan to keep the worst from the public because it is just so ugly! There is a danger in that, which parallels how bad people have kept the truth from us. I think it's incumbent on the good people to lay the cards on the table and then support the American people as they begin to understand and come to terms with what the heck has happened to their country and on behalf of their nation.

As US attorney general for President Trump (and formerly for George H. W. Bush), Bill Barr was one of those given an opportunity to come clean and did just enough to win the support of President Trump, but I don't think he will play a role in the new government because he didn't do everything he was asked to do. Barr was a clever tightrope walker.

Talking about the honorable side to this fight, we can't understand what God is because we're not gods. Even five-thousand- or six-thousand-year-old nonhuman entities believe in God, but they can't define Him, so perhaps they and we are not meant to? God is such that we can't see Him but might experience Him or see signs. The question is whether we actually understand what we've been shown. And if we do, how do we act upon it? It's all about choice. God is real. God is who created life and stands for 100 percent good.

One effort I'm involved with is deprogramming people who have been intentionally tortured as the way to control their minds, but that sort of help is not something a person can learn at college. If so, the CIA and others would lose a lot of their control. It seems God has given me an ability to do this. Because He individually gifts certain skills to each of us, we have to be brave enough to employ them, and then God will ensure we are able to do the work. Luckily, I've helped people who've gone on to handle elite jobs. Many victims of torture-induced mind control had it happen as preschool children. They didn't ask for it, so I am happy to help undo what the evil people did to them.

As far as what might end up as President Trump's greatest accomplishment, I don't believe he's done it yet, but upon his return he will help install the new financial system, which will really set people free. Another aspect of his work will be help with our worst threat—artificial intelligence.

I believe America needs to continue leading the world over the decades to come because it has been chosen by God—not as a policeman for the world but as the nation that sets the standard for treating people properly, an example of laws written correctly like those outlined in the US Constitution. The coming days will see a rejuvenation of America, again becoming a shining example for other nations.

I know the British people (like me) and average Americans have a solid bond as America does with Australia, but my heart goes out to the Canadian people because their government is far from an American mindset, so I would like the Canadian people to put a bit of pressure on their Canadian government.

Those Americas awake already, like many reading this, may have lost some trust from family and friends, but be strong and know you made the right choice. The sleepers have been wrong. You are right. They'll soon realize. And at that point, you must be available to support them, kindly helping to bring them back into the fold of those living in reality.

11

Mike Adams: Social Media Censorship and Luciferase

Mike Adams is best known as the Health Ranger, an outspoken consumer-health advocate, award-winning investigative journalist, internet activist, and science-lab director. Mike is the patriot founder and editor of NaturalNews.com, the internet's most trafficked natural-health news website, as well as Brighteon.com, a free-speech alternative to conservative-banning, truth-censoring YouTube. For flow and readability, the following is a paraphrase of my May 2021 interview. Here's Mike:

As far as what happened with the 2020 elections, Patrick Byrne (founder of Overstock.com) is a high-IQ individual, who is spot on with his analysis, even when it has been pessimistic at times like post-election when he expressed much discontent with the staffers surrounding President Trump. For example, Pat Cipollone was one of those running interference to keep Trump from learning and rightly dealing with the truth. It is a hopeful sign that Patrick now has a sense of optimism about the direction of this audit process, and I believe his analysis is accurate, but I'm not sure I dare hope the Supreme Court does the right thing because those justices face extreme pressure from the deep state. I know Chief Justice Roberts is compromised, as well as at least a few others. I've even seen bad decisions from the new Trump-appointed justices.

But a remedy might not have to involve SCOTUS if the states begin to revoke their votes that contributed to the so-called Biden victory. They can do that retroactively, bringing us to a contested election, two presidents simultaneously, and the American people literally up in arms; demanding a fresh paper-ballot vote, pressuring the military, and pushing the Supreme Court to render a decision in that direction. I think that possibility is probably where all this is headed.

And the health issue of the past year, their hugely ramped-up efforts to harm and kill people through vaccines, shows their desperation; they are accelerating the mass-murder agenda as Joe Biden works to cause an economic collapse through massive, unlimited money printing and the destruction of the dollar. They want to destroy America before anything happens that could override the election—it's a race against history right now.

Over three years ago, when I was one of the first to be deplatformed by YouTube, we wanted to continue getting honest information out, so I started the project to fund and build Brighteon.com. Even back then, before many became aware of the dangers, I was warning about vaccines. The key to securing free speech on our social media platform is that we own it entirely; venture capitalists were not involved. It's funded from our pockets. We have complete control. And Brighteon will never be a public offering where we sell shares on the open market for any nefarious group to get their hands on. We will also not have a board of directors that could end up corrupted—no board! Since I am the guy making decisions for our site, you get a proven Texas-patriot gun owner who is for America and our Constitution, as well as an advocate for natural health and freedom around the world. I will maintain control of the platform to provide freedom of speech to everybody who wants to participate. We have hundreds of thousands of users already and millions of videos available.

That said, we do not have the funding of video-sharing platforms like Rumble, but I am always concerned about an injection of money causing outside influence that most often leads to the yanking of the company's chain. For example, just look what happened to Parler after their huge infusion of funds, not long before all sorts of problems took them down. I do not trust outside investors, and we have to keep these technologies in the hands of dedicated, proven patriots. Frankly, the persecution of honesty has been so widespread that I don't trust anyone today who hasn't been attacked by the mainstream media and Wikipedia, an assault that is a badge of honor. And as far as I'm concerned, to be trusted, anyone with a significant following has to have been smeared by the *New York Times* and the *Washington Post*.

Of course, with all we know about the extreme dangers of vaccines, one pervasive question among patriots right now is why has President Trump been pushing vaccines since he began by promoting Operation Warp Speed? Well, I seem to have stumbled upon an answer: It appears that 90 percent of Democrats and only 60 percent of Republicans are taking the vaccines. If Dr. Luc Montagnier is correct and, unfortunately, those taking these vaccines die within the next two years, what do you think that does to change the 2022 and 2024 electorate and halting the theft of elections? I am not claiming patriots and Trump desire mass deaths, but I think Trump is using the left's own weapons against them. He may have pushed these vaccines into production, knowing that they would be harmful and mostly taken by Democrats who believe in the corrupt medical authority. And Trump's Warp Speed caused only emergency-use authorization for the vaccines, so the shots were not able to be made mandatory—people retained the choice. As soon as Biden was sworn in, suddenly those not trusting "Trump's" vaccines magically believed in Biden's shots, even though it was all the same injections. Did Trump, as a long-term thinker and strategist, anticipate that change in attitude?

One other area where Trump has thought ahead is through his social media platform launching this July. From experience, it is a complex project so I honestly think it stuttered a bit at first with many hiccups along the way, just like what happened in the past couple months to Mike Lindell's FrankSpeech.com. But over some time, the platform will smooth out and have a massive influence on future elections. I'll be happy to participate. I'll join any patriot platform. And I'll promote them!

Getting back to our food supply, which is more my area of expertise, personal sources are warning of extreme supply-chain disruptions. In fact, my operation buys pallets of food that cost us millions of dollars every year, and our firsthand experience right now is disruptions with food suppliers that have run out of stock; logistics and supply lines are in short supply, including rail, trucking, and shipping from overseas resources; and some suppliers are demanding full payment up front, instead of their usual willingness to extend credit.

Those issues, combined with the engineered drought in California and the continued COVID lockdowns of certain food-processing operations that exist in Democrat blue states, tell me we will continue to see price inflation of groceries through the end of this year and probably well into 2022 before we can hope for adequate supply to come back online. Even adding more aggravation to the rough situation is US dollar destruction. So, both problems combine to eat into incomes, especially those of low-wage earners and other poor people; the result may build toward food riots in America—this year!

My assessment of the immediate outlook for America is short-term hell and chaos, as part of mass economic collapse and deaths. But in the end, God and His people win. I am an optimist in the long run, but there is a lot of suffering between here and there.

As far as President Trump's greatest accomplishment, I would say that had to be forcing the swamp to expose itself, including their left-wing media, with its constant bias and lies that have been revealed for all to see. The fact that Trump even existed and sat in the Oval Office caused such insanity that the world now knows they can't trust the dying mainstream media, left-wing politicians, tech giants, and all the rest of the deep state apparatus. Trump's very existence brought all that out, and now there is no question it exists.

Right now, the greatest threat facing humanity is not a quick answer, but I would say this on a spiritual level: So much of these attacks on humanity are from satanism being practiced by those pushing Lucifer's agenda, which is apparent when you look at vaccines being designed to kill people. And they are more and more bold about it these days, not even hiding their devil worship when they give an occult name to new discoveries like "luciferase," a class of oxidative enzymes that produce bioluminescence (emit light).

What is behind the tech giants who censor the truth? Satan worship through demonic rituals is not just some fringe activity anymore; it's the way key creative players in the tech industry live, causing them to hate their own Creator, as well as His Bible, humanity, and the human body. This is why they are into transgenderism and the push to mutilate people's reproductive organs. They cannot stand a mother and father giving birth to another human that is created in God's image. It offends them. Luciferian satanism is our biggest threat. But God's on our side. God wins! We win! Though we are experiencing the epic struggle right now, just remember whose side we are on, which means we will come out okay in the end—we'll make it through this!

12

Jovan Pulitzer: Expert Information about How They Rigged Our 2020 Vote

Jovan Pulitzer is a winner of the National Medal of Technology and Innovation, the nation's highest honor for technological achievement, an award bestowed on America's leading innovators and handed to them by the president of the United States. The medal is awarded for outstanding contributions to our economic, environmental, and social well-being. Jovan is a laureate medal winner who is involved with augmented reality, artificial intelligence, machine learning, computer vision, general health care, mobile health care, engagement technologies, and the data-analysis industries. He has also created numerous product companies that have generated over a billion dollars in consumer sales, and his patents have been licensed to more than 330 companies, ranging from early stage firms to Fortune 100 industry leaders such as eBay, IBM, AOL, Cisco, Google, Walgreens, TiVo, and many, many others. As the winner of the 2001 Smithsonian Laureate Medal for "most likely to change society," Pulitzer's patents are part of case studies in over 140 universities, including Brown, Duke, Yale, Princeton, and Harvard.

Here is a paraphrase of Jovan Pulitzer from a late April interview in 2021, expertly discussing our 2020 electoral process and its lack of integrity:

Our American voting system does not have just a few flaws; it is riddled with issues and errors—100 percent broken. But don't just take my word for it; here is a simple test so you can decide for yourself: When you go into your precinct and fill out a ballot, before someone scans it in to a machine, have you voted? No, your vote is not counted until later. Most of us probably feel that our votes should be counted the moment they are cast, so ask yourself why the decision on your vote is withheld until later. That's a problem. Second, we've probably all thought these machines had to be flawless, but do you know they were made to even accept blank ballots and hold them in a file? An elementary school child these days could probably figure out how to kick those out, right? If we put a phony dollar in a vending machine, it immediately gets kicked back to us. Well, voting machines don't do that. They also won't warn you when they cannot read your vote, when a counterfeit ballot was fed in instead of an authentic one, or when the ballot was manufactured in another country, copied, or even created on a home printer.

Last but not least, why would a machine need the ability to allow adjudication (making a subjective judgment) of your vote? Whenever the machine determines something looks wrong, those votes are put aside in a file until someone else comes along to ultimately decide who those votes should count for. Why include that feature and not just kick it back like any old vending machine would? I think all of these are purposely created opportunities for nefarious activities to aid the stealing of elections.

Keep in mind that movements in these elections are not necessarily orchestrated by Dr. Evil and his minions in the cabal. Those conspirators are not even needed because these machines allow even blue-haired Mabel to make a few copies of any ballot she likes and then feed all of them into the machine. Keep that in mind as we look at the numbers for Fulton County (Atlanta), Georgia, with over a million people, a place where the election for president in 2020 was decided by only 9,250 votes. The area has about 2,500 voting precincts, so that comes out to less than four flipped votes needed in every precinct. Here's my question: Though the ability to cheat is a simple fix these days, but the machines have been made to take ballots that are blank, faked, copied, or counterfeited, could any random election worker who was passionate about their candidate slip at least four fraudulent votes in over the course of a twelve-hour voting day? Sure. No one would notice a few random pieces of paper tucked into a worker's stack.

So, these machines have plenty of opportunistic flaws available to be exploited, and let me tell you other interesting aspects of this recent election, discoveries I was asked to testify about in front of Georgia's Senate Subcommittee on Election Integrity. From statistics, the Democrat or Republican leaning of an area is known, even if many there do not vote—even Google knows. With the 2020 election in Fulton County, the Democrat-leaning area had ballots perfectly printed, but with no checksum, which is the ability to leave an electronic checkmark in the database after making sure the voter's signature has been verified. It was just gone, so signatures could not be authenticated even if the poll worker wanted to. A whole other issue happened for the Republican-leaning area where the machines reading ballots are not supposed to vary in their alignment by more than one to three millimeters—the Republican-area alignment was off 1,300 percent.

Look at that like a hunter peering through his high-power scope at a deer: if the scope had been calibrated correctly like it was in the Democrat area, a softly pulled trigger (catching the deer between breaths) would allow the shot to pass through the lungs and land just at the bottom of the heart for a clean kill that would drop his target on the spot. In the Republican area, the horribly calibrated scope pointed at the deer would cause his bullet to completely miss the deer and maybe hit a neighbor who was nowhere near the animal. And with these machines, they would not even tell you if you hit the deer or the neighbor. Once the voting machine is tricked into thinking that ballot is unreadable, it stores the Republican's vote for later adjudication by whoever controls each voting precinct. When the machine is that screwed up, it obviously dislikes a high percentage of the Republican ballots, so those votes will go the way the reviewer of that file decides.

Besides all that, for some inexplicable reason the machines are made with a feature that allows each precinct controller to set a percentage of votes they would personally like to adjudicate, whether that is 20 percent, 60 percent, or even 90 percent of all votes. Why would a voting machine have a feature that suspends and holds your and my vote until someone else decides whether to give our vote to Trump or Biden? That is sickening! So, when I exposed this to the Georgia Senate, the Republican secretary of state took action—he released a dishonest and brutal hit piece on me. And that following week, the Republicans who invited me to speak were all fired from the Election Integrity Committee.

I think the most important election components are physical ballots. If a country's vote involved information and manipulation done electronically through some other random place like Timbuktu, that injured nation would never get their hands on the computer server who committed the fraud. But if the only vote we have to deal with is paper ballots, we get physical forensic evidence of each vote, just like we use in the prosecution of counterfeit currency, stocks, bonds, passports, and so much else.

Here's what is really interesting when we think about today's voting system in America: You can be called to serve on a jury trial that has life-changing outcomes for those you will be judging, whether you're an electrician, cafeteria worker, landscaper, stay-at-home parent, or whoever. So, why does our election system with its voting machines take a computer scientist or engineer to understand? That seems to be totally upside down and nontransparent. Why must each of us fight to see how our vote was recorded? And why does our citizenry have to sue government or companies just to access the voting record that will tell us whether each American received equal protection under the law? That is absolutely nuts!

But don't think the problem is only a recent issue with the 2020 election; this has been going on at least since 1948 when Lyndon Baines Johnson lost his Senate race in Texas. The winner was about to be called when LBJ's campaign manager went to West Texas and magically "found" a box of ballots that were later labeled "ballot box 13." The race-changing box had 202 votes and gave the forty-year-old LBJ the 1948 Democrat primary, by only eighty-seven votes—out of almost one million cast. What is even more interesting is that every subsequent election has had magical boxes of ballots show up.

So, in our election system that the government does not want to discuss because fraud supposedly doesn't happen, the reality is that corrupt votes have been going on in America for a long time. There is case, after case, after case. During the 1970s in Miami-Dade County, Florida, one of the most prominent voter-fraud cases ever adjudicated showed that the media and politicians teamed up to hide fraud while claiming there is nothing to see. This has become the norm.

But here's the good news: America's eyes are open. And Democrats are right. Though that is not something normally coming out of my mouth, Democrats are always promoting the virtues of other countries while claiming America sucks. So, let's get on that Democratic chant as far as European election laws being better than ours. Europe kicked these election-stealing machines to the curb; they understand that method is completely compromised so they got rid of the fraud by going back to paper ballots, as we should.

Here's something else to think about, and please hear me out until the end: On February 23, 2021, headlines all across our nation announced that a Biden administration report claimed the vote had been the most fraudulent presidential election ever. Their study revealed that people were not allowed access to understand the vote count, that there were extra rogue ballot boxes, illegal counts had happened, votes were bought, there was intimidation to keep people from voting, and the vote was so bad that fourteen thousand extra troops had to be placed at the Capitol to protect the government. Does that sound familiar? Sounds like 2020 America, right? No. Biden cited the report to claim all those issues happened in Russia's 2012 presidential election of Vladimir Putin. So Democrats will acknowledge election fraud elsewhere but deny it in the United States—do as I say, not as I do. And through all the fraud, our corrupt media and politicians bank on the fact that Americans generally know nothing substantial about current political situations, which is the result of us being trained to only regurgitate whatever fake news headlines are put out in forty to a hundred characters—that's a supposedly informed citizenry. No, it's a joke.

The first US occurrence of fraud with mail-in ballots was during the Abraham Lincoln administration. So these election-stealing practices have been around a long, long time, but it is hushed up because our media is just as corrupt as the cheaters. That is why we're holding our "Defend the Vote" National Virtual Summit, which you can find at DefendOurUnion.org. The speakers include me, Mike Lindell, Patrick Byrne, Jim and Joe Hoft, Krisanne Hall, and others.

Here's what we must understand: Anyone who hasn't examined the history of America's voting and voting machines will be under the completely misled notion that our elections are fairly honest.

However, from having done that extensive homework, I am telling you that all our combined fascist social media companies are cleaner and more ethical than our elections.

This nation is in a critical voting crisis, and even if you want to strip away every theory put out by either party about what happened in the 2020 election, we can just look at the simple facts of neutral science. More than any other election ever on the face of this planet, the US 2020 general election saw $14 billion spent, many multiples over every previous election, or even many elections combined. Throughout history, this past election saw the most ballots ever printed, most mailed, most supposedly received back, most processed, and most counted.

However, in the aftermath of more cheating than ever before, we are seeing the beginning of election audits that will grow to be as grand as the election was. As the audits get us back to what happened, starting from ground zero, ballot evidence will be found and dealt with by honest Americans proceeding systematically, and in the correct manner, to let the science ferret out whatever was done, laying everything on the table. Then Democrats, who continually tell us to accept the science, will have to accept a scientific and honest outcome that they will not appreciate.

Here's another white-hat sledgehammer of truth that most people don't know: All paper in the United States, regardless of manufacturer, bears an identifying mark. Additionally, every printer that enters our country—whether owned by you, your company, FedEx, Kinko's, the little church on the corner, or whoever—has subfrequency detectable codes that our law requires. So, forensic science offers many ways to know where each piece of paper came from. If you decided to kidnap someone and print a ransom letter on your HP Color LaserJet, the right forensics team could put you away for quite a while.

Everything today is traceable, so there are only two outcomes to the 2020 election audits: Our nationwide vote and the down-ballot elections were either handled correctly, or those involved got it wrong. In the case of ballots, they were either used legally or illegally. If the former is true, the twenty verifiable markers will tell us we are seeing correct ballots and correct paper, all processed in the correct way and cast by the correct sort of vote-style system, which gave us the correct tally—or not!

Back in the 2000 election when we had that Bush/Gore hanging-chad controversy, the "kinematic artifact" (proof of a person's vote) was the partially or fully punched-out chad, which was examined by three George Bush people and the same number from Al Gore's camp. That group would argue over whether each ballot was a bit dimpled, ruffled, or had no sign of change. Whenever one looked untouched, I'm sure Al's group would point out that their Democrat snowflakes have little muscle, so the person must have pushed to make the impression but it came out too weak to see. That was the debate back then, where some supposedly neutral mediator would be called on whenever both sides got tired of arguing over a particular vote.

Two decades later, computer-vision technology involved with electronic manufacturing and artificial intelligence can drive cars and fly jets, advancements that are a million multiples harder than handling a simple vote count which verifies that each vote is a legal ballot, which has been cast the right way and done so with all the expected accompanying evidence—or it is not. There's no gray area.

We have to get back to an absolute, counterfeit-proof paper ballot, something our 2021 Congress is certainly working against because the House resolution they're trying to pass right now would eliminate paper ballots altogether. Remember, with no paper ballots, we will have no way to audit their fraudulent elections. So, having only reliable paper ballots is most important. The secondary requirement has to do with Moore's Law, which was given to us long ago by a guy named Gordon Moore, cofounder of the multinational Intel corporation. He said the speed of computers gets twice as fast every fifteen months, but the cost of those computer chips will be only half the current price. Well, those leaps now take just twenty days.

Even with that technology savings, our electronic voting system keeps growing and getting more expensive. Why? Because many in our government who are colluding with the companies that make election-stealing machines must justify more and more huge contracts handed out to rig our elections. Again, if you thought counting was fairly simple just in your head, how easy is it for today's computer systems? It should take only one small computer to tabulate every vote from a precinct, while easily making sure each ballot is authentic, the process has not been counterfeited, and a receipt is generated for each voter, showing their choice right there in his or her hand. A system with total confidence. It's what I would do. That's what is coming!

All these election issues aside, I will still declare that we Americans live in the greatest country on the planet. And I am not afraid to say so, even though these days my truth-telling has gotten me known as a fat, middle-aged, white, capitalist pig. I embrace it! Other than our current problems with the vote, we still have an amazing country and the election issues will be fixed, so this is not the end of America.

The most important goal we can have right now is to make every American's vote count. Otherwise, we fail first, and then the rest of the world. Refuse to give up and be quiet about all this election fraud because that only helps the cheaters. Patriots checking out allows them to win without even rigging the vote. So, get your mind in the game. Remember that it's not over until the fat lady sings, and I know her; she's a relative who has begun warming up. We have a long way to go, so keep your head up and do not allow the mental mush to melt your brain. This isn't over! We are America! The patriots win!

13

Mike Lindell: Introducing Colonel Phil Waldron's Damning Video that Explains How, Why, and Who Stole America's 2020 Elections

Alexandra Bruce is the founder and publisher of the popular alternative-news website <u>ForbiddenKnowledgeTV.net</u> and is a weekly contributor to *Making Sense of the Madness* on American Media Periscope (AMP). For consistency, flow, and readability in this book format, the following is a somewhat paraphrased version of Alexandra Bruce's report (<u>ForbiddenKnowledgeTV.net</u>) on an important part of Mike Lindell's three-day cyber symposium that was held in August 2021:

Early into the multiday event, Mike played a short video called *Unconventional and Information Warfare*, featuring retired army colonel Phil Waldron, who has been involved from the beginning with the forensic investigation of the 2020 election. Colonel Waldron speaks powerfully about the dire challenge America faces from China's stealth "unrestricted warfare" campaign being waged against

America with the help of the bankster elites and their puppets—our own corrupt politicians. Sadly, the majority of people are unable to see beyond the unrelenting propaganda from the mainstream media, not comprehending how the US is in the throes of a global information war that includes the coronavirus as part of the cover for a worldwide technocratic takeover.

Waldron begins by discussing the Chinese Communist Party's (CCP's) 75 percent ownership of Dominion Voting Systems, by way of UBS (Union Bank of Switzerland), and how the Spanish company Scytl declared bankruptcy in May 2020, after which it was purchased in a private equity deal by an Irish (European Union) company called Paragon. Scytl subsidiary ClarityElections.com is where about eight hundred US counties send their election data for processing, meaning these counties no longer own or control their voting data! Furthermore, Waldron mentions that Democrat operative Jonathan Brill serves as CEO, president, secretary, and treasurer of Scytl.

According to Americans for Innovation (Americans4innovation. blogspot.com) publisher Michael McKibben (and his forensic team), Scytl USA LLC was originally founded by CENTCOM (the US military's Central Command) in 2009. In 2010, 100 percent of the ownership was transferred to the Spanish corporation Scytl Election Technologies. McKibben describes Dominion and Paragon as "impenetrable corporate labyrinths"—the latter has 118 subsidiaries—which allow these company's leaders to feel they can get away with brazenly lying about their true ownership. McKibben's most shocking bombshell is his claim that CENTCOM orchestrated the theft of the 2020 election:

> "It's real clear...this was a Central Command operation and that it was specifically regarding election-rigging...What it looks like is that SOE Software [which was later acquired by Scytl] was hired by CENTCOM to build what would become the Scytl system, and get it ready for [elections] in 2010."

Is it a coincidence that Biden's secretary of defense, Lloyd Austin, was the commander of CENTCOM between March 2013 and March 2016? This is the same secretary of defense who decreed that all 1.4 million active-duty US troops must be "vaccinated" by September 15, 2021. It is Austin's plan to have all of our armed forces subjected to the same genocidal bioweapon that has killed tens of thousands of Americans in the past eight months (at least), and severely injured hundreds of thousands. CENTCOM and US Special Operations Command (USSOCOM) are each headquartered at Tampa's McDill Air Force Base.

The following is from the transcript of Colonel Phil Waldron's video presentation on how, why, and who stole our 2020 elections (for flow and readability in a book format, this is a paraphrased version):

In November 2020, multiple groups of Americans came together over something incredible they all observed in our nation's 2020 general election; they united to launch a full-scale investigation, led by former members of the US intelligence community, the Department of Defense, NASA, and US National Laboratories, as well as private-investigation companies, cybersecurity enterprises, and legal firms. Their intensively researched discoveries left everyone involved deeply concerned about the future of our nation and the rest of the world. While the constantly discredited US media will undoubtedly try to sweep this information under the rug by labeling it a "far-right conspiracy theory," the truth of this investigation is that those involved represent all colors, creeds, and political parties.

To ignore this message is to surrender to a government takeover that will gravely affect the lives of every man, woman, and child of every nation. If there ever was an authentic nonpartisan issue, this is it! In 1970, Henry Kissinger said,

"Who controls the food supply controls the people; who controls the energy can control whole continents; and who controls money can control the world."

Knowing the seriousness of that disclosure is critical to understanding the thinking of those who seek to cripple and control America. They strive to achieve their goal of domination over the US through disruption of families, dividing the races, destroying our small businesses, dismantling the middle class, and distorting the American dream of owning land, a home, and anything else that might be necessary for the pursuit of happiness and individual sovereignty.

In collusion with our foreign adversaries, these treasonous few are working hard to tear down the last-standing wall between them and their agenda of total, global control—which is we the America people and our Constitution. By focusing on specific election-system vulnerabilities, our investigation confirmed that the entire US vote is now subject to the whims of private equity firms and foreign money: UBS Securities LLC of New York and UBS Securities Company Limited of Beijing, China, injected hundreds of millions of dollars into Staple Street Capital, the current owner of Dominion Voting Systems, which are widely used across the United States. UBS currently holds the intellectual property of Dominion as their equity collateral.

Up until December 2020, UBS Securities of New York listed three senior Chinese Communist Party (CCP) members as being on the boards of both UBS Securities New York and UBS Securities Beijing, the latter being 75 percent owned by the Chinese government. Scytl, the parent company of Clarity Elections in Madrid, Spain, a data-management and early-election-night reporting company, went bankrupt in May 2020 and was subsequently purchased through a closed, private-equity deal by an Irish company called Paragon. The votes of numerous counties in the US go to the ClarityElections.com, so those areas of our country do not own or control their voting data. Instead,

Clarity Elections is headed up by Jonathan Brill, the company's CEO, president, secretary, treasurer, and occupier of a seat on Scytl's senior management team. Brill has run campaigns for Democratic Party candidates.

Contrary to the current, false, political narrative, our investigation learned that the election systems and their equipment were indeed connected to the internet, making them infinitely hackable. And just a short while ago, even Democrats admitted it: [Colonel Waldron shows a montage of Democrat politicians like Kamala Harris and Ted Lieu testifying that electronic voting machines are rife with fraud.] Through forensic analysis of election-management-system computers in Antrim County, Michigan, affidavits from numerous election officials in Georgia, and the operator's [computer software] manual for Dominion's Democracy Suite 5.5, our teams have gathered indisputable evidence that the entire system can be connected to the internet, hacked, and manipulated—which it was in our November 2020 elections.

Initiated by a court order, the Michigan investigation team obtained forensic access to a DS 200 tabulator, the machine that counts the votes, which had a Taiwan-manufactured Telit 4G-wireless chip embedded on its motherboard. And the voting-machine tapes clearly indicate modem engagement (internet connection) and transmission of election data.

Another anomaly we noticed with the 2020 general elections was how the five key battleground states (that all stopped counting votes around a common time frame on election night) were each using machines from Dominion, ES&S, or Smartmatic, and software like GEMS. All those counties stopped counting when President Trump was significantly ahead, and then had massive vote spikes for Joe Biden when the counting and reporting resumed.

Our teams also found significant financial transactions from non-profit organizations that had a severe impact on the 2020 elections. In fact, even a February 2021 article from *Time* magazine admitted that these individuals and organizations had been plotting to influence our elections since at least 2015. The diagram of this nonprofit network reveals the interrelationship of these groups' money, as well as key players and organizations: There were over two hundred non-profits in the network who all received substantial funding from a single source—George Soros. And this is not the first time Mr. Soros has been implicated in a plot to destroy nations. His cover organizations have been banned from several countries for hitting those nations with exactly what his groups are currently doing to America. The Philippines, Russia, Turkey, Poland, Pakistan, and even Soros's homeland of Hungary have learned the hard truth about the intentions of this ruthless multibillionaire. In 2006, Soros admitted to his malevolent intentions for America:

> *"The main obstacle to a stable and just world is the United States."*

A more accurate translation of his desires would be:

> *The main obstacle to me and my cohorts destabilizing the world is the United States.*

While Soros has often been accused of masterminding criminal organizations he had no part in, that should not deter from his plentiful guilt for heinous crimes against humanity, many of which he has kept hidden in plain sight. According to a white paper called "US Programs Strategy 2015–2018," the Soros-backed Open Society Foundation began funding radical Arizona and Georgia operations in 2015, efforts aimed at subverting America's 2020 presidential elections.

Through massive amounts of nonprofit funding and campaign contributions spread throughout the world, George Soros owns and controls countless public officials, university professors, teachers' unions, mayors, district attorneys, judges, congressmen, senators, secretaries of state, sheriffs, governors—and electronic-voting-machine companies.

In 2010, George Soros shocked even his most devout loyalists when he declared that China had a better-functioning government (the CCP) than the United States. While the Chinese people should be considered friends and allies, their CCP leaders have been plotting to take over the United States for the better part of this last century, all while their unconventional warfare tactics have barely been recognized by average Americans [in large part because our corrupt media has kept us in the dark about it].

While we were sleeping, their poisonous seeds planted in America took root long ago and are now in full bloom, part of which has been the CCP and their operatives buying up US property at an alarming rate. Through individual proxies and cover organizations, they have been purchasing our farms and businesses in massive volume while the CCP has also co-opted the US entertainment industry, owning several US entertainment companies and controlling more than eight thousand US theater screens. Hollywood scripts are often reviewed by the CCP and censored if they pose a threat to China's image. Besides all that, many of our professional sports teams are controlled in great part by the same CCP.

And China has been making big moves to control US port operations. It has already taken over the Panama Canal while also building 5G networks throughout Europe and the rest of the West, conduits put in place to gather our personal information and other sensitive data that is all relayed back to the CCP. Our private information is also extracted by their commercial software and apps that constantly spy on US citizens. In fact, estimates reveal that at least 80 percent of American adults have had their personal data harvested by China. Another issue is how multinational pharmaceutical companies (Big Pharma) have exported the vast majority of their production to China. Today, 97 percent of US antibiotics come from China, as well as 30 percent of personal protective equipment like the COVID face masks—from the same country that gave us COVID!

How else have our corrupt politicians allowed us to be compromised? Well, 80 percent of rare earth minerals come from China, including vital technology parts for our smartphones, electric cars, and even US military defenses. While China has dominated that supply, the US produced zero rare earths in 2017.

Another product supplied by China is 97 percent of the fentanyl smuggled into the US through China's partners in the Mexican drug cartels—crime syndicates that now have open access to our country because of Biden ending Trump's push for a secure southern border. Fentanyl is one of the most addictive and deadly drugs known to man.

Besides all that, China's decades-old unrestricted warfare on the US has involved computer hackers from the Chinese People's Liberation Army which has been executing unconstrained penetration, surveillance, theft, and offensive cyberattacks on US businesses, critical infrastructure, our intelligence apparatus—and the US election system.

Knowing the facts I've just presented you, all readers who go on to ignore these warnings are surrendering to the possible takeover of our US government, a reality that would gravely affect the lives of all humans of every class, culture, and nation. To counter that unthinkable outcome, our goal here is to reach and revive the heart of humanity while there is still time. *This is your wake-up call!*

14

Patel Patriot and Praying Medic: Evidence for "Devolution," the Probable Detailing of Trump, and the Q-Team's Plans

For consistency, flow, and readability in this book format, the following is a somewhat paraphrased version of Alexandra Bruce's report (ForbiddenKnowledgeTV.net) on Patel Patriot's first-ever, live-interview appearance, hosted in August 2021 by Sean Morgan and James Grundvig on American Media Periscope. During this discussion of evidence backing up his theory that President Trump purposefully allowed the election to be stolen—in what may turn out to be the greatest sting operation of all time—Patel Patriot revealed his face for the first time. Patel talked about how aspects of devolution are being accomplished through "Continuity of Government" protocols that have included Trump setting up eight separate shadow governments throughout the US. For the complete detailed explanation, visit PatelPatriot.substack.com/p/devolution, where he explains the reality and particulars of devolution.

As an author chronicling Trump and the Q-teams' covert, Q-post information operation, Praying Medic gives credence to Patel's devolution articles by pointing out how some of it matches many Trump and Q posts from the past four years, something Patel had not even looked into prior to this interview.

Before getting further into aspects of devolution, I want to give some context for that discussion: What we've been seeing at the Pentagon over the past few weeks is a US secretary of defense and our Joint Chiefs of Staff clearly serving their globalist masters, puppeteers who hold America and the US armed forces in contempt. The deception these military staffers are foisting on Americans (with help from their complicit mainstream media) reminds me of our US Supreme Court's complete dereliction of duty this past January, a travesty involving the stealing of our US elections that was probably brought about by the usual deep state blackmail and bribery of our American leaders.

And what geniuses thought it would be a good idea to leave Afghanistan's Bagram Air Force Base in the middle of the night on June 29, 2021? Why would we leave without at least notifying the Afghan armed forces? How could these military staffers allow the base to be looted by locals and then handed over to the Taliban just six weeks later? Does the Taliban answer to China? How might the Chinese Communist Party's (CCP's) unrestricted warfare campaign against the US figure in, a plan that seeks to take America out of the way so the globalists that control China can eventually put the entire world under their thumb?

Some of what we have learned along these lines came in October 2020, when Chinese defectors involved with Miles Guo's whistleblower movement (on GTV.org and GNEWS.org) published an overwhelming amount of potentially incriminating corruption evidence against Joe Biden and his family. These ex-Chinese they are in contact with provided America with evidence that has exposed the Bidens as a real threat to US national security. China Joe and family are the poster children of the CCP's unrestricted-warfare strategy, an effort working toward capturing the world through information control (censorship), money, and sexual blackmail. The defectors explained how the CCP has surreptitiously taken over the American mainstream media, social-media-technology companies, and other major corporations, as well as most members of the US federal and state governments and even bodies as small as local school boards.

This whistleblower group is warning us that the Biden family and other traitors have sold out American interests to China, inviting CCP-style censorship and their communist-fascist, social-credit system into the US. And because of how far along all these aspects of the war against the US have gotten, these honorable people blowing the whistle are warning us that America is on the precipice of being defeated by the CCP. They are concerned about the CCP's tactics of controlling people through the lowest aspects of human nature: fear, intimidation, bribery, and blackmail. It is no exaggeration to say their nefarious effort could eventually collapse human civilization. And because the CCP has succeeded in blackmailing such a high percentage of our American politicians and other important US influencers, this past seventeen months of insane COVID mandates seem to make sense because they've been imposed by puppet tyrants doing the globalists' bidding.

Of course, these crucial warnings have been kept from the American public by a big tech censorship that has been even more ferocious than what we've experienced with COVID disinformation. In fact, many truth-telling Twitter and Facebook users have been banned (deplatformed) just for posting GNEWS.org web addresses.

As far as Biden's son Hunter, multiple sources have confirmed that three extremely incriminating hard drives of his have been delivered to the FBI, computers that reveal many of Hunter's heinous acts.

But those understanding the long history of US agencies like the FBI and CIA instigating crimes and covering up criminal activity were not surprised when Chinese whistleblower Dong Jingwei did not hand over his information to either of those organizations. Instead, in June 2021, that ex-vice minister of the Chinese Ministry of State Security—who_had defected to the US in February 2021—presented himself to the Defense Intelligence Agency (DIA, or military intelligence). In addition to much else, Jingwei gave evidence of COVID's true Chinese-lab origins, allegedly forcing the Biden administration to change their stance on where the virus came from.

Now, knowing all that, let's explore what some individuals have brought to the world's attention with devolution: Around the same time as the Chinese whistleblowers were publishing their articles and videos, Carlos Osweda, aka Thomas Wictor, made the rather gutsy claim that Trump had already "drained the world swamp"—with the help of the Saudis and United Arab Emiratis. I lost track of Wictor after he and I were deplatformed by Twitter, but after hearing the internet's self-described radical iconoclast Clif High mention devolution a few times, I looked up the term and found that Wictor has been posting on the topic at QuodVerum.com since last March. Here is some of that:

> Trump and the Saudis began working on a plan [to deal with] China years ago. They understood that *genuine* global improvement was impossible with the power of the Chinese Communists to blackmail the entire world...Trump and the Saudis knew that the only way to take China out of the picture was to steal the blackmail database... They did it with...

military forces. They didn't shoot their way in and out. They used technology that we can't begin to comprehend.

Here is what I think: Trump convinced Congress that he had the votes to be president, but he also told them that he was willing to support "devolution." Devolution is the US military running the country under seven separate plans that are put into action when the civilian federal government ceases to exist. So, I think we're in a hybrid state of devolution *and* a shadow presidency. The military is making NO policy decisions, and Trump is preserving the national-security infrastructure, such as the economy.

I have no idea what the endgame is, but I never anticipated the current solution, which satisfies all sides and is legal and constitutional. This explains EVERYTHING, such as the FACT that Biden has never once ridden on ANY aircraft designated Air Force One [by Air Traffic Control]. It's clear that our foreign enemies interfered in the election. That would mean Biden could not be allowed to assume the presidency.

Trump created a counterattack that was MUCH SMARTER than simply exposing the theft before January 6. He took the mother of all calculated risks, but the payoff is incalculable. Under American devolution, the military DOES NOT replace the executive branch. If the executive branch DOES NOT EXIST, the military simply makes sure that all hell doesn't break loose. It can be argued that the Biden administration does not exist, due to election theft with the help of our enemies. The military would only take this extraordinary step if it KNEW that this had happened. And the way it knew was by using every single surveillance technology in its arsenal.

> The decision was made to NOT go public at this moment.
> Going public would have catastrophic global consequences.

So, if it's true that most of the entire world, including America's politicians, main allies, and trading partners, colluded to steal our nation's 2020 election—an act of war on par with a nuclear strike—what would be the appropriate response? Well, if we were to pursue a US armed forces remedy, Wictor rightly points out that "military coups are a sign of [a nation's] total instability" and would especially look bad for America economically, as the world's formerly largest economy.

Generally, devolution is a sometimes temporary form of administrative decentralization that grants a higher level of autonomy to devolved areas of a country. For example, Spain has a highly devolved government, which they call a "system of autonomies," where the federal government accounts for 18 percent of public spending and regional governments account for 38 percent. Doesn't that sound fabulous?

As an expert on Trump and the Q-team's 4,953 information-dissemination posts (since October 2017), the following quoted material is Praying Medic's (PrayingMedic.com) summary of Patel Patriot's devolution work, which Patel began in July 2021. Again, his entire *Devolution* series of articles can be found at PatelPatriot.substack. com/p/devolution. Even though much of Patel's devolution theory lines up well with the Q posts, he had not been a Q-team follower or even looked at the Q posts. And Patel has no trained expertise in any sort of information warfare. He is just a young American father working with the school system in the northern Midwest.

Here is Q-expert Praying Medic's evaluation of Patel Patriot's devolution explanation:

[Devolution] suggests that Trump and the military have established regional hubs of governmental authority, and this fact is known only to those who are directly involved. A number of people have uncovered documents and pieced together key events supporting the idea that Trump put in place a mechanism by which he could remain commander in chief, even as Joe Biden appears to be president.

The premise that Trump could do this is based on the idea that America has been in an undeclared war with China since at least January 2020. Trump has said on several occasions that when China allowed COVID-19 to escape Wuhan, they committed an act of war. When the US is at war—even when it is an undeclared war—the president has powers not available to him in peacetime. These powers do not require congressional approval, and many times when they are exercised, the public is not aware. The president can, in wartime, take whatever steps are deemed necessary to save the republic.

The devolution theory revolves around a number of presidential memoranda, executive orders, and odd personnel changes made in 2020 related to national security. The key players involved are Chris Miller, Kash Patel, and Ezra Cohen-Watnick, who held positions in the Pentagon and the National Counterterrorism Center prior to and after the election.

Central to the devolution theory is that Trump knew the election would be stolen by a foreign power, and he viewed this as an act of war. In response, he preemptively and covertly took steps to invalidate the outcome of the election. The measures he took are known only to a handful of people, but they effectively make him the true commander in chief. A decision was made to allow the public to believe Joe Biden is president, but at a later date, we will be informed of the truth.

Further, the theory proposes that a few key military assets around the country are covertly supporting Trump, while most of the military believes Biden is calling the shots. At a future time—perhaps when indisputable evidence of election fraud is made public—the military and Trump will make their big reveal.

15

Mel K and Benjamin Fulford: Unlocking Historical Truths You Probably Do Not Know

For consistency, flow, and readability in this book format, the following is a somewhat paraphrased version of Alexandra Bruce's report (ForbiddenKnowledgeTV.net) from June 2021, where she puts out these pieces of the worldwide cabal puzzle:

Patriot influencer Mel K (TheMelKShow.com) recently interviewed Japan-based Canadian journalist Benjamin Fulford (BenjaminFulford.net), who tells us forensic proof is available to be used in a court of law that will show how a group of about one million people make up the global "Kazarian Mafia," or "Sabbatean Frankists." Long ago, this cabal came to the conclusion that it was up to them to carry out the end-time prophecies of the Bible's New Testament, which means that they plan to wage war on all of the planet's people who are not part of their club in an effort to kill at least 90 percent, leaving the other 10 percent available to be their slaves.

According to Dutch researcher Janet Ossebaard, maker of the *Fall of the Cabal* video series that has been seen by millions, in 1776 the Sabbateans and Jesuits aligned with Adam Weishaupt to form the

Illuminati, after which they immediately set upon infiltrating all of the Masonic lodges of Europe.

Fulford traces the trail of this same group to our recent COVID-19 "scamdemic," which is just one act of world sabotage in their long line of lying, murder, and larceny against mankind, as seen in their financing of fascist Adolf Hitler and the communist regimes of Russia and China. They are behind the New World Order, Agenda 21, Agenda 2030, and the Great Financial Reset that they are trying to implement out of the global economic damage they have subjected us to through their fake pandemic. Klaus Schwab's World Economic Forum is their economic mouthpiece.

While putting the whole history of the cabal together, Fulford says a 1918 edition of *Forbes* magazine mentioned how John D. Rockefeller donated all of his money to a foundation, which allowed him to end any reporting of his finances—or paying tax on it—while maintaining control of how the money was spent, so he retained the power of that fortune, and his family still does to this day. The same method was used to shelter money for the cabal in over two hundred foundations, such as the Brookings Institute, Carnegie Foundation, etc. Besides that monumental mound of money to finance the deep state, the deep state has three gargantuan funds that are BlackRock, State Street Banking, and Vanguard. Through those foundations and massive funds, the cabal controls all of the world's Fortune 500 companies.

The end result: all of mankind today is being made subservient to a relatively small group of inbred families who own 90 percent of the multinational corporations. The cabal has a sort of politburo (the executive committee for a communist party) known as the Octagon group that resides in Switzerland and claims to be descendants of the Egyptian pharaohs. Here is Fulford outlining some past history and the current situation for just one of the cabal's long-time leaders:

It is well-documented history that the Rockefeller family took over Western medicine by setting up and financing medical associations. They suppressed, traditional, natural-based medicine in favor of petroleum and chemical-based medicine. Since Western medicine has long been structured as a military organization headed by "surgeon generals," it was easy to co-opt this system by taking control of its command structure. This is the WHO, the various medical associations, and assorted surgeon generals. Any doctor who dissents from this command structure will have their medical "license" removed and lose their access to a lucrative salary.

Since Rockefeller Jr. is ultimately responsible for the "pandemic" and the resultant campaign to vaccinate all humans with toxins, this makes him one of the worst mass murderers in human history. Rockefeller has been fingered by former Israeli prime minister Benyamin Netanyahu (who is now in protective custody) as the most senior member of the genocidal Octagon group. For this reason, a warning is being sent to the Swiss to either hand him over for questioning or face the complete destruction of Octagon group headquarters near Lake Geneva.

Rockefeller Jr. inherited not only control of the medical associations from David Rockefeller Sr., but also control of much of the so-called G7 power structure, including most of the Fortune 500 corporations. This is what they refer to as the "[Rockefeller] rules-based world order."

Fulford told Mel K that many years ago, he met with David Rockefeller Sr., after which the Italian P2 Freemasons sent Leo Zagami to meet with Fulford, inviting him to visit Italy where he could meet with some Freemason types, who informed him that they were going to fire Pope Benedict XVI and Italian Prime Minister Silvio Berlusconi.

161

Fulford was later impressed to see that they did indeed do so, and he says the P2 Freemasons claimed to follow orders from "aliens" in Switzerland. Fulford does not believe they are aliens, but that is what the Masons told him.

16

Alexandra Bruce:
Chinese Warfare

For consistency, flow, and readability in this book format, the following is a somewhat paraphrased version from one of Alexandra Bruce's (ForbiddenKnowledgeTV.net) regular appearances on *Making Sense of the Madness* at American Media Periscope (AMP). From April 2021, here are her comments related to research she has done on China's ongoing campaign of unrestricted warfare against the United States:

What we saw with the 2020 elections may mean the United States Postal Service (USPS) is the most thoroughly infiltrated agency by the Chinese Communist Party (CCP). Recall that a large part of the voter fraud was achieved through an unprecedented millions of counterfeited mail-in ballots—many printed by China. Patrick Byrne, founder of Overstock.com, published pictures of Chinese boxes with the US election ballots in them. They were postmarked from China and appear to be the CCP getting fake ballots to those six strategic counties that flipped the Electoral College, giving the 2021 election to Biden, whose family has corruption ties with China. An investigation by American Media Periscope host Lieutenant Scott Bennett revealed that the American Postal Workers Union, which is part of the AFL-CIO, is controlled by the Chinese Communist Party. And the AFL-CIO is the parent organization of all major unions in the United States, which is why we heard four years of celebrities from the Screen Actors Guild (union) screaming about how "the orange man" (Trump) is bad.

Americans needed to see the outlines of this covert war for themselves, including how the CCP has infiltrated and weaponized our government agencies against all US citizens. And complicit American saboteurs are being paid taxpayer dollars to undermine our entire country and its system of government. Besides that election-undermining corruption with our postal service, reports show that agency of our government has also been turned into a spying agency against the American people.

Another influential area of our society that the CCP has infiltrated is at the *New York Times*, where they have hired several editors, who self-describe as China apologists. For example, *Times* reporter Alex Marshall, who previously worked at the CCP's *China Daily*, is often seen praising the speeches of China Premier Xi Jinping on social media. The *New York Times* being infiltrated by the CCP explains so much about the downfall of the "Gray Lady" (NYT), which has not been the same kind of newspaper for many years.

We have heard about China's unrestricted warfare with its plan to take over the United States through infiltration instead of invasion. We need to be aware of how their attack is playing out here against our country, recognizing the contours of this infiltration and having better situational awareness. Another of the many institutions the CCP has infiltrated in the US has been our blackmailed politicians, such as forty-year-old US Congressman Eric Swalwell from California, a young nobody who just ran for president of the United States. Who the hell is he? Why run that guy? He hardly existed publicly! Two years ago, Swalwell was not even a twinkle in anyone's eye outside his district, so how did he get the backing to run for president in 2020?

I'm pointing all of this out because most people don't understand that we are already at war right now against a covert Chinese style of engagement. Everything weird that we have been experiencing with all the anti-freedom initiatives from so many of our institutions is just evidence that we are in the middle of a Chinese psychological operation (psyop) against America.

But to really understand our attacker, we must know that communist China with its CCP is just another product of the world's central bankers, who can identify as the cabal, the deep state, globalists, the one-world-government crowd, the Illuminati, or whatever other names this worldwide secret society of saboteurs goes by. They control the planet's currency and most of the largest multinational companies, which is why we in America had our extensive manufacturing industries moved out of the US, many going to China where a huge portion of the products we buy today are made.

The globalists are all on the same page, working toward the destruction of America as the world's leader. Their plan was designed many decades ago and has the ultimate goal of creating a one-party state here, so they can impose the CCP model of governance, with its surveillance state that would be illegal and unconstitutional in the United States. Yes, our National Security Agency (NSA) has been spying on its own citizens, but the cabal's plan has been gearing up for the eventuality of an America without the Constitution, which will help them fully implement their surveillance state, complete with artificial intelligence that is able to know everything about everyone for the purpose of labeling us all with an individual, social credit score—just what the Chinese people live under today. All that is connected to the cabal's push for a new digital currency, which will implement the new world order's complete financial hold on the world, unless the white hats institute their alternative plan.

THE WORLD AWAKENS

The deep state plan seems to be at least as old as the foundation of Chairman Mao's murderous, communist People's Republic of China that was formed in 1949. On Twitter in October 2020, @ JohnHereToHelp posted a great thread about this. Besides being a witness with information about the Seth Rich murder investigation, during an interview with influential attorney Lin Wood, John blew the whistle on corrupt public officials and gave details about the videos he has seen that were used as pedophilia blackmail, footage showing despicable acts against children by Supreme Court Justice John Roberts and Vice President Mike Pence. Here is that China-related post from October 2020 @JohnHereToHelp:

> China began a War against the US around 2002, with Bush Jr.'s help, and has not stopped—War by a "Million Ways"— economic, intellectual, medical, industrial. They have even weaponized tourism, from a tiny scale all the way up. They've had access/help from people on ALL SIDES.

The CCP's plan was written and published in 1999 by two Chinese army colonels, Qiao Liang and Wang Xiangsui. The book outlines the CCP's doctrine and tactics of unrestricted warfare, a tactic where China fights us without the military by infiltrating our institutions. They have been bribing our politicians, as well as planting their people in our big tech companies, universities, law firms, courtrooms, the medical profession, and manufacturing. With that last one, and through the help of people like the Bidens, the Chinese buy up US businesses that benefit them, after which they deliberately sell inferior products to their US competition so those competitors lose customers and go bankrupt, resulting in the Chinese winning either way. These tactics are known, and they do the same with food, medicine, clothing, and every other area of our society they can successfully sabotage. As an example, you may remember the 2007 widespread recall of cat and dog food imported from China, which contained melamine, something that was poisoning and killing our pets.

166

Today's China and its CCP seem to try whatever they think they can get away with in the undermining of American society, such as subjecting us to all the fentanyl (a powerful opioid drug) coming from China in amounts great enough to kill every US man, woman, and child—ten times each! Through all that, the Bidens have been happy profiteering off the planned demise of America. And they're just a few of the many treasonous US citizens who are taking money to conspire with our unrestricted-warfare enemies—the CCP. The same sabotage is being perpetrated by our large business entities like the NBA, MLB, and Coca-Cola. Why would these organizations scream about voting-security legislation like that passed in Georgia? The cabal's effort to make Washington, DC, a fifty-first state is another part of the plan.

As described by Patrick Byrne, the CCP's weapon of choice in their unrestricted warfare involves a subtle, long-term, Chinese assassin's mace. No fighter jets. Not one bomb. It's a stealth war. Clearly, the China-virus "plandemic" is part of it, a deception facilitated by their comrades running the UN, EU, NATO, the World Economic Forum, and all the other globalist entities that are in lockstep with the plan. And as just another cog in the globalist wheel, the controller of the cabal is not China, which is just one more puppet of the deep state that means to defeat America and its freedom-giving Constitution.

Patrick Byrne also mentioned that the CCP has been holding "information dominance" over our society, which means they have been able to whipsaw us into confusion by manipulating the information landscape. They have controlled much of the US media, allowing their propaganda to reach us by print and television, while also being able to censor patriots who are putting out honest information on social media. At Clay Clark's Health and Freedom Conference in Tulsa, Oklahoma, he asked who had been deplatformed or censored by big tech, to which at least half of the five thousand people raised their hand. The cabal has succeeded at spinning reality to such a ridiculous level these days, the best I can do to wake the public is just try to point out the many contours of this stealth war being waged against us.

As a quick side note to give you a feel for how long this undermining of America has been going on—and it's much longer than I will show here—my understanding is that the CIA was built out of British MI6 and Hitler's Nazi SS, both of which were financed by the banksters and money they extracted from taxpayers, the same financing that established China's first Communist leader Mao. It's always the same banking cabal that includes the black nobility, Rothschilds, Venetian banks, the British Crown, and others.

Another great comment from Patrick Byrne was that the twisted reality fed to us by the cabal claims fascism is a right-wing philosophy, but before becoming the dictator of Italy, Fascist Benito Mussolini was publisher of the biggest communist newspaper in Italy. A close look at fascism shows that it is just another form of collectivism, which is communism. And Nazi stands for National Socialist.

Completely contrary to that controlling communism, our republic's Constitution is about the rights of the individual. But the globalists don't want that for us, so they twist reality—the same way the Democrat Party rewrote their history to supposedly make themselves the party of civil rights, which is not what they were throughout their history. It was the Republican Party that was founded to abolish slavery and had to battle for it against opposition from the Democrats. The left is always demonizing the right and making the right look like they are evil because they want to dupe the public and are projecting their attitudes on Republicans. Luckily, the cabal's past and present lying seems to be coming out in spades lately, but they have been doing it for decades—if not centuries. It is stunning to realize how correct the Bible is when it tells us there is nothing new under the sun.

17

Doctor Steve Greer: The Coming UFO Cosmic Hoax

For consistency, flow, and readability in this book format, the following is a somewhat paraphrased version of Alexandra Bruce's (a regular contributor to American Media Periscope) report on her website, ForbiddenKnowledgeTV.net:

The latest film by Dr. Steven Greer, *Cosmic Hoax*, was released on July 4th, and it is a must-see documentary, with unprecedented interviews and testimonies, never-before-seen footage, and well-put-together photos, all of which make it a pleasure to watch. It delves back into the airships of the nineteenth century and brings us to the current fake alien invasion being staged by the likes of Christopher Mellon and Luis Elizondo.

Constitutional attorney and Greer's longtime "Disclosure Project" associate, Daniel Sheehan, believes that the official extraterrestrial (ET) narrative is controlled by an extrajudicial, extra-governmental group. Sheehan says:

> There is some other [organizational] structure. I have been persuaded by the evidence that,immediately after Roswell's recovery of a craft and bodies from a [crashed] UFO vehicle,

the Truman administration set up a [government-sponsored group] that was outside of the normal constitutional framework of our United States government, and it was made up of…people…viewed as the "real power elite."

It's sort of a shadow government within the government, not just in the United States but all around the world, and the kind of power they have financially, technologically, and…militarily is much greater than anything [wielded by] conventional military, government, or the president of the United States. Eisenhower knew and was very upset about it by the time he left office. One of the difficult things of the last six months was learning that the same group who had been feeding *false information to the public through* TTSA [To The Stars Academy] had their counterparts…going into our president's office, providing [him with]…a lot of disinformation.

Greer says something amazing that I've never heard before. He claims that the *entire* alien abduction phenomenon and animal mutilations (later, humans too) are conducted by this secret military. In other words, *all* reported alien abductions and animal mutilations have actually been done by people in order to stoke fear and loathing of the aliens, which is also what the latest UAP (Unidentified Aerospace Phenomena) propaganda push is intended to do. Greer adds that the UFO card has always been their "last card" in this globalist takeover:

The long-term defense strategy, from the late '40s and '50s forward, was informed by eventually using this last card to consolidate…global totalitarian military control of the population.

Sheehan jokes:

Those of us in the CE-5 [Close Encounters of the Fifth Kind] community, etc., need to establish some kind of level of discourse with Lue Elizondo and Chris Mellon. [They under-stand] we're obviously sophisticated enough to know that what they're saying publicly is not true. We have to be able to establish diplomatic relations with our *own* people if we're going to [do so] with an entire extraterrestrial civilization!

The film contains new UFO footage, as well as clips and revelations about Jacques Vallée that I have not seen before, part of which de-scribes the CIA's simulated "alien abductions" in 1992 that were used as psychological-warfare experiments in Brazil and Argentina. In an interview with Greer from 2019, this information is implicitly cor-roborated by Richard Doty, a special agent for counterintelligence with the Air Force Office of Special Investigations (AFOSI). When confronted with these details, Doty says, "That's pretty [classified]. I don't think I should talk about that."

Greer outlines three major lies involved with the media's current false flag disclosure concerning UFOs:

1) We do not know what UFOs are—first lie!

2) The US military does not have aircraft that can perform in the way these UFOs maneuver—second lie!

3) They are a threat to national security—third lie!

Greer says, "The only threat to national security and world peace are unacknowledged projects using man-made UFOs and other tech-nologies to hoax alien events—period! And yet, we are inundated with messages about the threat to national security posed by UFOs."

The final twenty minutes of this film is great and I won't blow it for you; it's definitely worth a watch.

18

Alexandra Bruce: Was January 6, 2021, a False Flag FBI Operation on Our Washington, DC, Capitol, as a Way to Implicate Innocent Patriots?

For consistency, flow, and readability in this book format, the following is a somewhat paraphrased version from one of Alexandra Bruce's (a regular contributor to American Media Periscope) reports on her website, ForbiddenKnowledgeTV.net:

YouTuber "Mr. Reagan" elaborates on the work of <u>Darren Beattie</u> at *Revolver.News*, who says the leader of the Oath Keepers, Stewart Rhodes, is an FBI operative, which explains why he has not been charged, even though Oath Keepers is the main militia group being charged with orchestrating the January 6, 2021, Washington, DC, Capitol riot. Further, it appears that the Oath Keepers group was founded by Rhodes for the purpose of entrapping "right-wing extremists" on behalf of the FBI, much in the same way that the FBI has planned terror attacks and set up Islamic extremists over the past twenty years. In other words, the FBI staged January 6th!

Here is Mr. Reagan:

The particularly disturbing thing about Stewart Rhodes is that he appears to have encouraged his members to storm the Capitol, and using incendiary rhetoric, he implied that they should take some drastic action against DC politicians. Also, a lot of the claims coming out of the FBI and media have been predicated on things that Rhodes said, rhetoric that he was likely instructed by the FBI to use to agitate members of his organization. They are creating the illusion of crimes.

The _Revolver_ article details one particularly egregious case where a guy named George Tanios was arrested and charged with nine counts because he had bear spray in his backpack that he never used. At one point on January 6th, Tanios's friend Julian Cotter reached into the backpack to grab the bear spray, and Tanios said, "Hold on, not yet." Now, keep in mind that this bear spray was never used, so who knows what Tanios meant; it was probably more like "Hold on, not yet...[because I brought that for self-defense in case something really dangerous goes down."] Yet, his words are being used as evidence to suggest he's a dangerous extremist who planned on using bear spray to viciously attack people. And bear spray is a nonlethal defense spray used specifically to avoid permanently hurting someone—what a monster.

The FBI is clearly distorting events to paint a picture that is entirely fictional, so they can lock up innocent Americans as part of crafting their false narrative. Clearly, the most important revelation to come out of the _Revolver_ story is that it appears our FBI planned and executed the riot that happened at the Capitol on January 6th.

If the FBI is creating various domestic terror plots, inviting people to join their efforts, and then arresting them on the flimsiest of evidence—charging them with serious crimes and threatening decades of prison time—no one involved in the January 6th protests, who were members of the groups infiltrated by federal agents, should be able to be convicted of anything.

I'm not a lawyer, but isn't there something in America called the "entrapment defense"? Every time the FBI does these sorts of things, they are engaged in entrapment. About that, the Cornell Legal Institute's website states it must be proven beyond a reasonable doubt that the defendant was disposed to commit the criminal act prior to first being approached by government agents. Clearly, this was not the case with anyone accused of the more serious crimes on January 6th.

But this also means the selfie-taking MAGA Moms, who've been charged with trespassing in the Capitol, actually have it worse because they can't argue entrapment. They are just victims of an overly aggressive, highly politicized FBI that no longer thinks it needs to work within the bounds of the law, ethics, or reason. There was no insurrection, and none of these crimes are legitimate. It's all phony. It's all fake. It's all a show. This is all being done to make the FBI look good and to give credibility to the ridiculous notion that white supremacy and white men are the great threat to America.

19

Donald S. McAlvany: Undercurrents of Globalism, including World Wars, Surveillance, and the Rising Populist Awakening

This is a somewhat edited version (for readability and flow in this book format) of the lead article in a monthly newsletter of the *McAlvany Intelligence Advisor* (June 2021 issue), which can be found at McAlvanyIntelligenceAdvisor.com:

I. A Historical Perspective of Upheaval: Global Wars, Proxy Wars, and the Race to World Government—Part IV

"Veterans know better than anyone else the price of freedom, for they've suffered the scars of war. We can offer them no better tribute than to protect what they have won for us." –Ronald Reagan, 1983

"As long as there are sovereign nations possessing great power, war is inevitable."—Albert Einstein

"In the councils of government, we must guard against the acquisition of unwarranted influence, whether sought or unsought, by the military-industrial complex. The potential for the disastrous rise of misplaced power exists and will persist."—President Dwight D. Eisenhower, Farewell Address, 1961

"There are few historians who would challenge the fact that the funding of World War I, World War II, the Korean War, and the Vietnam War was accomplished...through the Federal Reserve System. An overview of all wars since the establishment of the Bank of England in 1694 suggests that most of them would have been greatly reduced in severity, or perhaps not even fought at all, without fiat money."— G. Edward Griffin, *The Creature from Jekyll Island: A Second Look at the Federal Reserve*

"Is there any means known to man more effective than war to alter the life of an entire people?"—Carnegie Endowment for International Peace, meeting notes, 1911

Introduction

Conflict is rooted in the nature of man separate from his Creator. The quest for power, the love of money, the race for resources, economic competition, and the contest between ideas, ideologies, and religions all contribute to this conflict, one that did not begin in the modern era but traces its roots back to the Garden of Eden, the desire to be like God, and the first murder (one brother killing another). Modern tools, such as finance, statecraft, communication, transportation, and military technology, and the cult-like ideologies of communism and globalism have only made modern wars more destructive and deadly, and provide the same capabilities for a now-emerging, next world war.

In 1911, the globalist Carnegie Endowment for International Peace found that war was indeed the most effective means to "alter the life of an entire people." Though a massively successful businessman, industrialist, and philanthropist, Andrew Carnegie mistakenly believed that world peace could indeed be accomplished by a one-world government, as he wrote during World War I, "The longer that this war continues and the more terrible its results, the stronger the argument for permanent world peace."

While Carnegie was wrong to believe that a one-world order created by globalists could transform the corrupted heart of man, he was right to assert that war leaves its mark on society. For example, far more civilians died in the Russian civil war than did soldiers (an estimated 12 million civilians compared to 1.5 million soldiers). Those living in Italy during Emperor Justinian's reconquest in the A.D. sixth century found themselves successively ravaged by war, famine, and disease (see "A Historical Perspective of Pandemics," a past article in the *McAlvany Intelligence Advisory*). Over 13 million Syrians (out of a population of 22 million) have been displaced in the past decade since fighting began in the 2011 Arab Spring.

Warriors and their families sacrifice much, often paying a horrific price. More Vietnam veterans have taken their lives since the war than died in the Vietnam War. Veterans have had to cope with PTSD (in all wars), Agent Orange (Vietnam), Gulf War syndrome, and other physical and psychological afflictions (not to mention the bodily injuries sustained). American soldiers held in Japanese prison camps during World War II suffered the highest death rates in American history—a staggering 40 percent! But at the same time, war tests and forges character. In America, those who lived and served through the Great Depression and World War II were called "the Greatest Generation" for their tenacity, heroism, and sacrifice.

Globalists have called for three world wars, out of which they hope their world government will rise like a phoenix from the ashes. Before we can understand the race to world war three we must first reflect on

177

history. (1) What can we learn from past conflicts? (2) How does globalist ideology directly impact war? (3) How have globalists used (or even provoked) war to advance global government, including in the two World Wars and conflicts since then? (4) What valuable lessons can we learn from brave individuals who sacrificed for their country?

A. Lessons from Past Conflicts

Wars are fought for many overlapping reasons, including economic, territorial, religious, and national. However, every war of the past has almost always had a strong underlying economic element. Further, large-scale conflicts often pit an emerging power against a waning power that leads the global order (e.g., French vs. British, British vs. Dutch).

1. The Peloponnesian War—Thucydides called the conflict the most momentous war up to that time. From 431 to 404 BC, it engulfed nearly all of the Greek city-states, led by Athens on one side, with its financial and sea advantages, and Sparta on the other, with its land advantage. During the First Peloponnesian War, Athens suffered a plague when all of the surrounding inhabitants crowded into the city.

2. The Mongol Wars—The Mongols conquered much of Asia, stretching from China to the Middle East to Russia, creating the Pax Mongolica and the Silk Road, and killing up to an estimated 60 million in the process! The Black Death may have originated in the Mongol Empire and spread to Europe. Today, only 3.3 million live in Mongolia, the country which bears the name of the once-mighty dominion.

3. The Thirty Years' War—Fought from 1618 to 1648 and sparked by religion, the Thirty Years' War was one of the most destructive in European history. Between roughly 4.5 million and 8

million perished, up to 60 percent of the population in some parts of Germany. The war also encompassed the conflict between the Austrian/Spanish Habsburg and French Bourbon dynasties.

4. The Seven Years' War (the first global war)—Winston Churchill later called it "the first world war." The Seven Years' War included all the great European powers of the day (Britain, Prussia, France, Austria, Russia, Spain, and Portugal), and took place in North America (the French and Indian War), India, the Philippines, West Africa, Central America, and Europe. The war claimed up to 1.4 million lives and propelled Great Britain to its status as a great global power.

5. The Napoleonic Wars—Revolution within a nation can spill over into mass conflict with other nations. The Napoleonic Wars mark the first time that mass conscription via the draft was instituted. Six and a half million died in these wars.

6. The American Civil War (The War Between the States)—Slavery, state's rights, economic interests, and cultural conflict contributed to America's deadliest war, in which over 650,000 Americans died.

B. The Globalist Blueprint for World War and World Government

"The world is governed by very different personages from what is imagined by those who are not behind the scenes."—English Prime Minister Benjamin Disraeli, 1844

"Who controls the food supply controls the people; who controls the energy can control whole continents; who controls money can control the world."—Henry Kissinger

1. Modern Banking: A Tool for World Government—With modern banking came the rise of the modern state, modern wars, and modern globalism. The influential Rothschild family, whose dynasty began in the mid-eighteenth century with Mayer Amschel Bauer, the son of a goldsmith and the "founding father of international finance," got their start safeguarding gold and then lending it out to individuals.

   In 1815, Nathan Rothschild had a special courier, Rothworth, stationed at Waterloo to observe the battle. Arriving in London twenty-four hours before Wellington's courier, Rothworth relayed the news to Rothschild. Nathan Rothschild then took his usual place at the stock market. G. Edward Griffin writes, "All eyes were upon him as he slumped dejectedly, staring at the floor. Then, he raised his gaze and, with a pained expression, began to sell. The whisper went through the crowded room, 'Nathan is selling?' 'Nathan is selling!' 'Wellington must have lost.' 'Our government bonds will never be repaid.' 'Sell them now. Sell. Sell!'" This panicked selling allowed Rothschild's planted agents to buy up these bonds at dirt cheap prices, leading to Rothschild's control of the Bank of England.

   With his power firmly established, Rothschild would reportedly later boast, "I care not what puppet is placed on the throne of England to rule the Empire. The man who controls Britain's money supply controls the British Empire, and I control the British money supply." Rothschild biographer Frederic Morton concluded that the Rothschild dynasty had "conquered the world more thoroughly, more cunningly, and much more lastingly than all the Caesars before or all the Hitlers after them."

   Even Napoleon Bonaparte, who was dependent on private loans to finance his army, recognized that the power of bankers had superseded that of governments. "When a government is dependent upon bankers for money, they and not the leaders of the government control the situation, since the hand that gives is above the hand that takes...Money has no motherland; financiers are without patriotism and without decency; their sole object is gain."

Thomas Jefferson reportedly warned in 1816, "I sincerely believe that banking establishments are more dangerous than standing armies."

2. The Occult: The Reason for World Government—In pursuit of global government, an ideal as old as Babel, the Rothschilds helped organize the Organization and Sect of the Illuminati, founded in Bavaria in 1776 by Adam Weishaupt. This group merged with the Freemasons in 1782. They were called the "Illuminati" because they claimed to be illumined by Lucifer. Their goal was the destruction of national governments to be replaced with global government. To achieve those ends, the Illuminati proposed controlling money by installing central banks in countries.

Many globalists were deeply inspired by occult writers, including the founder of the Theosophical Society, Helena Blavatsky (1831–1891), who believed that enlightenment and salvation could come through freemasonry. Blavatsky declared that Satan is "the God of our planet and our only God" and saw The Fall as having opened man's knowledge to his own divinity through the indwelling of Lucifer! Blavatsky's ideas have been credited with inspiring both Adolf Hitler and the New Age movement.

3. Cecil Rhodes: A Plan for World Government—Cecil Rhodes's vision came on the day he became a member of the Oxford

University Apollo Chapter of the Masonic Order. Rhodes wrote, "The idea gleaming and dancing before one's eyes like a will-o'-the-wisp at last frames itself into a plan. Why should we not form a secret society with but one object—the furtherance of the British Empire and the bringing of the whole uncivilized world under British rule for the recovery of the United States for the making the Anglo-Saxon race but one Empire?" (The blueprint would later change for the United States to take the lead role in global government, with Britain accepting the junior position.) To this end, Rhodes worked for the religious, political, and economic unification of the world. After his death, his "Society of the Elect" carried on his mission with devastating success. For more on Rhodes's secret society, read" Reviewing the Rhodes Legacy" by William F. Jasper (*New American*, February 1995).

4. Global War: The Path to Global Government and "Peace"—Leading Freemason general Albert Pike (1809–1891), who was also head of the Illuminati, called for three world wars, believing that out of the third would rise the new world order. The Communists (funded by globalists) declared that a perpetual state of war exists between them and free countries, which cannot cease until absolute victory is achieved, at which point the world will enjoy "peace." In 1954, the Reece Commission discovered the meeting notes from a 1911 meeting of the Carnegie Endowment for National Peace, which was held to discuss the question, "Is there any means known to man more effective than war to alter the life of an entire people?" After agreeing that war was the best preparation for "world peace" and world government, the Endowment then resolved to influence the US State Department in the direction of war.

5. How Globalists Use War to Expand Power—First, war can enrich the well-connected, as big banks and businesses in

America discovered during World War I. Second, war can restructure the global chessboard to remove rulers from power and remake boundaries of power. Third, war (especially total war) can transform a nation and expand a government's power over its people. Ultimately, a world war is a world problem that requires a world solution. Global elites love war and any "global crisis" (like COVID and climate change) that brings them closer to their satanically inspired quest for world government.

C. Globalist Agendas in World War I

At its core, the unification of Germany in 1871, following France's defeat in the Franco-Prussian war, upended the British-led economic and geopolitical order, which had remained relatively stable since the defeat of Napoleon in 1815 at Waterloo. George Friedman notes that as Germany "became Europe's dominant economic power, and as it began to modernize its military, concern grew. Germany sought to create a continental alliance." The assassination of Archduke Franz Ferdinand in 1914 was the spark that set the entire continent ablaze, beginning, as Woodrow Wilson described it, "the war to end all wars." World War I would claim up to 11 million military and 13 million civilian lives.

Behind the scenes, internationalist forces worked to exploit conflict and reshape the geopolitical order in pursuit of their vision.

1. American Loans and Supplies to the Allies—American bankers, who had been shut out of Germany's economic rise, were heavily invested on the side of the Allies. In 1914, Andrew Carnegie became one of the cosigners of a $500 million loan from J. P. Morgan and Company to the Anglo/French Commission. This was the largest foreign loan in Wall Street history. By 1917, the Allies had borrowed around $2.3 billion

from Morgan and other Wall Street banks. Only $27 million had been loaned to the Germans.

J. P. Morgan acted as a sales agent for English and French bonds and as a purchasing agent to buy war materials with the bond proceeds in the States. His lucrative commissions amounted to $30 million with France and England alone! Morgan was also heavily invested in production companies that sold military supplies to the Allies. However, J. P. Morgan's sale of Allied war bonds quickly dried up when the war began to go badly for England and France. An Allied loss would have devastated Morgan's loans and production companies.

2. A False Flag Operation: The Sinking of the Lusitania— Unsuspecting Americans were not informed that the ship was transporting six million rounds of ammunition and other military munitions to Britain, including six hundred tons of pyroxyline explosive, six million rounds of .303 bullets, and 1,248 cases of shrapnel shells. The Germans, who were aware of the Lusitania's cargo, posted newspaper notices warning travelers not to set foot on the vessel. Steaming slowly in a straight line and without a naval escort, the Lusitania was, in the words of G. Edward Griffin, "virtually a floating ammunition depot."

When the German U-boat fired upon the Lusitania, two explosions occurred. Many researchers believe the second was caused by the ship's explosive cargo. Tragically, 1,195 perished, including 128 Americans and 94 children (31 of them mere babies).

The sinking of the Lusitania was the major catalyst that brought America into the war, conveniently ensuring that loans to American bankers would be repaid at the cost of over fifty thousand American lives, a reminder that the globalists and financiers viewed brave American doughboys as expendable assets in their greater agenda. In 1936, Senator Gerald Nye of North Dakota stated, "We didn't win a thing we set out for in the last war. We merely succeeded, with tremendous loss of life, to make secure the loans of private bankers to the Allies."

3. Activating the Propaganda Machine: Persuading the American Public to Go to War—Woodrow Wilson, who won narrow re-election in 1916 on the slogan "He Kept Us Out of War," used the incident to draw America into the conflict, which enjoyed much less popular support than did World War II. After the sinking of the Lusitania, controlled newspapers began publishing stories chronicling the atrocities of the barbaric "Hun."

    The father of modern "public relations" (propaganda), Edward Bernays cut his teeth working for Wilson's Committee on Public Information, which worked to shape American opinion in favor of war. Bernays would later write, "The conscious and intelligent manipulation of the organized habits and opinions of the masses is an important element in democratic society. Those who manipulate this unseen mechanism of society constitute an invisible government, which is the true ruling power of our country. We are governed, our minds are molded, our tastes formed, our ideas suggested, largely by men we have never heard of."

4. The Rise of the Military Industrial Complex—By 1918, military spending constituted 22 percent of GNP, primarily benefiting US Steel, Bethlehem Steel, Du Pont Chemical, Kennecott, and General Electric, all related to the House of Morgan. Highly decorated major general Smedley D. Butler, who served in the US military from 1898 to 1931, wrote in his book, *War Is a Racket*, "I spent thirty-three years and four months in active military service, and during that period I spent most of my

time as a high-class muscle man for big business, for Wall Street and the bankers." Butler would also write, "War is a racket...It is the only one in which the profits are reckoned in dollars and the losses in lives."

5. The League of Nations—Wilson's envisioned League of Nations for international government would have realized Cecil Rhodes's vision, with the United States at the head of the new order. After campaigning vigorously to drum up public support for the League, Wilson suffered a severe stroke and was further devastated when the American Senate rejected his treaty. Leading the opposition, Senator Henry Cabot Lodge said the League would make Wilson "the president of the world." Warren G. Harding's landslide platform included a strong condemnation of the League while Democrats endorsed it.

6. Globalist Goals of World War I—One of the most important goals was the establishment of communism in Russia (funded by Wall Street). Whitaker Chambers wrote, "The chief fruit of the First World War was the Russian Revolution and the rise of communism as a national power."

Another fruit of World War I was World War II, as the Treaty of Versailles left many important issues unresolved. Adolf Hitler would cleverly use the Versailles treaty to stir up the German people.

World War I set the stage for US interventionist foreign policy for the next one hundred years. For more information, read "World War I, Rather Than World War II, Is Key for US Foreign Policy" by Ivan Eland, PhD, July 8, 2014.

In 1921, the Council on Foreign Relations was established as a means to align America's foreign policy with Federal

Reserve policy. It was founded by bankers, businessmen, and politicians connected to and controlled by the Rockefellers, Rothschilds, and Morgans. In its inaugural edition in 1922, *Foreign Affairs*, the mouthpiece of the CFR, condemned "the dubious doctrines expressed by such phrases of 'safety first' and 'America first'." Today, almost every major bank and corporation is a member of the CFR, along with many prominent politicians, Republican and Democrat.

Under Woodrow Wilson, World War I massively expanded the power and reach of the federal government over individuals and businesses.

D. Globalist Agendas in World War II

"To involve a country in war or the threat of war, it will be necessary for it to have enemies with credible military might. If such enemies already exist, all the better. If they exist but lack military strength, it will be necessary to provide them the money to build their war machine. If an enemy does not exist at all, then it will be necessary to create one by financing the rise of a hostile regime."—G. Edward Griffin, commenting on the globalist blueprint for instigating war

Some have called the world wars a single conflict that began in 1914 and ended in 1945, with a twenty-year truce in between. Seventy million to 85 million perished in World War II, history's deadliest conflict.

1. German Economic Recovery (funded by Wall Street)—Wall Street banks and corporations enabled Germany's rapid economic recovery, as detailed in Anthony Sutton's *Wall Street and the Rise of Hitler* (July 8, 2014). As one example, I. G. Farben (which had both German and American branches) received a $30 million loan from Rockefeller's National City

Bank. Farben produced 100 percent of Germany's synthetic oil, 100 percent of its lubricating oil, and 84 percent of its explosives. Thirty percent of the tires produced in Henry Ford's factories ended up being used in the German Wehrmacht. The Bank of International Settlements, opened in 1930, in Basil, Switzerland, with J. P. Morgan among its founders, also aided German recovery.

2. Hitler, Hyperinflation, and the Occult—Adolf Hitler was immersed in the occult—an obsession that began at a very young age—as was his inner circle. Nazism was more than an ideology; it was a religion. The massive hyperinflation in Weimar Germany created the conditions necessary for Hitler's rise (See "A Historical Perspective of Financial Upheaval," in the *McAlvany Intelligence Advisory* newsletter).

3. War in Europe—Lloyd George predicted of Germany's border with Poland that it "must in my judgment lead sooner or later to a new war in the east of Europe." The city of Danzig was 97 percent German, creating a tension point between Poland and Germany. Poland, which had previously helped Hitler divide Czechoslovakia (as the British and French stood by) was invaded by the German blitzkrieg on September 1 (after a series of false flag incidents instigated by the Germans) and by the Soviet Union on September 17. Though Stalin (who slaughtered 20 million of his own people) and the Russians helped Germany carve up Poland, Britain, and France, they only declared war on Germany.

4. The Rise of Japan—Japan's industrial modernization and military expansion began in 1868 with the Meiji Restoration and accelerated with their invasion of China in 1937. Under Shintoism, the Japanese were taught that their emperor had descended from the gods. Warriors fought by the code of

bushido, which inspired Kamikaze suicide missions and included the command to "never surrender."

5. The Council on Foreign Relations Prepares America for War—The CFR took the lead in shaping American public opinion in favor of war and in discussing a proposed United Nations for the aftermath. The CFR held 362 meetings and prepared 682 papers for the State Department. Its War and Studies project was funded by the Rockefellers. Like Wilson, FDR promised in campaigns not to bring America into war, but had war plans laid up two years before the US entered World War II. War, not the New Deal, finally brought America out of the Depression.

6. Economic and Military War with Japan—Already strained US/Japanese relations rapidly deteriorated in 1939 with continued Japanese expansion. Robert Higgs argues that Pearl Harbor should be viewed as Japan's military response to provocative US economic action. In July 1941, FDR imposed a crippling trade embargo of oil, rubber, scrap metal, and steel to Japan, while the British and Dutch enacted oil embargoes. Japan lost three-fourths of its overseas trade and 88 percent of its imported oil. FDR also froze all Japanese financial assets in the US and closed the Panama Canal to Japanese ships.

On July 31, 1941, Japan's foreign minister, Teijirō Toyoda, communicated the following message to Kichisaburo Nomura, Japan's ambassador to the United States: "Commercial and economic relations between Japan and third countries, led by England and the United States, are gradually becoming so horribly strained that we cannot endure it much longer. Consequently, our empire, to save its very life, must take measures to secure the raw materials of the South Seas."

Researcher and World War II US Navy veteran Robert Stinnett contends that FDR did indeed know about the Pearl Harbor attack beforehand but withheld the information from military commanders in Hawaii.

7. Globalist Goals of World War II—The globalists massively strengthened the fledgling Soviet Union. First, through lend-lease, America propped up the Soviets economically, militarily, and technologically. Secondly, during the war, the US government and media hid from the American people the atrocities of Stalin, including Stalin's murder of 20 mil- lion of his own people, exposing Nazi atrocities but not Soviet atrocities. Third, at the Yalta Conference, FDR agreed with Stalin to hand over two million Soviet dissidents who had fled communism (Operation Keelhaul). Many of these people committed suicide or perished in the gulag. Fourth, Stalin was handed control of Eastern Europe, which would remain beneath the Iron Curtain for decades. Fifth, the Soviets were sent plans for the atomic bomb as revealed in Major Jordan's diaries. Robert Higgs believes, "In 1945, we merely traded one set of aggressive enemies [Nazis and Japanese] for another [the Soviets]." For more information, read *American Betrayal*, by Diana West, September 2, 2014.

In addition to building up the Soviet Union, the globalists (by funding mass-murdering Mao Tse-tung) established China as the second bastion for communism in the wake of World War II. Returning from China in 1973, globalist David Rockefeller would opine in the *New York Times*, "Whatever the price of the Chinese Revolution, it has obviously succeeded not only in producing more efficient and dedicated administration, but also in fostering high morale and community of purpose." Whatever the price? The price was a staggering 65 million slaughtered! Rockefeller would further state, "The social experiment in China under Chairman Mao's leadership is one of the most important and successful in human history." Far from "making the world safe for democracy," the globalists created two powerful enemies who could challenge the United States in a future world war.

Last, the establishment of the United Nations succeeded where the League had failed. UN plans were drawn up in 1943 by the Council on Foreign Relations and funded by the Rockefellers as a means to control the world's weapons, courts, wars, economy, and taxes.

8. The Heroes of World War II—The greatest war heroes are the ordinary men and women who fought on the battlefield and who sacrificed at home. In the words of JFK, "The cost of freedom is always high, but Americans have always paid it." These men and women were ordinary individuals who became extraordinary heroes. They were not privy to the counsels of those who launched and directed the wars, but they sacrificed everything because they wanted to preserve freedom and the American ideal.

The strong character and indomitable perseverance of the American people won World War II, [as outlined in an article you can find at *https://vetmc.org/just79tearsago,* where they note that—during] just 3½ years—"we the people" produced the following:

- 22 aircraft carriers
- 8 battleships
- 48 cruisers
- 349 destroyers
- 420 destroyer escorts
- 203 submarines

- 34 million tons of merchant ships
- 100,000 fighter aircraft
- 98,000 bombers
- 24,000 transport aircraft
- 58,000 training aircraft
- 93,000 tanks
- 257,000 artillery pieces
- 105,000 mortars
- 3 million machine guns and
- 2,500,000 military trucks

"We put 16.1 million men in uniform in the various armed services, invaded Africa, invaded Sicily and Italy, won the battle for the Atlantic, planned and executed D-Day, marched across the Pacific and Europe, developed the atomic bomb and, ultimately, conquered Japan and Germany."

Sadly, evil global elites spurned these heroic individuals, viewing them as simple pawns (a means to an end) to be expended in their drive for world domination. The same is true today. Many Americans living in comfort easily forget the sacrifice of past heroes and fail to recognize that freedom always demands a price. However, such ingratitude can never diminish the courage and sacrifice of America's true heroes.

E. Other Conflicts that Advanced the Global Agenda—Since World Wars I and II, proxy wars and localized conflicts have played a role in rebalancing power in line with the globalist strategy.

   1. The Korean War—According to the *Encyclopedia Britannica*, at least 2.5 million died in the Korean War, including between forty thousand and fifty-four thousand US soldiers. After orchestrating the impossible amphibious landing/assault at Inchon, General Douglas MacArthur drove North Korean

troops back to the Chinese border. At that point, a massive Chinese force hurled themselves against the American lines, pushing them back into South Korea. Under attack from China, MacArthur asked for permission to bomb China and to coordinate with Nationalist troops from Taiwan, but he was denied by President Truman and ultimately removed from command. Of course, MacArthur likely didn't know that the State Department had funded Mao and was not about to let Chinese communism be defeated. In his memoir, *Reminiscences*, MacArthur (January 1, 1964) said that he believed the United States could have won the Korean War. MacArthur also warned, "I am concerned for the security of our great nation, not so much because of any threat from without, but because of the insidious forces working from within."

2. Vietnam—The globalists wanted the Communists to win in Vietnam. Once again, the United States was not allowed to win a war, although fifty-eight thousand Americans perished in the conflict. For more information, see *The Naked Truth* by Dr. James C. Bowers (November 15, 2011).

3. The Gulf War and Iraq—G. Edward Griffin writes, "In the Gulf War, every effort was made to ensure that [Saddam] Hussein's regime was contained but not destroyed...His military infrastructure and most of his weapons were spared. After the cease-fire, he was allowed to keep his fleet of helicopter gunships, which he promptly used to put down a large-scale internal revolt." Griffin continues, "The big pill to swallow is that, for many years, Hussein was an asset to the global planners in the West, and they did everything possible to keep him in power. It was only when he refused to allow US companies to dominate Iraqi oil production that he was seriously targeted. Prior to that, he was untouchable precisely because he was widely perceived as a perfect, despicable enemy."

4. Afghanistan—Beneath the surface, there were strong geo-political and economic reasons for invading Afghanistan. Afghanistan produces 90 percent of the world's illicit heroin and contains rich natural resources, including mineral deposits, natural gas, and oil.

5. The Arab Spring and Syria—For more information, see "A Historical Perspective of Revolutions."

Predictive Analysis

With a solid understanding of the past in mind, what should we expect moving forward?

First, carefully follow the narrative, led by the conversation and rhetoric emanating from prominent think tanks and organizations (e.g., the Council on Foreign Relations, the Atlantic Council, Project Syndicate, and John Hopkins University). Who are these globalist entities painting to be the enemies of democracy? Often, such proposals find their way into mainstream media (where they shape public opinion) and into political discourse (where they become state and military policy).

At the same time, observe the key players in big business, high finance, high tech, and the military-industrial complex. What strings do these players pull? What outcomes are they planning for?

Third, watch the shaping of economic and military alliances (e.g., Russia, China, and Iran; the Quadrilateral Security Dialogue, including the United States, Japan, India, and Australia). Evaluate the flash points of conflict, including the Middle East, the South China Sea, and Eastern Europe (See Global Outlook).

Fourth, carefully observe today's use of unconventional unrestricted warfare, which can include biological warfare (COVID-19), technological warfare, spy craft, and ideological subversion.

Lastly, recognize that the globalist blueprint for global war and global government has not changed. Globalists remain committed to global depopulation (they want an optimum population of 500 million or less, which is why they always promote death through wars, abortion, eugenics, and now COVID injections) and relentlessly pursue global government by any means possible. If attaining their goal requires immense bloodshed, mass propaganda, and global destruction, those following "the father of lies" whose aim is to "kill, steal, and destroy" will feel no remorse.

20

Cyrus A. Parsa: God, China, America, and Artificial Intelligence

Cyrus Parsa is the author of several books and an expert in artificial intelligence (AI), quantum physics, 5G, national security, and relations between the United States, China, and Iran. He is the founder, CEO, and director of creative analysis and defensive innovations for the AI Organization (TheAIOrganization.com). Cyrus has a bachelor's degree in international security and master's in homeland security. He lived in China and trained with Buddhist-Taoist fighting monks to learn Wudang (named for a mountain range in China) arts and meditation (also called Qigong).

Cyrus has researched and investigated more than a thousand companies involved with AI, robotics, 5G, cybernetics, and other technologies. For many years he has been warning the public about the impending danger from diseases like coronaviruses being used as a bioweapon by the Chinese Communist Party (CCP). He has also alerted people all over the world to possible technology-aided attacks that may lead to regional conflicts, AI enslavement, famines, and misuse of biotech, as well as potential civil wars, world wars, and other threats to human lives.

Parsa has worked hard to get his research out to the public, part of which was publishing two books in 2019: The first was *AI, Trump, China & the Weaponization of Robotics with 5G* (August 24, 2019), and his second was *Artificial Intelligence Dangers to Humanity* (October 20, 2019). Of course, his warnings have been largely ignored, censored, or berated by mainstream and social media. Both books are available on his website mentioned above. Had Cyrus been given a platform earlier, countless lives may have been saved, much chaos averted, and potentially trillions of dollars saved.

The following is a paraphrase of the transcript from my December 2020 interview of Cyrus on American Media Periscope. Parsa shares some of his key research, warnings, future predictions, and advice for getting humanity back on track. Again, this content has been modified for the readability and flow, though the meanings remain the same. Here is Cyrus Parsa:

Let's start with a general overview of AI, which scientists classify in three stages (or levels): Artificial narrow intelligence (ANI) includes smartphones, as well as the "internet of things" (computing devices that enable sending and receiving data) that connect to Apple's Siri, Amazon's Alexa, or other chatbots designed to simulate interactions with humans. At this ANI level, we have those sorts of devices in our homes, just like mini "robots," which don't always work like the classical example but encompass all the products that watch us and help in our homes—technology we have to allow to invade our privacy because we've been socially engineered to believe they are beneficial.

Level two is artificial general intelligence (AGI). Where AI seems so human that we considered it to have "real life" like you and me, an AGI can have emotions, likes, dislikes, and free thoughts. Of course, the third level is most complex, which means a full understanding would require you to read a book like my *Artificial Intelligence Dangers to Humanity*. This stage is called artificial super intelligence (ASI) that uses human biometrics like facial and voice recognition, along with your other personal data, information that big-tech companies like Google, Apple, Microsoft, and those in social media have been mining and collecting for the past two decades. It has all been pulled together in their data against our free will, or at least without our informed consent, to create a quantum machine controlled by ASI.

That whole industry is a major concern because AI should be controlled by humans—not just within itself. Throughout history, the faith and philosophies of God and man have governed the world and its inhabitants. Before now, these important aspects of society have not been entrusted to AI systems or other internet-related machinery that is able to control our minds. Why would big tech team up with governments to hand dominion over our thoughts to AGI and ASI systems?

Human identification is the most common way AI is used today, and a modern example is how the CCP (Chinese Communist Party) tracks every aspect of their citizens' lives, including whether each is in compliance with their COVID-19 vaccines. They have been using facial and voice recognition, along with other biometric systems and algorithms, to identify those not buying into every CCP policy.

Just like the 1984 movie *Terminator,* starring Arnold Schwarzenegger, our reality today is AI technology that can police societies by targeting individuals in the exact way that film portrayed. Arnold was a cyborg assassin sent back to the 1980s from his home time that was twenty-five years in the future. As a terminator robot, he had an internal-targeting system that could decode and identify anyone by scanning past their skin to analyze a person's skeleton. That technology is available today! Big tech has it, so do many others. Along with facial and voice recognition, today's AI can track your gaze, physical stance, the way you walk, and your skin appearance, combining all of that data to predict (in varying degrees) what you will do next. My second book of 2019, *Artificial Intelligence Dangers to Humanity,* will help us prepare against and fight those kinds of AI abilities—together.

AI also powers facial recognition drones that check us out as they fly by, deciding on the spot if we are complying with social directives, or if we are wanted for any reason, and then some can even be equipped to deal with us violently, if needed. Speaking of future threats, another aspect of AI to be mindful of are AI robots that simulate human, animal, bird, and insect traits. Boston Dynamics is one company deeply into these very physical machines that are mechanical replicas of soldiers, horses, dogs, cheetahs, and many other living things. Another company makes bionic robot bats. The wilds of nature are being engineered into robots powered by AI.

By studying thousands of companies, I discovered that the whole spectrum of technology has been mostly engineered to connect together into a massive matrix. For example, we think of 5G (fifth generation telecommunications) as just a helpful way to increase the speed of wireless internet connections. But it was not invented for use in households. Instead, 5G was created to be used as a military weapon, including mobilizing drones and other complex systems of machines. Now that it is connected to AI, their hard push of 5G is extremely concerning because the technology is harmful to humans, potentially mutating our bodies in a few different ways.

We saw this effect in China where they have a company called Huawei laying wiring and installing parts for their 5G network. This one business serves 3 billion people and 1,500 networks, even though they are known for issues like using poor-quality products, fiber that emits five-millimeter waves, and harmful radiation coming from their towers. That last one messes with human skin and other biological functions, which throw our nervous system out of whack, making cells morph and divide. For healthy bodies that normally fight viruses fairly well, those sorts of radiation and millimeter waves can mutate a virus, while reducing the effectiveness of our immune system at the same time. That sort of interference with our biological systems can even mutate a virus that has been sitting dormant in us for thirty years; 5G has the ability to activate those sorts of harmful elements—turn them back on!

The human body is extremely complex, and I probably know more about it than most doctors, mostly because of so much research but also from training with monks in China, learning a form of ancient martial arts known as Qigong, which uses body posture, movement, and breathing for balance and energy flow. Discipline allows a Qigong practitioner to become attuned to his or her body; experienced followers can sense what is happening to themselves internally, even when the best technology is not able to. I incorporated Qigong into my research, combined it with biometric tools, and then used open-source information sharing to get input from other researchers, which is how we came up with many theories that later turned out to be true.

In the spring of 2020, most of us saw Chinese-supplied videos of Wuhan residents walking along normally and then suddenly falling over face-first on the sidewalk—instantly dead. That was part of the scare operation against the world, something that was accomplished through Wuhan's 5G network that either reinforced the viral effects inside those people, or attacked them by interacting with their biology in some other way. That same sort of reaction would not have happened in the United States because our 5G is a bit better. However, as I mentioned, it is made for machines, not people! The 5G system would be needed for things like the flying cars portrayed in the 1960s sitcom cartoon called *The Jetsons*. In fact, Western countries already have cars with wings that will someday fly by using 5G, and also 6G when we naturally transition to that at some point. Unfortunately, though, the horrific problem with 5G is how globalists plan to use it for forced morphing of people—making transhumans.

In fact, through extensive research I was able to pinpoint "extinction codes" in the majority of humans, part of our makeup that can be exploited to depopulate the planet, while claiming the large number of deaths was caused by natural occurrences like famines, viruses, or wars. Those extinction codes have to do with technology's ability to change a person's DNA by merging him or her with machines, changing them so they are no longer fully made in our Creator's image—not human—thus, transhuman.

As far as potential conflict with China, in most regards they are not as technologically advanced as the US, but in some ways, they are much more so. China has 1.5 billion people, so they've been able to send millions out across the planet for espionage as spies stealing technology from the US, Europe, the Far East, and everywhere. They have learned and stolen from the best scientists around the world, and brought that information straight back to the CCP. Besides that, China has hundreds of times more people than other countries, so think of how many more they can have working on AI research, especially since they often force certain careers on their citizens because it is a controlling, collectivist system. Knowing all China has dedicated to AI, also bear in mind that the CCP has a communist Marxist ideology, so they have no moral compass, meaning they will happily create new or upgraded viruses just because they are irresponsible. Is it safe for a regime like that to have artificial intelligence? What about the people? They've been indoctrinated and brainwashed. So, no!

In the books, I outline the many, many atrocities that the Chinese Communist regime has committed, which is why they are doomed to fall! I completely believe that our Creator God built a code into the universe that, over time, causes evil humans to be punished and taken out. The world used to have a much greater percentage of those who had faith in God, but today science has become an extremely popular religion. And many of those who still profess faith in God today don't feel it at the level folks did hundreds of years ago or at any other time in history. A lot of the issue is how science and technology have invaded people's minds and spirits, controlling them mentally, spiritually, and emotionally.

Today we often hear adamant opinions about what is true, even though those views come from no real evidence, only something claimed by a person they like or admire. They do not seek evidence from God and His Bible, which is extensive. And they also don't believe in God because they've allowed their actions and thoughts to be controlled by science, making people dependent on technology at just the time AI comes along to create the greatest ever threat to mankind, which is why I wrote *Artificial Intelligence Dangers to Humanity*.

In 2002, I began investigating companies after having a vision about global depopulation that I recounted to a few higher-ups at Homeland Security and Secret Service, who confirmed that what I saw was exactly accurate to the plan they knew about. However, since people won't trust someone who claims to know the future from a vision, I started investigating depopulation, which led me to the conclusion that our world is in danger—the new world order's plans for depopulation are real. My research uncovered how the globalists are building an AI system that connects to a digital brain for mobilizing the internet of things on a 5G-grid system. This AI-powered matrix will introduce drones and robots into our lives that have facial and voice recognition, as well as capabilities like delivering vaccines. Further down the transhuman road, their plan is for us to be converted toward a cyborg existence where each person is connected to the controlled, fake-news media, which will be in our heads for constant brainwashing. And through use of a method I call "biodigital social programming," they have conditioned us to accept all their technological advances.

After investigating the companies for my second book, I began a lawsuit against many of them because of what I found. It is clear that big tech is connected to Marxist communism. The whole system is being powered by AI, and it will become what the Bible's last chapter, Revelation, tells us will be the Antichrist's beast system, which completely takes away the freedom of the world, controlling everywhere and everyone. Even the way they write their programming code is anti-faith, anti-God, and anti-conservative, while also promoting transhumanism in many ways—their algorithms promote bestiality. With such an in-depth look at these companies, I could see the demonic presence working at controlling the world, wanting to bring in its system and rid the world of most humans. In fact, I had a vision of President Trump in power and fighting that beast system.

Speaking of Trump, I could go on and on about his great accomplishments, but I think the best thing he did was to go after China, especially ending their theft of our intellectual property (IP), such as weapons systems that would endanger the whole world if allowed to fall into CCP hands. China has also bought up a huge amount of assets in the US. Trump's second most important accomplishment was to expose the worldwide network of corruption, whether you call them the globalists, cabal, deep state, or whatever.

Getting back to 5G, I think it can be done in a safe way, but there are also numerous dangers, including its impact on human health, so I would suggest we all write our members of Congress, as well as get communities and mayors involved to expose the uncertainty of 5G, especially since we do not know the long-term effects five and ten years out. It must be studied for at least ten years, but I think smart cities can be built with 5G that are not Orwellian like *1984* (author George Orwell's dystopian account of a future totalitarian state), as long as it is not placed close to homes. We can have a *Jetsons* sort of future, and that's what Trump's administration was working at, reducing risks and improving on what had already been started. Of course, many dangers still exist because Trump can't simultaneously battle a thousand fronts, but pain is coming for these nefarious players in big tech who've done very bad things. They are going to feel it.

As most know, America's Founding Fathers were geniuses. The Fourth Amendment of the US Constitution guarantees "the right of the people to be secure against unreasonable searches [spying] and seizures." It certainly can be used for protection against government agencies spying on us, most of the time in collusion with big tech. Our founders set the country up so that everything would connect back and be checked by the Constitution—today, we don't do that. I could build a 5G and AI system based on our Constitution, something not understood or appreciated by those currently building it.

On top of that, there are techies all over the world who are signing million- and billion-dollar contracts with advisers, consultants, and big tech companies, and these contracts can eventually be worth trillions. This is going on in so many sectors of our economy that are vital, such as health care and security, yet technology people don't think like we do: They often do not concern themselves with the dangerous effects of their work or what deep state entity they might be creating it for. They only see what is on their list to do and how the creation or use of technology will bring them money.

One AI plan promises to help us eventually live for two hundred, five hundred, or even one thousand years by transferring people's consciousness into a cloned, humanoid machine. They think they'll basically capture and transfer souls through their data migration, but that is not possible. For a lot of money, they will put your memory into another body, but the result will not be you because your brain and its memory are not your soul.

As far as unreasonable spying on us, big tech companies have been using GeoLocation (locating us by use of the internet) and Lidar (targeting the location of objects by bouncing a laser off them), which both tie into our smartphones and many other personal devices. These companies and municipalities have been constantly violating our Fourth Amendment rights for a long, long time. We must stop this and hold them accountable for illegally spying on us!

Big-tech spying is being done by governments at all levels, and I'm not against limited government and its workers, but some who get into that system of massive funding and power only care about their own clique, family, and friends. It's in our human makeup from a history of living separately in families, neighborhoods, tribes, and villages. We have many who are part of ranches, teams, communities, towns, and cities who focus just on their group. But now, the whole world is being globalized, so does it make sense to have an entire country operated by just a few people at the top who use the resources of the masses to make sure their families, friends, and associates are enriched and empowered, while the rest of us struggle to get equal treatment in their rigged system? We have let that happen, but it can't be allowed to go on. The world needs at least ten thousand separate monitors, or kingdoms.

Obviously, the major issue with technology is how it is being used to supersede and bypass the Fourth Amendment—and our entire Bill of Rights—in multiple ways, interconnecting all aspects of society, including media, entertainment, education, government, and health care. As all that comes more and more under AI, human beings increasingly lose control. Even assuming a politician like Trump is trying to do the right thing by the people, think about how laws get passed in the technology sector. Some guy who might not even be too bright, and probably had a communist upbringing in our public schools, sits in Trump's AI department where he signs for important government initiatives all the time, making technology decisions for our president. Even comprehensive technology-related legislation, involving millions and billions of taxpayer dollars, is often brought about by guys around a president who vouch for the merits, so he just signs it into law without investigating well because he's dealing with so many decisions every day. And probably none of his people really understand the technology, especially the bigger picture of cause and effect for these green-lighted initiatives that begin branching out like a tree to affect a thousand other areas of our lives.

Those are some of the crucial issues to be worked out right away because AI will outsmart the entire human race, and that's what Elon Musk (billionaire involved with Neuralink, SpaceX, Tesla, OpenAI, and more) meant when he said we have been summoning the demons and it's now too late. For three years Musk has been posting messages like these on social media:

> "If you can't beat them, join them. It's too late; AI is here, and we must merge with it to survive."

Completely contrary to big tech's atheistic view, I've been trying to warn people that these advancements threaten the morality of nations. But any country blessed and protected by God will continue to enjoy that status as long as its inhabitants are virtuous and moral. Just look back at every extinct society. The people had become morally bankrupt. It happened to the Babylonians, Persians, Greeks, Romans, and on, and on. Destruction would often come about after two hundred years, which is a threshold the US passed a while ago.

Can we be saved from going the way of those others? Yes! Definitely! Here's how: We all point to certain countries and people as the sources of our world's problems, whether deep state groups like the CCP and international bankers, or individuals like George Soros, Bill Gates, Obama, the Clintons, and Joe Biden. And some just blame the universal cabal as the entire issue, but the foundation of our troubles is not really them—it is us! I don't think of myself as conservative politically, but more so ethically and morally. Conservatives point at liberals as the problem, but where were we over the last many decades of changing morality? What did we do? Did we allow evil? How did it take over? I will say that most of us are guilty because we have not done our due diligence.

Over the last hundred years and more, even the few brave voices standing up to warn everyone got pounded down when they were not joined by other honorable people; instead, they were left to be lone voices led to the slaughter. Our Founding Fathers like Benjamin Franklin and George Washington let us know that every American has the duty to protect this country from enemies, both foreign and domestic. We especially have the ongoing responsibility to hire politicians of high moral character, and stay that way ourselves as a society, because moral decline and eventual bankruptcy follow those who are not diligent! Our founders were adamant that character was the most important issue to base our vote on—so far, we have failed.

Think about this: Who in their right mind would allow our public schools to teach very young children how to sexually touch themselves? What kind of broken society lets that happen? And ten years ago, my own doctoral degree program taught that it is perfectly normal for an older man to have feelings for a little boy. And then I see footage from Pixar that shows a bearded older man in bed, holding and hugging an unrelated small boy. What subliminal message does that send?

On top of those issues, we allow abortion to enter society and grow to the point where we are now allowing all sorts of ungodly ideas and practices for our bodies that have been made in God's image. We are told not to procreate, and instead we need to embrace cloning, robots, and transhumanism. So, humanity is extinguishing itself because so much of it has arrived at an unsustainable level of moral bankruptcy. I know what I say is blunt, but we are at the point where the solution needs to be stressed; the issues we face today have to do with you, me, and our morals.

There are thousands of problems that all tie back to morals, which is part of a relationship with, and faith in, God. People are afraid to even use the word "God" today, but President Trump wasn't—and he is exactly right to do so! How dare any American be afraid to mention God. Our founders were clear: *one nation under God!* It's in our Constitution!

As we get back to God, the grand solution should involve exposing the CCP, other communism, Marxism, socialism, and all the rest of the satanically inspired, collectivist ideologies. Even we capitalists need to stop being socialists! We have crony capitalism—a system where people in business and government collude to take and redistribute money they have not earned—on an unbelievable scale. God has a law of the universe that does not respect liberal, conservative, atheist, or person of faith. Whenever you steal, harm, plagiarize, or lie, God will not support you—we must get back to respecting that.

I am completely against liberals or conservatives who support those that steal intellectual property (IP), including authors like me, who have paid for an extensive education and spent decades researching, all to write books that get plagiarized. That is straight-up IP theft. Many of those blaming China for IP theft are the ones stealing my stuff, so think about how even our Christian nation has become completely corrupt! Of course, that means the whole world has issues. When I moved to the US in 1987, this country had a wonderful society with a beautiful feel in the air, especially at Christmas. But as great as it still was, that decade involved a continuation of the same downslide toward socialism that had started to seep in after the 1950s.

America had a lot of moral fiber in the 1930s and 1940s, a time when the majority of this nation could be trusted—their word meant something—but now it's not that way here. Our people are not even in control of themselves because this entire nation, people's minds, and their families' have been destroyed by moral decline and ever-increasing collectivist ideology. I saw this country's decline in the 1980s, 1990s, and 2000s, with heavy drug use taking a toll. That's why I can see that today's liberals are yesterday's Communists, and today's conservatives are yesterday's liberals. The world's story feels so much like a science fiction movie playing out about how the new world order marches toward their takeover. In fact, I believe our own morally bankrupt nation and the rest of the planet's degraded people would have been destroyed in any number of ways decades ago, if not for God's grace.

Today, many of us attend church but still don't truly believe in God. If our hearts had enough faith to know God is real, we would understand that we all have a soul, so everyone is going to live for eternity—we are all already immortal! Instead of false narratives from compromised news sources and other lying media, if the entire world's population could be informed with true knowledge of God, we would again act right toward each other.

I'm encouraged that there appears to be a real great awakening to the evil works of this world's deviant controllers and what they have been doing. Once enough of us learn that truth, many will choose God over the reality of the uncovered evil they will have to come face-to-face with. That will cause huge portions of mankind, long-time unbelievers, to pick faith and relationship with our Creator God—and the resulting great awakening of faith in Him will see massive swathes of humanity saved!

The Goals of the Illuminati

The following is a much-less-detailed version of Dr. John Coleman's 1993 list called Twenty-One Goals of the Illuminati and the Committee of 300:

Establish a one-world government/new world order with a unified church and monetary system under their direction; bring about the utter destruction of all national identity and national pride; engineer and bring about the destruction of religion, and more especially, the Christian religion; establish the ability to control each and every person through means of mind control; bring about the end to all industrialization; encourage and eventually legalize the use of drugs and make pornography an "art form," which will be widely accepted and, eventually, become quite commonplace; bring about depopulation of large cities, *according to the trial run carried out by the Pol Pot regime in Cambodia; and suppress all scientific development except for those deemed beneficial by the Illuminati.*

Cause, by means of A) limited wars in the advanced countries, and B) by means of starvation and diseases in the Third World countries, the death of three billion people by the year 2050, people they call "useless eaters"; weaken the moral fiber of the nation and demoralize workers in the labor class by creating mass unemployment; keep people everywhere from deciding their own destinies by means of one created crisis after another and then "managing" such crises; introduce new cults and continue to boost those already functioning; press for the spread of religious cults; export "religious liberation" ideas around the world so as to undermine all existing religions, but more especially the Christian religion; and cause a total collapse of the world's economies and engender total political chaos.

Take control of all foreign and domestic policies of the US; give the fullest support to supranational institutions, *such as the United Nations, the International Monetary Fund (IMF), the Bank of International Settlements, [and] the World Court; penetrate and subvert all governments, and work from within them to destroy the sovereign integrity of the nations represented by them; organize a worldwide terrorist apparatus; and take control of education in America with the intent and purpose of utterly and completely destroying it.*

21

Mary Fanning: Stealing America

Most of the following introduction of Mary Fanning was taken from SarahWestall.com: Mary Fanning is an investigative journalist who has collaborated with another of the same profession, Alan Jones, to expose a series of breaking national security stories. You will find their work at theAmericanReport.org. The beginning of this interview will get right into how this August 2020 book from Fanning and Jones exposed the "Hammer and Scorecard" vote-stealing computer system:

> *The Hammer Is the Key to the Coup "The Political Crime of the Century": How Obama, Brennan, Clapper, and the CIA Spied on President Trump, General Flynn...and Everyone Else*

Fanning and Jones were the first reporters to connect President Trump's 2017 tweet, which accused President Obama of wiretapping Trump Tower, to the case of CIA whistleblower Dennis Montgomery, who asserted that President Obama's director of the CIA, John Brennan, and his director of national intelligence, James Clapper, illegally spied on Trump. They used an illegal, super-surveillance system known as the Hammer.

Mary and Alan also uncovered the connections between rogue Iraqi nuclear physicist Dr. Jafar Dhia Jafar and a 2014 Port Canaveral

(Florida shipping port) Project Pelican cargo container. This terminal, which the US had leased to Gulftainer (a Middle Eastern port management company), helped the Obama administration bypass the required national security threat analysis that is normally done through CFIUS (Committee on Foreign Investment in the US). Dr. Jafar was the scientific mastermind behind Saddam Hussein's nuclear weapons program. Fanning and Jones subsequently connected Project Pelican to the Clintons, the Clinton Foundation, the Clinton Global Initiative, and Russia's Klub-K Container Missile System.

Mary and Alan were also the first reporters to expose the Jafar family's connections to the now-collapsed Middle Eastern hedge fund called the Abraaj Group, along with the connections of Barack Obama's college roommates to the Abraaj Group and the Jafar family. Fanning and Jones uncovered ties between Hawaii's director of health Loretta Fuddy, Chicago Communists' SUBUD (Susila Budhi Dharma), and the Soviet Silvermaster spy ring. Fuddy had released a copy of Barack Obama's birth certificate to the White House before she was reportedly killed in a plane crash.

Mary Fanning is known for her *Betrayal Papers* series that exposed the infiltration of the Muslim Brotherhood into the highest levels of American government. Along with retired US Army Major General Paul E. Vallely, Mary created a coalition of concerned Americans who have exposed the influence that the Muslim Brotherhood exerted over the Obama administration, members of Congress, and American policy—both foreign and domestic. In her *Qatar Awareness* series, Mary showed the penetration by Qatar, home of the Muslim Brotherhood, into US universities and corporate America. Mary's work has appeared on the websites of the Center for Security Policy, Breitbart News, Community Digital News, Lifezette, The Gateway Pundit, 1776 Channel, and The American Report.

Here is author and researcher Mary Fanning from a December 2020 interview by me on American Media Periscope. This is a paraphrase of the content, while retaining Mary's meanings:

As a brief explanation of *Hammer and Scorecard*, the Hammer is an electronic surveillance tool built by the CIA in 2003, through a contractor named Doug Montgomery, the man who designed it for then CIA Director John Brennan and former Director of National Intelligence James Clapper. The Hammer originally belonged to the Department of Defense. Montgomery turned whistleblower when he found out that the machine was not only being used for *foreign* surveillance to keep America safe after 9/11, but also for illegal *domestic* spying. In 2015, Montgomery provided sworn testimony to the FBI and the DOJ about the Hammer and its Scorecard software having the ability to hack into US *domestic* election systems. Allegations of the Hammer's utilization for stealing elections goes back to being used against Trump in 2016, to help Obama and Biden win Florida in 2012, and in support of the Democrats stealing the presidential primary for Hillary Clinton, away from Bernie Sanders.

Montgomery also built multiple "exploits," which you know as your smartphone's applications, or "apps." One of those was Scorecard, an app Doug had originally built to *secure* elections against those like Communists who would attempt to take over nations through stolen votes. Instead, Hammer and Scorecard was turned on America to steal our elections like what we saw in November 2020, a massive steal by domestic traitors working with foreign enemies like China, Iran, and Russia, all colluding through cyberwarfare facilitated by the Dominion voting machines. Imagine that, our adversaries are actually accessing our voting systems and stealing American elections to place their puppets in power.

As part of the Hammer, the Scorecard application uses a prismatic scoring algorithm to steal votes at internet transfer points like when electronic votes leave a secretary of state's server. Even if a nation, state, or county uses paper ballots, various totals throughout the process that are sent over the internet can be intercepted and changed by the Scorecard software. In November 2020, as a landslide for President Trump was coming through, these nefarious vote stealers were not able to keep up with the high count for Trump, so they began copying, or cloning, large blocks of votes in at least five swing states that we know of here in December 2020.

Getting back to the history, as part of blackmail and leverage operation using the Hammer, it was moved to Fort Washington, Maryland, where it was employed for spying on Americans like Donald Trump and General Michael Flynn, members of Congress, and business leaders, as well as 156 District, Federal Circuit, and Supreme Court judges. Imagine a situation where the new administration coming in faces a country that has been turned into a police state, spying on anyone and everyone. In fact, (former) Attorney General Bill Barr characterized it as *spying* because there was no better word. After General Flynn's long court battle, General McInerney and I participated with Flynn in his first interview, a forum where he strongly characterized the 2020 election this way:

"You are still watching a coup d'état in progress."

Again, John Brennan and James Clapper illegally commandeered (stole) the Hammer surveillance tool and inserted an encrypted virtual private network (VPN) that connected directly to the Obama White House, so the vote stealers could have access at will. The existence of the Hammer was first exposed when Federal Judge G. Murray Snow, chief district judge for Arizona (Maricopa County), released audiotapes of sworn testimony that whistleblower Montgomery gave to the FBI and DoD in Snow's courtroom during 2015. The "whistleblower tapes," as Alan and I dubbed them, talked about illegal surveillance taking place and how people were being recorded, unbeknownst to them. According to the man who illegally recorded all these people,

Montgomery's whistleblower tapes were never intended to be made public, but "somehow" got out from under Judge Snow's nose.

Alan and I transcribed those tapes and published them in a March 2017 article, which is when the public first started hearing about this. In fact, just thirty hours after we published that piece, WikiLeaks dropped CIA Vault 7, their largest ever publication of confidential documents from that agency, which included confirmation of the Hammer's existence. Hammer and Scorecard became more widely known when General Thomas McInerney—a widely respected man of sterling character, who was the three-star general in charge of NORAD (North American Aerospace Defense Command) and our Pentagon nuclear weapons— along with four-star Admiral James "Ace" Lyons came forward with our transcripts, reading them verbatim on a March 2017 radio program. The very next day, James Comey launched the Russian collusion investigation (hoax!) against Donald Trump.

Something else interesting happened at that same time: A year later, text messages were revealed by US Inspector General Michael Horowitz that matched up with that March 2017 time, communications between (former) FBI Agent Peter Strzok and his then-lover, (former) FBI attorney Lisa Page, who had been texting each other within a few minutes of General McInerney's appearance on the radio. Strzok and Page were texting about Dennis Montgomery and his attorney, the very people that McInerney was speaking about on a radio program. And again, it was the next day that Strzok's boss at the FBI, James Comey, launched the Russian collusion hoax against Trump—and Comey put Strzok in charge of it! I am assuming we can rule out the minute chance that either Strzok or Page just happened to be listening to that specific radio station at the exact time McInerney popped on, so there is more proof they had been using the Hammer for surveillance of people like the general. As I mentioned, they have been turning it on the American people, including judges, company executives, members of Congress, and even President Donald Trump.

All this becomes even more problematic when we look into the background of John Brennan, who says he converted to Islam, and his family's long history as Communists. In fact, Brennan supported Gus Hall for American president, a guy who was head of the US Communist Party, an entity long thought to be answering to communist Russia. It was also reported in the *New Yorker* magazine that James Comey used to be a Communist, but now claims he doesn't know what he is. So, under Obama, the heads of the CIA and FBI were both self-proclaimed Communists!

As General Michael Flynn charged, we are not just looking at voter theft; this is about cyberwarfare, something our Founding Fathers may not have known about, but they could certainly recognize tyranny when they saw it—and this is it! We're also looking at "man-in-the-middle" technology, where an attacker secretly relays and possibly alters the communications between two parties who don't know their messages are being deleted and changed. General McInerney states that cyberwarfare is, of course, just like any other act of war. Foreign adversaries, with the aid of domestic traitors, have been breaching and stealing our elections. A recent example was easy to see when Joe Biden, who rarely came out of his basement and was not drooling at the same time, supposedly beat President Trump, even though Biden could hardly get a dozen supporters to listen to anything he *attempted* to say. In fact, they attempted to get away with stealing a landslide reelection from Trump. There is absolutely no way Joe Biden won the November 2020 election, but as usual the American people are being lied to by the mockingbird media.

[When the Cold War was getting started in the late 1040's, the CIA implemented a program called Operation Mockingbird, with the objective to purchase control and influence of many major media outlets. The CIA also planned to have reporters and journalists on the CIA payroll (dannyboylimerick.wordpress.com).]

Today, Donald Trump is standing up for this country as a sovereign nation, while Joe Biden has been bought and paid for by the CCP (Chinese Communist Party). How do we know the latter? Well, for one, it's been reported and proven that Hunter Biden traveled to China with his father on Air Force Two, after which the Chinese paid him $1.5 billion, and then Hunter hit the Ukraine with his dad for a another billion dollars, which his father bragged about during a guest appearance at the Atlantic Council (an American think tank for international matters). When the Ukraine attempted to investigate and stop Hunter from taking their people's money, Papa Joe called the Ukraine to demand the official looking into Hunter be fired. Imagine what they think they've gotten away with: The family of a US vice president being paid off by Red China and the Ukraine to the tune of $2.5 billion, after which the head of the family attempts to steal a presidential election from the present president that the people actually want. And who was assisting all this? China, Iran, and Russia.

As far as that possible US Special Operations raid in Frankfurt, Germany, during November 2020, General McInerney says it does appear they obtained computer servers from a secret CIA facility, but he had gotten no confirmation of any firefight. There were also some strange characters in Europe who claimed to be with an American military magazine, but they turned out to be Norwegians.

On the night of the 2020 election, you may remember President Trump foreshadowing when he said he didn't want to start seeing vote theft by 4:00 a.m. Sure enough, at 4:00 a.m., a huge block of 112,000 votes were delivered in Wisconsin, at the same time as 135,000 got added to the tally in Michigan—and both blocks were 100 percent for Biden. These were just a couple examples of the massive vote stealing they had to employ, which also included the vote theft by Dominion machines used in twenty-eight states. Those electronic voting systems apparently come with instructions on how to steal elections.

On top of all that, we saw multiple fraud operations with paper ballots, the most disturbing being stolen ballots from our soldiers, many of whom were away battling in foreign nations, so they had to submit votes by mail, only to have them trashed, or changed from Trump to Biden. And getting back to Hammer and Scorecard, it's important to note that Sidney Powell (US attorney, former federal prosecutor, and author of *Licensed to Lie: Exposing Corruption in the Department of Justice*), submitted an affidavit from a US contractor, Dr. Navid Keshavarz-Nia, who worked for defense intelligence agencies like the CIA, National Security Agency (NSA), and the Department of Homeland Security. He came forward to disclose that they had indeed used Hammer and Scorecard to steal the 2020 election. And even the far-left *New York Times* confirmed that Dr. Navid is the smartest man in any room, which is how most people describe him.

We also know about something called the "Kraken," possibly out of the 305th military intelligence battalion located at Fort Huachuca, Arizona. They seem to be some of those looking into all this cyber activity, most likely to be among the future groups who will eventually expose it. Most likely related, General Flynn's attorney, Sidney Powell, was on *Lou Dobbs Tonight* in November 2020, when she "let loose" this statement:

"I'm going to release the Kraken."

One of our deeply established problems today is the mockingbird media only presenting us with propaganda, a basket of falsehoods, and wall-to-wall lies. General McInerney rightly characterizes their work as aiding and abetting the treasonous theft of our elections, with the assistance of China, Iran, and Russia. Donald Trump won the people's 2020 vote by a landslide, while these Communists have been all about stealing America. And if they had been successful, we would have never gotten it back.

Luckily though, the American people have awakened and they are saying to Washington, DC, "You...work...for...us! This country belongs to its people, and we will not let you steal it!" The attempted theft was so obvious because, to win, they knew they must commit fraud in a massive way. They had to cover up all their past crimes, fearing what would come their way if Trump got back in again. And they should be scared because the American people *are* coming at them right now! We will not stand down as our country is stolen from the likes of Red-China-Communist Joe Biden.

Here in December 2020, we know that the Dominion voting machines were purchased in part by China, which is hard to fathom—letting another nation run the vote in our country—especially a communist adversary! If the American people can't get a free and fair vote, there will no longer be a rule of law. We will end up like China's people today, living in some sort of social-credit-score system or gulag-like labor camp.

"Social credit" is a sort of national blacklist being installed by the CCP in China, which is meant to assess the economic and social reputation of businesses and citizens. It has also been described as a system where citizens are evaluated for trustworthiness.

I hope the American people will stand up and fight against having their country stolen by the likes of Red China, a country that has been known to put its elderly Wuhan residents in body bags—while still alive—and then throw them into furnaces!

In defending our honorable rule of law, the world is watching what America will do now. Ronald Reagan was right when he warned:

> *"If we lose freedom here, there is no place to escape to. This is the last stand on earth."*

22

Amapola Hansberger: Legal Immigrants for America

The following is taken from a June 2021 interview of Amapola Hansberger by American Media Periscope host Sean Morgan. The meaning remains the same, while the verbiage has been altered for readability. The first three paragraphs are an introduction to her organization:

As a legal immigrant from Nicaragua, Amapola Hansberger is the founder and president of Legal Immigrants for America (GoLIFA. com), whose mission includes educating the public about the differences between legal immigrants and illegal aliens, representing American citizens who have migrated to the United States legally, and giving voice to the voiceless legal immigrants who have not had one until now. LIFA envisions a nation where our immigration laws are respected, abuses prosecuted, and borders defended.

LIFA has three core values: First, they believe national sovereignty is a fundamental right of any nation, so we need protection of our borders, which involves support for four things: our brave ICE (Immigration and Customs Enforcement) officers and border patrol, enforcement of existing immigration laws, building a wall on our southern border, and English as the common language of all legal immigrants.

Second, LIFA believes our rights are given by God, including life, liberty, and the pursuit of happiness, which means they value the concerns of existing American citizens, defunding of sanctuary cities, an end to H-1B visa abuse, respect for the US Constitution as the law of the land (regardless of religious beliefs), and encouragement of legal immigration from countries and cultures that share our Judeo-Christian world and life view. Third, LIFA believes life is the most fundamental right given from God to man, so they oppose human trafficking and policies that encourage it, value the protection of all humans, and support the vetting of legal immigrants, particularly those from countries that have proven to be hotbeds of radical Islamic terrorism.

Here is Amapola:

I love America because it is uniquely a beacon of freedom, which makes me sad that many born in the United States do not know the benefit of being a citizen here. The US is exceptional, especially because of those Christians who have gone out to evangelize the nations of the world, how our founding fathers sacrificed everything to create this amazing Christian country that has been blessed by the Lord, and the fact that America has had so many in our military sacrifice and die, not only in the defense of us but also for many other countries around the planet.

Compare that to socialism and communism around the world in places like my birth country of Nicaragua, where President Daniel Ortega is abhorrently attacking and apprehending all of his opponents for the presidency. We Nicaraguans are not for that, but it is being allowed to happen because people all over the world these days are not taught who the real Karl Marx was and what his Marxist communism is truly about. He advocated for communist revolutions all over the world, which are always hindered by the Christian Bible and love of God, country, and neighbors. Because Communists fear those aspects of freedom the most, they want to destroy Christianity. They are God's enemies, just as all communist Leninists and communist Marxists are. Here is the first leader of Russian communism, Vladimir Lenin, who advocated for dividing people, the same tactic used by Socialists and Communists today:

> *"Among the masses, we can and must...sow hate, revulsion, and scorn toward those who disagree with us."*

Except for parents who were already "good" Communists, Lenin advocated teaching the world's children to hate their fathers and mothers. Anatole Lunarcharsky, the former Soviet Russian head of education, admitted this:

> *"We hate Christians and Christianity. Even the best of them must be considered our worst enemies. They preach love of one's neighbor and mercy, which is contrary to our principles. Christian love is an obstacle to the development of the Revolution. Down with love of our neighbor! What we want is hate...Only then can we conquer the universe."*

Today, illegal immigration is a Marxist, communist tool—just like "critical race theory," which teaches society that whites are born racists. Those are two of about forty-five steps Communists outline for conquering nations. Overwhelming a country with immigrants is part of that nefarious effort, and it plays on the unattainable goal that no nation can take on—absorbing all of the poor around our planet. Having worked most of our lives and paid into the tax system, it is also unfair to make Americans support the needy of the world, whether each individual is willing or not. Instead, we should help those living in poverty to vote for leaders who will promote freedom like our founders did.

Years ago, our LIFA organization saw President Trump as a unique, gifted, special person anointed by God, so we worked to make sure he would be elected, passing out an English and Spanish "freedom card" that contrasted communism with free-living capitalism. Marx claimed the purpose for his life was to destroy capitalism. He was a diabolical enemy of God with a PhD in philosophy, but he never went to work, which probably contributed to two of his children committing suicide and three others dying of starvation. Further demonstrating that Marx was not someone to learn from, his cowriter of the *Communist Manifesto*, Friedrich Engels, had to give Marx money to survive because that arrogant man was also lazy and dirty. Those who were unlucky enough to hear him speak in person could not believe their ears, so he was booted out of countries like France and Belgium, as well as even his home country of Germany. Responsible adults could not stand his philosophy.

Today we need parents to be sure their children are taught the contrast between capitalism and Marxism, which is explained well by a couple of books that Moms and Dads should read and discuss with their kids: *The Naked Communist*, by Christian author W. Cleon Skousen, and *The Making of Modern Economics: The Lives and Ideas of the Great Thinkers*, by Mark Skousen, W. Cleon's nephew. The latter talks about Adam Smith, who wrote *The Wealth of Nations*; Karl Marx; John Maynard Keynes; Ludwig von Mises; Milton Friedman; and many other prominent economists of history—some excellent, others terrible like Marx.

Of course, the most important book to read is the Bible, but all three together will tell you all you want to know about why so many English-speaking countries like America, Australia, New Zealand, and England have been prosperous, which has to do with how much they prayed to the Lord, something especially American because our founders came here to escape persecution for being Christians. Out of that great struggle came the creation of the greatest document that ever existed outside of the scriptures—the Constitution of the United States of America. There has never been a better constitution anywhere else in the world. Just like the Bible, it had to have been inspired by God because the men who came together to write it were not wise old statesmen. Instead, most were smart young soldiers in their twenties, thirties and forties.

23

Laura Logan: A Veteran Mainstream Reporter Gives Some New-Media-Type Truth about the Global Threat

The following is taken from a June 2021 interview of Lara Logan (LaraLogan.com) by Glenn Beck (GlennBeck.com). As mainstream media figures go, the South African-born, fifty-year-old journalist is a familiar, highly-respected, long-time television and radio personality. Besides reporting projects for all the networks, as well as other news organizations, she was the chief foreign affairs correspondent at CBS News for sixteen years, which included work on *60 Minutes*, the *CBS Evening News*, *The Early Show*, *Face the Nation*, and many others.

Here is Lara Logan's warning for our world about the globalist threat:

We talk a lot about left and right, and for obvious reasons, because, right now, this is lining up as a left-right fight. But if you look at the Open Society Foundations, Kellogg Foundation, Ford Foundation, Tides Foundation, Thousand Currents, Sunrise Movement, and all of these organizations, their ultimate goal is not Marxism and communism; it is a global world where everything is about using euphemisms to hide your real agenda. So, when they say "sustainable develop-ment," they mean "We tell you what you can and can't grow, we tell you what you can and can't eat, and we control the food supply. And, by the way, you can have no fuel, and you are going to be geographi-cally isolated." With "net zero emissions," no one asks what happens to global air travel. Right? Of course, there won't be global air travel for you and me, but they will still have whatever they need. So, we will be graphically isolated.

And using technology, these ideas have been spread, incubated, nurtured, and sustained all across the world. Everywhere you look, whether it's South Africa or Bosnia or the Soviet Union, there are activists and nongovernmental organizations that hide; they use their nongovernmental and charitable status to hide behind a sinister agen-da. They even use Marxism and communism as recruitment and orga-nizing tools. But the world that they imagine in the end isn't one that is Marxist or communist; it's one in which a tiny group of powerful people control everything, and we are the monitored class—they use the technology to surveil and control us.

Anyone who does not pay attention to this, who dismisses it as a con-spiracy theory, is delusional. Beyond the public eye, there are some very serious things going on in this country.

24

Editor's Supplement: Lord Willing, After We Have Helped God Stomp Out Much Evil in Our Time, What Comes Next Biblically?

Christ said something that may have been meant for our time:

> *"There is nothing hidden that will not be disclosed, and nothing concealed that will not be known or brought out into the open" (Luke 8:17).*

Every act of sabotage that the hidden, satanic cabal has subjected us to is being revealed in these last days of mankind before Jesus returns, and each new revelation leads to ten more. That is a lot to stomach, but I think it means we are headed for a period of long-standing peace and prosperity, which God is bringing in because it involves uncovering the evil. Much of our world today is neutral on God and does not believe in a real Satan, even though the Bible mentions hell many more times than heaven. Either way, these Luciferians believe in the devil, and they are worshipping him through the death and destruction of those made in God's image—they hate us and God. But when mankind soon comes face-to-face with the horrific practices these child sacrificers carry out in the name of their demon guides and Satan, it will cause the world to choose a side—a vast number will pick God.

However, we know from the Bible's book of Revelation that this approaching peace and prosperity is only a window of time, especially since all Christians will be raptured off this planet any day now—in the blink of an eye. If you don't believe that, make the effort to research it in the Bible. Even God's enemies know it to be true. Look up the satanic New Age movement's teachings about the same event; though they lie about it, they claim the Christians' departure will be a good thing because Christians are holding the world back from "ascending to the next level." Satan knows Bible prophecy better than anyone, and even his followers are predicting the imminent, sudden disappearance of millions around the world—all the Christians.

Just reading basic Bible prophecy shows how that event has no more preconditions; it is imminent in our day. (See *The Rapture: Don't Be Deceived,* by Pastor Billy Crone at GetALifeMedia.com or *The Now Prophecies,* by Bill Salus at ProphecyDepotMinistries.net.)

Two thousand separate times throughout man's history of six thousand years, God's word in the Bible has specifically and successfully predicted the future. Psychics are frauds that tend to predict in generalities like "I see you meeting someone new today." Yeah, ya think? Dwelling outside the dimension of time that He created for us to live in, only God knows the exact future from the beginning, and He put those proofs in His Bible, so we would gain confidence in our scriptures, as we read His detailed prophecies that have since come true in detail, exactly the way He said they would—100 percent of the time.

Over a hundred years ago, most all church-attending Christians were taught Bible prophecy, resulting in no doubts that their scriptures were divinely inspired, divinely written, and divinely given to us by God through men. Their faith remained strong because they did not wonder if they could trust God's word completely. When you put time in to do the homework, you will find that the last five hundred Bible prophecies are about events obviously lining up right now. Unfortunately, the vast major of Christian pastors today are figuratively ripping God's perfect record of predications out of their Bibles—and their congregation's Bibles. They refuse to teach it!

Besides the definitive proof of Bible prophecy, how else do we know the Bible is from God? Former atheist and investigative reporter Josh McDowell set out to prove the Bible and Jesus are frauds. From his resulting book, *The Case for Christ*, here is part of what he found that caused him to become a Christian and trust his Bible completely:

> [The Bible was] written over a 1,500-year span; over 40 different generations; written by more than 40 authors, from every walk of life—including kings, peasants, philosophers, fishermen, poets, statesmen, scholars, etc. Moses was a political leader trained in the universities of Egypt, [Peter was a fisherman,] Amos, a herdsman, Joshua, a military general, Nehemiah, a cup-bearer, Daniel, a prime minister, Luke, a doctor, Solomon, a king, Matthew, a tax collector, and Paul, a rabbi. [The Bible was] written in different places: Moses in the wilderness, Jeremiah in a dungeon, Daniel on a hillside and in a palace, Paul inside prison walls, Luke while traveling, John on the island of Patmos, [and] others in the rigors of military campaigns. [The Bible was] written at different times: David in times of war [and] Solomon in times of peace. [The Bible was] written during different moods [with] some writings from the heights of joy and others from the depths of sorrow and despair. [The Bible was] written on three continents:

> Asia, Africa, and Europe, [as well as] in three languages;
> Hebrew, [some portion in] Aramaic, and the New Testament
> language, [Koine] Greek.

Pastor Billy Crone, a former head-banging guitarist and demon-possessed adherent to New Age teachings, is a rare, biblically sound Christian pastor today, and he gives God all the glory for that. At his Sunrise Bible Church in Las Vegas (SunriseLV.com), as well as on his ministry website (GetALifeMedia.com/videos), with tens of thousands of followers all over the world and hundreds of free teaching videos, he is a man of God who still preaches the whole Bible, here at a time when most pastors only fill their congregations with fluffy, feel-good, self-help messages. Pastor Billy adds this to what we quoted from Josh McDowell:

> Also, these people mostly didn't know each other, especially since they were from different generations. They could not cross-reference their writings. And yet, the Bible never once contradicts itself and has the same message throughout, which is about God's redemption of man through Christ's work on the cross.

As Pastor B knows from personal experience, escaping the false teachings of New Age (after it had driven him to attempt suicide three times, including the last being a bullet shot into his own chest), the New Age movement is looking for a new ascension, a new light—a new age. But as the Bible warns, those beliefs play right into the Antichrist's hand. Satan is called the "light bearer" by his satanic cabal followers, just like the Bible describes him as a supposedly benevolent but deceptively evil, camouflaged, saboteur "angel of light." As the ultimate source of lies and murder, the devil knows he is doomed for eternity, so his only purpose is to take all he can with him. He is like the cornered bank robber that is so evil he kills all his hostages before being captured.

Doomed for eternity, Satan has only one remaining purpose with non-Christians: to distract you away from finding Jesus, just long enough to see you die before choosing a relationship with Christ. That way Lucifer knows you too will end up where he and his demons are bound for, instead of with your Creator and Savior who loves you (and all of mankind) more than any human ever could. But God gives you free will to make that choice, instead of forcing you to love Him. Would you force your family to love you? No. And if you never heard that before, while reading this you have been given the choice, so you are now without the excuse of not knowing. Right now, make the choice to be with Jesus, or risk eternal separation from Him at your death that can happen any minute, leaving you eternally apart—by your own choice. It's up to you. God or no God. Heaven or hell.

Satan also has just one purpose for us Christians, an evil goal of his that I will mention in a minute, but first we Christians must realize that we can never lose that free gift we truly accepted from Jesus. Every true Christian has become so by genuinely humbling him- or herself before God. Christians know they have no way to reach heaven on their own deeds because they are sinners in their perfect-Creator's eyes. But by receiving what Christ did for him or her on the cross to wipe away their sins in God's eyes, they've been given God's pardon through Jesus's sacrifice of Himself. Romans 10:9 tells every man, woman, and child how to become a Christian:

> *"If you declare with your mouth, 'Jesus is Lord,' and believe in your heart that God raised him from the dead, you will be saved."*

And here is the best part: If you heartily agree with Romans 10:9, the free gift can never be taken away. Can something given be required back? No! Once saved for eternity and born again as a believing child of Christ, can you be unsaved and unborn? Can a newborn baby become unborn? No! The Bible declares that once you have made that commitment to become a Christian, not even you can snatch yourself out of God's hand. Your future in heaven is secured—no matter what!

So, as a secure Christian, get busy! Because the devil's goal for Christians is to keep them thinking of self instead of saving others. *All* man-made religions have their followers constantly "work for their own salvation." Also, by man's design, even with all that work, the adherents never truly know if they will make it to heaven until the moment they die and end up in hell because they rejected humbling themselves to accept Christ's sacrifice on the cross as full payment for their sins. That work prescribed by man's religions and cults normally involves giving time and money to the organization, as a way to sup-posedly earn one's own way into heaven.

So, that becomes the focus and false hope of your life, and it will not even lead to heaven if you have not humbled yourself to accept biblical Christianity that is not a religion but just a simple relationship with your Creator, Jesus, who asks no time or money in order to be saved and spend eternity with Him. However—and this is where the Bible's teaching on works do come in—God would like you to accept the free gift, becoming totally secure in your own magnificent future after this life, and then get busy earning heavenly rewards that you will receive when you get there, rewards you can lay at Jesus's feet to show your appreciation for what He did by dying for God's glory, as well as the forgiveness of our sins.

How do you earn rewards? That is your life's purpose (while also glo-rifying God so that others will look to Him for everything in life). Help others get to heaven with you! Help Jesus save them. Hell is real and eternal. And Satan's goal with Christians, using unbiblical man-made religions that Christians can be drawn to, is to keep you busy working to get yourself to heaven. But doing so, you are figuratively climbing up on the cross, slapping Jesus in the face, and asking Him why He was not good enough to save you all by Himself. Defeat Satan by

accepting Christ's free gift, and then thank Christ by getting busy saving others, all while you become a serious discipled learner of your
entire Bible, scripture divinely given by God, having no error from
front to back—we know that from Bible prophecy!

Speaking of God's word proclaiming our future, during these end
days with the Rapture of Christ's church an imminent event, Lord
willing, we will have this time where evil is uncovered and we can
lead a great harvest of suddenly evil-recognizing humanity to Jesus.
However, this will be just a window of time. As the book of Revelation
and other prophecy scriptures tell us, eventually the Antichrist teams
up with technology that facilitates demonic signs and wonders, all
surrounding the coming full disclosure of what they will disclose as
real "UFO's and aliens among us." The Satanists need something to
take the place of today's bankrupt idea of evolution, which is only a
guess that does not even qualify as scientific theory.

That long-planned great deception will claim that these demonic beings, along with complicit Satan-worshipping human helpers and
technology, are mankind's originators, the ones who planted us on
earth thousands of years ago—another bad guess called "pansper-
mia"—or at least here to "help" us. And most all people on the earth
at that time, besides Christians, will fall for this well-crafted false narrative. The vast majority of men and women on earth will buy into the
temporary peace that follows, wrongly believing it will lead to some
supposed ascension of mankind. But populations around the world
will completely turn away from any more thoughts of Jesus returning,
and instead they will decide to follow the devil and this supernatural
Antichrist, who will, one day, suddenly show himself as the wolf in
sheep's clothing that he is.

Possibly even before the Rapture of Christ's church, a contented mankind might let evil people back in power, just as the Old Testament Jews
often did, many times just a few generations or less after God saved

them from another self-inflicted, catastrophic situation. Consider that God's people defied Him and built their occult Tower of Babel just a couple hundred years after the worldwide flood had wiped out all but eight of mankind. Borrowing from evil pre-flood teachings, the devil, and his demons, that tower-building Babylonian population gave us the widespread occultism we are battling on a massive scale today, with its witchcraft and satanism.

In the meantime, the only reason Jesus has not come back yet as a roaring lion that wipes out evil on the earth (this time after three and a half years of God's wrath being poured out on this rebellious creation of His) is that He has been extremely patient with us, so that more will have time to choose a relationship with God before they die. You, I, and everyone else have one epic purpose in this life: to help others come to heaven with us. Using the free will God gave us, He wants more than just you and me to choose a relationship with our Savior, instead of rejecting Him and ending up separated from Him by our own choice, doomed to spend the rest of eternity with the foul creatures, Satan, and the demons that God will send to hell. But people who know about what Jesus did will only suffer away from God for eternity if they have not repented and chosen Christ before their death.

This fast-approaching time when people will see evil up close—all around the planet—is God giving us the perfect opportunity to tell the world about Jesus. Every human, whether honorable or extremely evil, can be saved from their sins and go to heaven—people who would otherwise spend their afterlife with the Satanists and their de-mon lords because they used the free will God gave them to choose to be away from Him. At some point during that window of time, while enjoying true freedom and prosperity, a contented population will allow the future fascist technocracy to crack down on the world again, something that will at least become imminent when every Christian on earth disappears in an instant at the Rapture. For those remaining, the ones who knew about Jesus but did not pick Him, He says this in Matthew 24:12 about their fate:

"For then there will be great distress, unequaled from the beginning of the world until now—and never to be equaled again."

That will be the time of the Antichrist, who will come in preaching peace, safety, and prosperity, but eventually set himself up as God in the new multireligion Jewish temple (to be built in Jerusalem). The Israelites have already prepared everything to build and equip that temple. They are just waiting to begin. First Thessalonians 5:3 gives this warning for a future contented society that will claim to no longer need their Creator:

"When people are saying, 'Everything is peaceful and secure,' then disaster will fall on them as suddenly as a pregnant woman's labor pains begin. And there will be no escape."

Luckily, we all have a way out today and it is something simple anyone can remember to do and tell others about. For this present time, as well as those quickly approaching days when evil will be uncovered and punished—a time when everyone will come to know real evil exists in this world—much of mankind that never before thought a lot about the Bible and the real God will be promoted to choose a relationship with Jesus. He is waiting. Here in Romans 10:6 and 9 is what Paul tells us all to do so we can be sure to spend eternity in heaven with Jesus, instead of choosing an afterlife of torment with Satan and his demons:

"Righteousness…is by faith…If you declare with your mouth, 'Jesus is Lord,' and believe in your heart that God raised him from the dead, you will be saved."

That's it! Too many have been taught they have to work their own way to heaven. But it is a free gift made available to everyone, no matter what you've ever done that you are not proud of. God came to live among us as Jesus, making Him still fully God but also fully man. He then offered Himself to die on the cross as payment for our sins. He was the only person ever without sin, so this was the perfect sacrifice.

However, the hard part for us arrogant humans is to humble ourselves and admit we need a savior because we have sinned against the law of our Creator and need Jesus's free gift to be reunited with a sinless God. A perfect God cannot be in the presence of a sinful, unsaved person. And once we have sincerely accepted what Christ did, that gift cannot be taken back; it would not be a gift. How can someone born again become unborn? God says not even you can snatch yourself out of God's hand from that point forward—forever. But first you must humble yourself enough to really mean that Romans 10 passage, from your heart. Tomorrow is promised to no one. If you believe, why not take this opportunity to let God know? The Creator of the entire universe is waiting patiently for you to say yes to having a close personal relationship with Him.

The complete intentions of our Creator will not happen on this planet until the Second Coming of Christ when we enter a thousand years of living with Jesus here on earth—as it was intended from the beginning. C. S. Lewis, the man who wrote *The Chronicles of Narnia* and one of the greatest biblically sound Christian thinkers of all time, taught this (from the Bible) about mankind's feeble attempts to create a utopia on earth before Jesus comes back:

> *"You and I have need...to wake from the evil enchantment of worldliness which has been laid upon us for nearly a hundred years. Almost our whole education [and] modern philosophies have been devised to convince us that the good of man is to be found on this earth."*

Completely contrary to the idea that man will create his own utopia on this planet before the Second Coming of Jesus, the Bible tells us man's heart has been deceitfully wicked ever since we went the way of the original sinner: Satan. Everyone has at least once lied, stolen, lusted, hated, idolized, or coveted, just to name a few of God's laws. That is all it takes. Our choice to sin keeps us separate from God, as long as we won't make that one decision to accept what Jesus did for us on the cross, thereby receiving forgiveness from God.

> "The human heart is the most deceitful of all things, and desperately wicked" (Jeremiah 17:9).

That is why we must trust in Jesus's work on the cross as the voluntary Savior who took the penalty for our acts of sin against our Creator.

Again, we will have a window of time to improve life, becoming more like God's desire for us, rooting out evil and showing it to a previously lethargic public that has forgotten God, but will remember to turn to Him when faced with the kind of evil that is being uncovered now. Before all that is brought into the open (Lord willing), we have a mess we've allowed, so let's help make it right—while also helping Jesus bring more to heaven to be with Him.

25

John Michael Chambers: If It's Not Okay, It's Not the End (Part Four)

My sudden ownership of this quickly growing news network was another process that had to have been divinely planned. While touring around the Southeast US, talking to mostly Floridian patriot groups, I was asked to be interviewed by Will Johnson of Unite America First (UniteAmericaFirst.com). Someone had given Will my book at the Washington, DC, "Mother of All Rallies" (September 2017). That one interview was seen by 725,000 people while I had been driving all over Florida sleeping in hotels and only speaking to fifty or one hundred at a time. Of course, it made sense that I could get in front of a camera and instantly reach more people, so I launched a YouTube channel in January 2020. After eight months of building a following and beginning to monetize those efforts, I woke up one day to learn that I had been deplatformed. The deep state's fascist YouTube would no longer allow my free speech after letting the same sorts of content earn them money for eight hundred to one thousand hours of my life and heart being invested in this battle, along with nearly $100,000 in various costs for studios, rents, and technology. After two days of dealing with that gut punch, I did what President Trump always does: counterpunch! I doubled down by forming American

Media Periscope where we are now getting 5 to 10 million collective views per month [updated at the start of January 2022].

Much is happening that does not get reported, but the huge barge I'm using to represent American society is no longer headed in exactly the wrong direction. I think we've made a ninety-degree turn, and every day we are seeing it veer more and more in the right direction. The worst development for the cabal, the one scenario they had to prevent at all costs, was to have their sabotage exposed. But it is happening with millions waking up and many of those stepping up to help wake others.

The globalista power structure revolves around the City of London, the Vatican, and Washington, DC, wielding cabal control of world finance, religion, and military might, in that order. But their grand ideas for a more controlling future will be thwarted. Again, I leave that up to God's timing because most of us with the independent media have been dead wrong a time or two when attempting to pick dates for significant changes. It doesn't mean we're bad people. This is an information war with disinformation coming from the fake news as always, but also from the white hats who want the cabal to expend their ammunition on misleading intelligence that is purposely released publicly. Through this fog of war, we with the patriot media are working hard to try putting out the truth, while jeopardizing ourselves and our families—risking life, fortune, and sacred honor at the tip of the spear. We can get it wrong.

The Q team has been absent since December 2020, just as President Trump is no longer out there each day as the voice of the patriot movement. For all intents and purposes, the patriot movement does not have one current leader, so we keep going back to the Q boards that contain all those previous posts of intel that were left behind to help us connect dots. The broad time frame that appears when we analyze those shows us at the precipice right now, in the middle of a near-death experience where good people are dying from the cabal's mass murders using dirty bioweapon vaccines, among other widespread increases in death from their lockdowns. Was the deep state's release of a China virus just the bait used to prompt society into taking their illness-causing operating systems into our bodies through jabs in our arms—their ultimate weapon to make us sick? I think so.

Our freedoms are being taken away more each day as they come after our guns, set up physical and social-media tracking, censor conservatives, and otherwise cancel our voices in whatever way the can, destroying innocent people and even putting some in prison. They're setting up false flags and blaming it on Trump supporters in an effort to take us out from top to bottom. Americans and good people around the planet are risking their health and lives by taking deadly cabal injections to gain back freedoms only promised to those earning their "vaccine passport." Show me your papers! But mass illness caused by those vaccines will be deceptively labeled as "virus variances" that supposedly necessitate taking more and more of our freedoms away over time. Either way, the Fascists have set it up so their power would constantly grow from this point, if it weren't for white hats willing to step in and say, "Hell no!"

And speaking of travel, I am grateful that my calling to help the patriot movement has not impacted me as negatively as some in this country, but I will also honestly disclose that I have a life previously lived in a foreign country, where there are people I cannot go back to because I will not take the cabal's phony and toxic no-vaccine vaccine. They have our lives on hold while they work at corralling us to eventually slaughter the vast majority of civilization, which is their ultimate plan involving the reduction of the world's population from almost eight billion now, down to just half a million. You can read about that in the memoirs of prominent globalistas, as well as check out the structures they crafted to brag about their plans like their writings on buildings, portraits in airports (like Denver), and monuments outlining our demise (like the anonymously funded slabs of granite called the Georgia Guidestones). In their sick, satanic-cult minds, whether they announce it cryptically or outright, letting us know what they have in store for society makes them feel justified to harm those they control because we were too dumb to do anything about it. And silencing dissent or exposure of their evil plans is straight out of Communist Chinese Chairman Mao Zedong's playbook, a mass murderer of his own people who gave the Asians today's Chinese Communist Party (CCP), which was spawned by the teachings of Communist Karl Marx, the inspiration for massacring tens of millions in the twentieth century. That same communism is exactly what the deep state is trying to shoehorn America and the rest of the world into through their Green New Deal, Agenda 21, Agenda 2030, the World Economic Forum with Klaus Schwab, and Joe Biden—just another cabal puppet.

On that last one, the lecherous, old, belligerent occupier, remember that I mentioned having dinner with a high-level CIA gentlemen, a patriot intel officer who served at least as far back as President Ronald Reagan. Again, he told me there are at least three different Bidens that he has identified. So, nothing is as it seems in this circus full of anomalies surrounding the fake presidency of Biden, another aspect of this whole election travesty that is soon coming to an end.

But before that happens completely, we are experiencing the precipice of destruction during this season of false flags performed by a deep state that knows they have been caught on everything, including the stolen election, drug running, human trafficking, and pedophilia, along with taking trillions from the American people, and something else the "big guy" (Joe Biden) was involved with: he sent his son to collect money from foreign governments, after which crooked Joe would take his cut. Even I have extremely incriminating videos of Hunter Biden's wrongdoing on my computer, as many people do, so don't you think the NSA must have it all too?

But because they are desperate right now, false flag season has ramped up, something that involves cabal use of the Hegelian Dialectic. For those who may not be clear on what exactly that means, the "false" part does not mean the incident never happened. Instead, the deception comes from the deep state claiming some fictitious motivation for a shooting (or other heinous crime) that is then falsely reported by their complicit mainstream media. The Hegelian Dialectic, with its "problem, reaction, solution," is the method used to accomplish their one-world government goals. False flags have been run by militaries for centuries; acceptable clandestine operations to help win wars fought between nations. However, it is not something governments should use against their unsuspecting citizens. But the cabal has turned that tactic on innocent populations of the world, just as our own CIA has for decades, an agency tasked with protecting us from foreign adversaries, but instead they spy on Americans and carry out all sorts of secret criminal operations around the planet.

The man who created the "Hegelian Dialectic," meaning "Hegel's dialogue," was a German idealist named Georg Wilhelm Friedrich Hegel, who died in 1831. Employing his method, the shadow government causes fear and anger among the public by first creating a *problem* that they provide by pulling off a mass shooting, bombing, assassination, shipwreck, or other shocking tragedy. Then they blame someone else for the harm and murder they committed. Anticipating the *reaction* that will follow this staged incident, they present their *solution*, which usually sounds helpful but mostly leads to more loss of our freedoms. For example, (and I don't mean to sound crass), school shootings are the problem of dead children that the cabal carries out to create an extremely fearful population where a large portion of society has children or grandchildren that could have been there when that crazy "lone gunman" (yeah, right) murdered those poor little ones. So, what is the freedom-losing solution they have lined up in many of those cases? To restore our kids' safety, they must take our guns, just as every dictatorship has done before mass-murdering their own people. And their willing fake news accomplices turn the lie into another false narrative they pitch to an unsuspecting public. Our worldwide mainstream media is part of the cabal, so they are happy to lend a helping hand to take away more and more of our freedoms, while also finding another way to divide and conquer us. When we're divided, we fight each other and continue to ignore what they are doing to us. And our fellow citizens, the fake-news-indoctrinated left, agree that we all must disarm because those hunks of metal kill kids. But gun-owning protectors of liberty rightly point out that only murderers are responsible for shooting people, so Fascists will only get the guns over our dead bodies. On and on it goes.

Famous false flags in our American history are more prevalent than honestly reported major events. The October 2017 Las Vegas shooting, which could never have been pulled off by a lone gunman, was staged by the cabal to go after our guns. Notice how these mass shootings are always done when they have a chance to pass gun legislation, something they had no opportunity to do during Trump's years. But false flag shootings ramped up before and after Trump's presidency because they are desperate to pass gun legislation quickly in anticipation of potentially losing power again. President John F. Kennedy's assassination came right after he laid out his plans to take down the cabal.

Even as far back as the Titanic, three of the richest men in the world (who also happened to be dead set against the private banksters putting their central bank in the US), died on that ship after being invited to sail that maiden voyage by the owner of the ship: JP Morgan, a card-carrying, cabal-club member. As planned by the globalistas, Morgan backed out at the last minute, sending those men to death with all the rest. The next year we were given a central bank. And what sailed out of port wasn't even the Titanic. The real Titanic had its badging switched out with a sister ship, the Olympic, that had taken its place because the Olympic already ran with its severely compromised hull from a previous collision with a military ship as they were passing close to port (see *Kid by the Side of the Road* from Juan O Savin). The most recent false flag events are of course COVID and all that entails, as well as Washington, DC's, no-insurrection "insurrection" of January 6 2021.

Having no concern for lives other than those of their bloodline families, the deep state will often use murderous false flags as mere distractions from damaging revelations that have just, or soon will be, revealed to expose some part of their evil operations. The storming of the Capitol building on January 6, 2021, was not carried out by those peaceful, weaponless Trump supporters who were waved into that congressional building by capital police. The violence and destruction that day came at the hands of goons from the cabal's Antifa and Black Lives Matter. On my *Making Sense of the Madness* show, General Michael Flynn declared January 6th to be a false flag operation. That day, President Trump had a gathering of peaceful, freedom-minded patriots to talk about the election theft. The deep state knew he was going to lay it all down so well that they would need to distract from those truths. And their false flag invasion of the Capitol (the *problem* they created) was successful because the news cycle carried little of his comments—if any—only fabricating their preplanned *reaction*, a narrative that claimed Trump supporters held an unforgivable insurrection. It was the cabal's false flags used to gain two results (desired *solutions*): distract from the election fraud Trump pointed out that day, and push a manufactured story that paints patriots as dangerous, furthering their efforts to label all patriots as potential domestic terrorists, instead of just honest, peace-loving people who are loyal to their country, and not blind globalism. False flags have been constantly used to push a misguided public opinion through murders carried out by saboteur globlistas and their minions.

Getting back to the 2017 mass shooting in Las Vegas, that story came and went in five minutes, a farce that said some sixty-four-year-old guy got a huge pile of ammunition and artillery up to the thirty-second floor of the Mandalay Bay Hotel, a casino covered with security cameras and personnel. Then all by himself he spent ten to thirty minutes gunning people down with a thousand rounds of ammunition. Just another false flag. Their story was nonsense! No way! One other incident where they used the Hegelian Dialectic was that distraction they threw out after losing the circus they instigated surrounding Supreme Court Justice Brett Kavanaugh's confirmation. The following few days should have been a news cycle that pinned those lying losers against the wall, holding them accountable for the nonsense of those hearings. Instead, they gunned down Jewish people in a Pennsylvania synagogue just to divert attention.

I could go on and on with past examples, but we all need to keep a sharp eye out (see something, say something) because false flag season is still upon us as we fight this information war. And the shadow government will only get more desperate as we pile up victories with audits in those states and counties that swung the election, as well as social media wins with the launching of uncensored platforms from patriots like President Trump, Mike Lindell, Juan O Savin, and others. The cabal is panicking, which means they will be unleashing more false flags. So, we patriots need to stay safe and not fall for any more bait like what they set up for us as a trap at the Capitol building on January sixth. They will take every opportunity to mischaracterize our peaceful protests. We must continue to gather but be smart, careful, and take comfort in what the Q team assured us of in a post from January 13, 2018:

"YOU and YOUR FAMILIES are SAFE. PROMISE."

That should take some fear away, at least for those who follow and subscribe to what Trump and his Q team put out—which you should.

What is the greatest threat facing humanity today? There are many answers but the common denominator with all of them is ignorance. We could point at problems with China and their deep state masters, and maybe the fact that God has been removed from our government and public lives, but in the end it all stems from most folks being oblivious to the corruption surrounding us. In most cases honorable people purposely ignore the signs because they feel too busy, and part of the problem is ignorant Americans produced through the indoctrination of our children that has been going on for generations in our public schools. Foul, politically correct curriculum taught through that bankrupt institution also serves to dumb down society by leaving out the sound classical education we used to have over a hundred years ago. The US was the only country that had 100 percent literacy for American women, and the hardworking men were not much lower than that. Butchers and bakers could use their classical education, problem-solving skills, and critical-thinking lessons to debate engineers and doctors about the great works of literature, the origins of life, biblical realities, fanciful philosophies, or any number of interesting intellectual topics. Contrast that with this latest generation that has been raised by the lying globalistas like Obama and Google. It's not their fault, but they are still responsible to wake up now. Still, we can't help but rouse them by getting in their faces and shouting how wrong they are. We must wake people up by showing them the truth, something Dave at the *X22 Report* (X22Report.com) does very well. Before having my own show, Dave was one of my main alternative news sources. So, don't beat up sleepers! Do not make them wrong. Just show them. Anything that helps the deep state divide and conquer us is just falling into the enemy's trap.

That includes being careful not to stoke tensions between patriots inside the movement. Knock that off, agree to disagree, move on, and unify to fight the real enemy. This great awakening is taking place within the human spirit, and it is global. People from over thirty countries email and message us at American Media Periscope. Everyone is watching the developments in America's fight to rid ourselves of these one-world globalists—it all hangs on what happens here. If the US is defeated in this information war, there is no other place to turn to for help; the rest of mankind will also lose it all! The cabal will move on us like wolves on sheep, clamping down with total control this time, especially since they have already put their fascist plans in place, which include the technocracy with its transhumanism and artificial intelligence that they desire to use for the takeover of our lives, replacing our God with a few bloodline families that are loyal to Satan. They attempt to play God and replace God.

But their despicable deeds are being exposed more each day now, so they're rushing to accelerate their battle plans like Agenda 2030. They had no choice after Trump won their first formidable challenge, especially when he began waking us to what they have been building to further snare the world's free people. Again, the deep state's worst fear is an awakened population! And now that so many of us have woken up, they are moving with reckless abandon toward the fruition of their reprehensible plans against us. That greatly backed effort from these satanic, human-sacrificing, bankster pedophiles at the top is all hitting us right now, and our worst response would be fear and retreat. Again, follow the example of Lin Wood who is one man we should all be listening to throughout this ordeal, a great patriot bravely doing God's work.

And speaking of work for the Lord, I think Trump's top accomplishment was massively waking the world to our cabal controllers. We could also talk about his orchestration of the greatest economy in modern history, safety at the border, and keeping his promises. If you do a search for Trump promises made and kept, you'll find a long list that even surpassed what Ronald Reagan did for the people. Since the media would not report that truth, Trump's camp had to compile the record, which is broken down by categories that include ending endless wars, not starting even one war, clamping down on human trafficking, exceeding 3 percent growth for the first time in more than a decade, supplying millions of jobs, worker development, raised incomes for the poor and middle class, increased optimism, support for small businesses, deregulation, tax cuts, domestic infrastructure, health care, combatting opioids, law and order, border security and immigration reform, trade, energy, foreign policy, building our military defense back up, help for our veterans, and on, and on when you analyze each of those areas further. But his most profound accomplishment was waking the people. Everyone who finally sees what the deep state is doing cannot go back to sleep. When he or she gets away from the lying media's false narrative, added facts fit nicely with the rest of the truth they have already learned.

Besides waking Americans, as well as masses of others around the world, Trump ushered in the peace and prosperity that people obviously want. He also promoted the right-to-life movement against abortion, and did so all throughout his years, including being the only president to attend the Washington, DC, March for Life. Of course, this satanic death cult doesn't want anyone to promote life because they are about destroying God's children. The media and others involved with the cabal have brainwashed the world using Wi-Fi frequencies, hypnotic propaganda on "tell-a-visions," MK-Ultra programming, dumbed-down education, fluoride to clog our thinking and perception, street drugs, nonstop medicines, and horrible synthetic and processed substances they call food, but which harm us because our bodies don't recognize much of it as real food. Now add in all the entertainment presented at our figure tips by hand-held computers, and the result is a population that has completely stopped thinking for themselves. Again, whether we realize it or not, this youngest generation has been raised on Google and Obama, while artificial intelligence has taken over control of most information we are allowed to see.

That brings us back to Trump, who is just one of us who has not joined their deep state club, though he is tougher skinned than most and will go down as the greatest president this country has ever had—certainly in modern history. That is my opinion, and I'll add that all future presidents will be compared to him. I love Ronald Reagan and what he did for us as another rare president who was not in the one-world-government club, but the coming generation will size up candidates by how they compare to Donald Trump. The best is yet to come. It is a historic presidency. And he's just getting started. If you listen closely to what Trump said after the 2020 election, you'll find he has never conceded because that vote-count process is not over, and he let us know he would be back soon, though it may be in another way. Does he mean that the usurping US Service Corporation is, or will be, gone? Does Trump end up being the first new president of our US Republic since 1871? Will Trump be number nineteen in our history after Ulysses S. Grant? What we know for sure right now is that Donald Trump does what he promises and plainly told us he would be coming back.

For strength through this time, we need to surround ourselves with like-minded people, and those who have faith should pray like never before. Along those lines, in my first book I called myself a political atheist. But that phrase seemed to be misunderstood by some. If I could pluck those words out of the first edition I would because it was meant as nothing more than a poetic play on words, an indictment of our tyrannical two-party system that gives us only bad choices. Both these present-day parties are captured operations that have taken us to this disastrous point. Sure, I voted for papa and baby Bush back then—as the lesser of two evils. But the bottom line is that I now know all about the Bushes, starting with Prescott Bush, who helped fund Hitler, and then his son George H. W. Bush, who was a pedophile and drug runner (check the research). H. W.'s son George W. was the president when 9/11 happened, and it was under his watch that the Saudis, who might have been involved, were allowed to leave this country right after that orchestrated mass murder by the cabal. Their false flag allowed accomplishment of deep state goals to transform and control another part of the Middle East. They were also excited to feed billions of our money to their military-industrial complex, cause displaced populations that included children who could be used for their human trafficking, rid themselves of a noncooperative Saddam Hussein in Iraq, and take over the Afghanistan opium operation. Of course, neither Bush voted for their Republican presidential candidate, Donald Trump. They did not support or endorse the future president, but they did trash him. That's because they have been long-time members of the fascist, globalista, bloodline club, the group that despises us Americans that Trump fights for. Millions around the world have woken up to the plots and schemes of the Bushes.

Lord willing, what the future holds a decade from now will obviously depend on how we meet this present challenge involving a paradigm shift of gargantuan proportions. We continue living through these past six millennia of good constantly having to fight evil; it is still God, peace, and joy against sin, depravity, and death. But now white hats are bringing our modern-day version of the latter out of its hiding places, making all the controlled populations of the world look evil in the face so they can no longer deny its existence, and forcing today's lukewarm mankind to pick a side, which I believe will overwhelmingly result in vast numbers of new relationships with God, (as outlined in the previous chapter).

Getting back to this window of time where God will give the whole world an opportunity to get right with Him in massive numbers, here at this biblical end of days, we are heading to a period when wars will end and no one will live under communism. I know those things sound crazy, but I lived in China for eighteen months—under the Chinese Communist Party (CCP). I had a Chinese/American wife. I'm divorced now. But I studied a bit about the CCP and understand what they are. In certain intelligence circles, we are hearing that Xi Jinping and Vladimir Putin are working with Donald Trump against our evil, deep state enemies. That means the CCP is coming apart behind the scenes, which goes along with my long-standing prediction that communism will end in our lifetime. Charlie Ward supported that notion and even claimed it has already happened. I'll need to see more evidence of that, but I respect Charlie and always tend toward a glass-half-full mentality, so I believe it very well could be, especially when we know God always wins in the end. I don't believe this time is meant to wake up the whole world only to get plowed back under right away. We, Trump, the Q team, many in our military, and the rest of the white hats are just getting started!

The key human on this planet right now is President Donald Trump, a man with the most influence over the minds and hearts of humanity. But like Trump, the duty lands on all of us to help further God's kingdom on earth. As rosy as this takedown of evil sounds, I believe we will first go through some challenging days because a switch will not suddenly get flipped and all these criminals will be in Gitmo (Guantanamo Bay, Cuba's, US Naval Base prison). It won't suddenly be "Happy days are here again!" Instead, this will most likely take years, but the ocean barge we've all been riding on is rotating in the right direction, so if Jesus does not return sooner, the decades to come will see the world with this window of time where we will all live in a much better place. And part of that will be the revealing of suppressed technologies to heal diseases that have plagued man for a long time, as well as an end to scarcity of the life support needed in any way—a new existence where we are involved with the natural order of things, rather than the cabals made-up reality.

It's all coming, folks. But first we have the battles between deep evil and God's pure light, a defining time that will have us use our God-given free will to pick which side of the fence to be on. You are either teaming up with the rest of God's people or helping those who have been enslaving mankind. I believe the summer and early fall of 2022 will see an extraordinary awakening. At the age of sixty-three, that is not just being glib because I'm truly optimistic that my good Lord may decide to have me stick around long enough to see the fruition of these white hat efforts to face today's monumental challenges. I believe the worst history we've had to live through, where this satanic cabal has been hanging over our heads, is behind us—at least for some significant window of time. But many battles are still before us during this paradigm shift with billions continuing to wake up. And it all makes for an extraordinary time to be alive, so we need to get unstuck from any fear, a state of mind facilitated by gathering with like-minded patriots.

Some wonder why the ultimate patriot, President Trump, didn't disclose a greater amount of classified information in his first four years. First, I would say more was revealed under his watch than what I have seen in the rest of my lifetime. And the second reason has to do with responsibility, which has a simple but often-overlooked definition: "the ability to withhold." Think about a five-year-old waiting for Christmas morning when Santa will come down the chimney again and leave him or her some exciting presents. But then that morning the parents crush the child's fun by disclosing that Santa Claus is a lie, and it was just Mom and Dad going to get the gifts at a store. That would be irresponsible. You have to have the ability to withhold information. If President Trump suddenly dropped all the truth bombs, it might cave society under. As Trump's Q team did for three years through a buildup of information, we can be properly prepared, strategically awakened, and made aware of our true reality because the psychological damage of rapid disclosure can be too much for many of us. Disruptive, uncomfortable truths have to be given out in a responsible way. There are also other political and strategic moves needed during an information war involving the type of intelligence battles we've been fighting. Some revelations might be better saved for later—one shock at a time.

I have faith and trust in the very active white hats planted all over our intel community right now, and I do not think Special Council John Durham's role is finished yet. All will come out when it's supposed to, and at that time the hammer of justice will drop hard on the criminal cabal, sending many to be confronted by their Creator. Coming up in this life, or at least after death, if they have not already repented and gotten right with God, these people will stand in front of Jesus, as we all will, and meet justice there. Again, it will happen in God's time.

But getting back to the future world I anticipate after all these truths are revealed in a responsible manner, after we've gotten through these very dark and challenging times that will get worse before they get better, I think we get to *love*. That will absolutely be a time of brotherly love. We've forgotten what that feels like, but it almost brings me to tears thinking about love at the cellular level, so much so that we won't know how to handle it all, the intense camaraderie we will feel for our patriot brothers and sisters all over this planet. If you went to a Trump rally, you felt it there, where twenty to thirty thousand people who didn't know each other, folks from all walks of life, races, religions, colors, and even some that admitted to having been Democrats, stood there feeling the great love in those crowds. It was off the charts!

I'm not embarrassed to admit that I am an emotional man, just like General Flynn who tears up a lot these days when he gets into some of the trauma the cabal put him and his family through. Whenever he does though, it comes with this warning: "Don't let that tear indicate a sign of weakness!" I may mention that too as I tear up from time to time during this epic struggle. But love and camaraderie are what's truly intended for us on this planet, and that is part of what we look forward to. We'll have a window of time without scarcity. Instead, we'll experience a taste of prosperity, morals, and ethics. I think we get to an amazing place that is closer to what God intended six thousand years ago (again, this was detailed in the previous chapter).

Up until now, our lives have been so rigged by our deep state captures that we spend most of time just dodging bullets to keep a roof over our head, grab more food for our stomachs, and learn to hate others so much that we are leery to even speak with strangers. During this COVID crackdown, our overlords have ramped that up by working to limit us from normal amounts of talking, walking, or even being able to breathe enough oxygen because of the face diapers they force on us. Those same fascist masks have caused the average person to breathe in our body's waste product, carbon dioxide, one hundred times the normal amount. Carbon dioxide in our air is minuscule compared with the huge, ongoing amount those masks make us constantly consume, which is part of the complete insanity we are living through at this precipice, our near-death experience. But soon we will throw their shackles off that mountain cliff and head back down to a place where we can enjoy our lives, neighbors, friends, family, and God—in reverse order. That's where we are, and it is why I am optimistic about a future full of forgiveness, kindness, and love.

People sometimes ask my religion, and if that means placing me in a category, I will surely profess to being Christian, but I also want to say my philosophy is simple: be nice to people. The last message I would urge all of us to keep in mind through this minefield that is our present information war is to *never give up*! God is in control. And His nature is pure love, as well as faith, hope, joy, peace, kindness, goodness, faithfulness, gentleness, and our source of self-control through every shadowy valley. Keep in mind that Trump has never broken his word to us. Unlike all those previous, globalist presidents from both deep state parties, Trump delivered everything he pledged on the campaign trail—and more. He has not left us. He's not gone anywhere. Together, we'll take this back! I don't want to get really preachy here, and I work hard to practice what I preach, but we patriots need to cut out any infighting, have faith, and do something each day to move ourselves away from reacting to cabal-caused events that are constantly plastered on the fake news, and move toward having our own effect on what happens in our communities, as well as farther away from home.

If you still pay attention to mainstream daily "news," or other sources of information coming from the deep state, knock it off! You don't feel mentally well because you're listening to a bunch of bunk—lie, after lie, after lie—along with other vicious, psychologically harmful programming, which especially includes their stupid commercials. Turn it all off! At least in terms of news, my televisions remain dark. I will sometimes check out programs on Roku or cable, but that's it. How do we detect the truth from lies in the age of fake news? Turn that off! Find a few alternative sources of information that make sense for you, and those should be outlets that empower you to be connected with like-minded patriots, providing truth while also just making you feel better. And I mean cut out Fox News too! Certainly stay away from CNN, the networks, MSNBC, and all that other nonsense like most Hollywood movies, an activity I have not engaged in for quite a while and am very selective with when I do.

Also, most modern music is not for me. This satanic cabal has been buying up everything for decades, so they have us coming and going these days, both outright and subliminally. Turn it all off! You will begin to feel better when you keep out their crud and instead take daily injections of the truth, getting properly informed so you realize we are winning this war. Yes, it's still dangerous out there, but we're coming after the globalistas with a mighty and widespread force of honest humanity, and the saboteurs are feeling that extreme heat. So, again, once you have gotten rid of the toxic input and surrounded yourself with honest people, get busy helping us take this country back. Move to action and you will feel notches higher, whether it's sharing truth on social media by joining the new uncensored platforms, or spreading facts through friends, neighbors, and even strangers, including the anomalies happening all through this sketchy "presidency" of Biden's. Use some of those suggestions I mentioned to gently wake them up a bit.

A more aggressive contribution would be to run for city council, your school board, or even mayor. And I absolutely encourage everyone to visit Lieutenant Scott Bennett's show on AMP, and specifically the episode from May 6, 2021. There you will find his marching orders for average citizens who want to go to their city councils, commissioners, and mayors to inform them in a way that puts them in a position to either act against these unconstitutional executive orders and laws coming into our backyards, or risk being held for treason. People are doing this all over the country.

Again, turn off the fake news, surround yourself with like-minded patriots, get active, and pray! And for those who have some money, the cabal is coming after it, so protect your savings by diversifying away from their phony paper and into tangible assets like gold and silver that hold their value.

This is an information war, an intelligence battle, a colliding course correction. And there is a plan unfolding. Trust the plan and fight for what's right. We are under a wartime command structure, and we don't know what we don't know, but everything will be okay in the end; if it's not okay, it's not the end. Pick a lane and hold the line, patriots—hold the line. Victory is ours! And remember, WWG1WGA.

Lightning Source UK Ltd.
Milton Keynes UK
UKHW011849090223
416719UK00004B/444/J